*For Charlie, my BH.*
*And for my beloved daughters*
*Clemmie and Flora.*

*Frostquake* n. a seismic event caused by a sudden cracking action in frozen soil. As water drains into the ground, it may freeze and expand, putting stress on its surroundings. This stress builds up until relieved explosively in the form of a frostquake.

In the dark time of the year. Between melting and freezing
The soul's sap quivers.

T. S. Eliot, 'Little Gidding', *Four Quartets*

Well, I know now. I know a little more how much a simple thing like a snowfall can mean to a person.

Sylvia Plath

# Contents

# Introduction

The winter of 1962–3 was one of the coldest Britain has ever known. After a week of catastrophic, lung-clogging smog in early December in which many hundreds of people lost their lives, snow began to fall on Boxing Day 1962 . . . and did not stop for the next ten weeks. With blizzards, treacherous ice and temperatures lower than -20°C, the winter of 1962 was even colder, longer and more life-impacting than the remarkable winter of 1947. At times the entire country was paralysed. Aeroplanes were grounded. Trains, lorries and cars came to a halt. Bicycles, tractors and even snowploughs failed to make their way through huge wind-swept drifts. Animals and birds struggled to survive. Food was rationed. Many, especially the elderly, found themselves confined to their homes. Schools were closed. Families were separated, unable to travel to see each other in such exceptional weather.

For many of those who had fought in or lived through one or both world wars this interminable winter felt fearful, like the ending of a way of life, the loss of familiarity, of certainty, of the old way of doing things. And for those who had been hopeful about the new decade, a new beginning, a sloughing off of the old, the very real prospect of another – and even more terrifying – world conflict was starting to shake their optimism. When John F. Kennedy became President of the United States in 1961 he was warned that a nuclear war with Russia would probably kill a third of humanity, with most of those deaths concentrated in the USA, the Soviet Union, China and Europe. Even after Kennedy's negotiations with the Soviet Union leader Nikita Khrushchev in October 1962 had defused the Cuban Missile Crisis, the nuclear threat and the fragility of world peace continued to monopolise domestic and international agendas as well as private thoughts and terrors.

The winter crystallised a growing tension between the old and the new. Although a December 1962 Gallup poll found that sixteen to eighteen year olds considered Winston Churchill, who had just celebrated his eighty-eighth birthday, to be Britain's most respected adult, this loyalty to the old ways was an exception. In his 1959 novel *Absolute Beginners*, Colin MacInnes describes the divide between teenagers and those referred to as 'squares' by the eighteen-year-old unnamed hero. 'Every time I open a newspaper or pick up a paperback,' he says, with scorn in his voice, 'I hear nothing but war, war, war. You pensioners certainly seem to love that old, old struggle.'

Wherever possible, post-war Britain was trying to catch up with the pacy, modern, convenient world we saw across the

Atlantic. As the old industries of steel and shipping declined and Victorian factories gave way to scientific advances, office blocks of shining glass and chrome were built in the rubble-filled spaces left by bombs that had dropped twenty years earlier. Ownership of television sets, refrigerators and other labour-saving gadgets was on the rise. John Bloom, opportunist and direct-mail marketer, cut out the middle-man shopkeeper and sold washing machines bought cheaply in Belgium directly to newly-weds and housewives. By 1962, at the age of thirty-one, Bloom had become a millionaire four times over. With a Rolls-Royce the colour of a black tulip, two yachts, a villa in the South of France, a flat in London's Park Lane, a swagger and a neat little goatee beard, his marriage to Anne was celebrated in the Savoy Hotel. Two huge wedding cakes dominated the ceremony, one in the shape of a washing machine and the other a spin dryer.

But in the inner cities of Britain and in the countryside alike, laundry was still done by hand and the contrast between the affluent and the struggling was as acute as it had been immediately after the war. In 1961 fifteen million people still lacked a plumbed-in bathroom, with many washing in a tin bath in front of a coal fire. In 1963 six million Britons shared a lavatory with others in their street. Three million people, or nearly 7 per cent of the population, were estimated to be living in slums. In London, 155,000 households were confined to one room each.[1]

And yet, and yet . . . beneath the frozen surface a process of incubation was taking place. Just as the spring bulbs were stirring under the earth, the ground was cracking imperceptibly beneath the ice, and society was preparing for the moment when a different landscape would emerge. This was a winter in which despair and hardship both personal and political contrasted with a burgeoning sense of liberation and opportunity. It was a winter in which the old structural pillars of class and entitlement – a world in which swings in public playgrounds were locked up on Sundays and a nation's sense of joyfulness felt wanting – were starting to fragment and crumble.

Throughout the early winter months of 1962–3 rumours about a government minister said to have betrayed state secrets through his relationship with a twenty-year-old 'model' swirled and eddied. Like snowflakes they sometimes melted in the air as they fell, but sometimes they settled on the hard ground of credibility, attaching themselves to a new generation disillusioned by privileged self-protection and hungry for change. As the momentum of this scandal grew, one unchallenged rule for the elite and another for the bulk of the population began to feel increasingly wrong. This was a winter in which a fertile silence gave birth to a summer alive with sexuality and song. Old institutions and old viewpoints no longer made sense; what had been 'correct' – the acceptable norm around clothes and accents and sex and class – was being upturned. By the end of ten astonishing weeks the circumstances of the rich, the immigrant, the homosexual, the musician, the politician, the woman and above all the young had been spotlit and shaken up. Eager to seize their moment, the new generation was bent on dismantling archaic prejudices, injustices, hypocrisy and restrictions, and on creating a world of inclusivity and opportunity. As Ian

McEwan wrote in *On Chesil Beach*, his 2007 novel set in the early 1960s, being young was no longer 'a social encumbrance, a mark of irrelevance, a faintly embarrassing condition for which marriage was the beginning of a cure'. Suddenly youth was a state to be envied.

I was eight years old that winter and can remember the feeling of living on an edge. I knew my parents were unhappy with each other, even though my mother was expecting her third child in the spring. The prospect of new life in the new season was the energy that propelled her forward. And I was aware of secrets being kept from me when I overheard exchanges that were sometimes subdued, sometimes tearful, rarely cheerful. More publicly, the prospect of a third war was never far from my parents' discussions or from my own thoughts. Like images flashing past a train window, these overheard conversations remain vivid in my mind. And we were living with my recently widowed grandfather, who, like so many of his generation, was bemused and confused by a world that he found unrecognisable, grieving for his wife and struggling to understand his part in a new environment. His despair was my education in the power of compassion.

At the same time we had just moved to a place that seemed to me the loveliest on earth. And by the autumn of 1963, along with almost everyone else on the planet of whatever age, I had fallen flat in love with four irreverent, exuberant singers from the grimy streets of Liverpool. After five years of hanging around seedy basement cellars, the few outside their home city who had heard of them before the snow began falling on Boxing

Day 1962 considered the band to be little more than an uncategorisable novelty act. By the end of the winter they had become the most famous band in Britain.

There are moments when society, however embedded, shifts on its axis. The long and lingering hardships of the paralysing winter of 1962–3 encouraged, even enabled, change; the very effect of shutting down empowered a thawing. Forces of social change that had been building over many years now found their moment of release as they broke through the icy surface. As the country froze it melted.

# Chapter One

## *Driving through mustard*

On the morning of Monday 3 December 1962 Paulene Stone was driving her blue Mini across London from her flat in South Kensington.[1] Her boyfriend knew something about paint and had sprayed the car her favourite colour. As she turned into the Mall the roads were almost empty and the smog was so thick and yellow that it was like driving through mustard. Slowly Paulene edged her way round the small island on which the statue of a seated Queen Victoria reigned serene, impervious to the appalling weather, her marble skirts spread out gracefully in front of her. Paulene was on her way to meet her photographer boyfriend at his house in Petty France, even though she had heard the man on the wireless warning people not to go outside unless it was absolutely necessary. Cars should only be driven in an emergency: visibility in some places was down to fifteen feet.

Paulene went everywhere in her Mini, her independent, nineteen-year-old mind very much her own. And today would be no different, whatever the BBC said. She was proud of her little car, complete with its sun roof and its distinctive colour, and confident of her status as one of the new, beautiful, breezy young models who turned every head on the King's Road. Their fashionable androgyny was maintained by a diet of Ryvita, the wheat-based biscuits which made you feel full up and ensured a willowy figure, as did Limmits, the brand-new cellulose crackers that promised in a television advertisement that you could 'eat and be thin'. No matter whether you chose the mint, chocolate, orange or cheese variety, Paulene admitted, 'they all tasted of cardboard' but would swell up inside you and replace the need for at least two meals a day.

Paulene's mother, an expert dressmaker, sewed all her daughter's clothes so Paulene had never owned a shop-bought dress and had no idea of her frock size when in 1959 she won a modelling competition run by *Woman's Own* magazine. She had made her name in 1960 with a photograph taken for a *Daily Express* feature called 'Autumn Girl' by David Bailey, a twenty-two-year-old up-and-comer from the East End of London. At the shoot, Bailey (always known by surname alone), described by the newspaper as 'a cocky, confident, energetic, handsome lad' in a black leather jacket, asked Paulene to crouch down on the floor. Wearing a fluffy sweater and a tight skirt that ended above the knee, Paulene was invited to flirt with a 'live' squirrel (it was actually stuffed). The combination of the pretty young redhead and the lens of 'David Bailey who makes love daily', as the tabloids had begun to chant, was dynamite.

Paulene never took the Underground; why would you when the London traffic moved at a steady speed and the pavement provided convenient off-road parking right outside the door of any destination? Reaching her journey's end, slightly surprised that in her rear-view mirror she could still just make out the reflected outline of the regal statue at the top of the Mall, she passed a figure in an abnormally elongated fur hat, some impressive railings and a wide-open gate that she did not recognise. A blue cloth sleeve with shiny buttons straight out of television's current police drama, *Dixon of Dock Green*, suddenly rapped on her window. 'Ere, ere, ere? What do you think you're doing? You can't park here.'

'Am I in Petty France?' she asked, confused.

As the policeman told her quite firmly to turn round and take her Mini straight back into the smog in the direction from which she had just come, she realised she was talking to him from the parade ground inside the forecourt of Buckingham Palace.

It was that time of year when daylight hours decrease with dispiriting speed and it is dark by teatime. And during that first week of December the noxious fog veiled the prominent buildings of the city, obliterating the white lines in the roads and disorientating Paulene Stone. Temperatures nose-dived and half a million coal fires began to burn in fireplaces across the capital. Sulphur dioxide filled the air, suffocating ninety people to death in twenty-four hours before it spread outwards to twenty-two further counties. The Ministry of Health warned those with heart and chest problems to 'stay indoors and rest as much as possible'. *The Times* reported on 4 December that the only aeroplane given permission to land at London airport came from the Blind Landing Experimental Unit at Bedford. The delighted pilot jumped at the chance to try out his new automatic landing equipment in optimum conditions. However, on 6 December Richard A. Prindle, an American medical researcher on a business trip to London's St Bartholomew's Hospital to discuss potential links between cancer and air pollution, was able to land at Gatwick. The moment Prindle's plane door opened the 'overwhelming' combination of sulphur and coal hit him and on reaching the city he was confronted by 'a continual metallic taste in the mouth and irritation of the nose, pharynx and eyes'. However much Prindle blew and coughed, he could not get rid of the taste as the 'misty gray-brown fog that was cold and made one cough' rolled though the streets edging its noxious way into every crevice.[2]

London was almost empty. It was as if some dreadful warning bell had sounded, telling people to remain inside. The Ministry of Health issued further advice to vulnerable citizens to wear home-made masks, and Prindle passed a few determined people with handkerchiefs tied across their mouths. As he watched them feel their way along street railings, they were brought to a complete standstill, lost in the smoggy environment, choking on engine fumes expelled by car-owners flouting the official advice not to drive. A very few, very ancient Londoners told *The Times* they still remembered first hand the old Dickensian fogs that had turned the ethereal violet hour a still deeper purple. The newspaper speculated that the Victorian novelist's 'master-hand might have exaggerated those famously dense nineteenth-century pea soupers known as the "London Particulars".' But this smog was no fiction. The sulphur levels were even higher than in December 1952, when an estimated 12,000 had died from smog-induced illnesses and a further 150,000 had been hospitalised. On 8 December the *Times* leader, headlined 'Poisoned Air', criticised the 'atmosphere of lethargy' and the 'failure to move promptly over the creation of effective smoke control areas' as outlined in the 1956 Clean Air Act. But everyone knew that the new smokeless fuel laws were often not observed and not monitored. As visibility in the city dropped to ten yards, four lives were lost in impossible driving conditions on motorways. The air smelled old and stale, sluggish and worn out. The smarting in Richard Prindle's eyes reminded him of peeling onions and he was disappointed to find that smoking cigarettes in such an environment had suddenly 'lost all its usual pleasure'. By the end of a smoggy four days, 106 people were dead and 235 had been admitted to hospital. A red warning was sent out by London's Emergency Bed Service that many more were going to be needed.

Up in Leeds sulphur dioxide levels also rose dramatically and in Glasgow pneumonia cases were three times higher than usual. In Salford the smoke pollution was 400 per cent above average for the time of year. Diana Reich, an undergraduate at Manchester University, already weak with chicken pox, felt the polluted air begin to settle on her chest. Within days she was diagnosed with pneumonia and rescued by her parents to recover at home. Concern over pollution had been spreading especially for those like Diana with a weakness that could be further compromised by the contaminated air.[3]

Harold Evans, known to everyone as Harry, was the thirty-two-year-old crusading editor of Durham's *Northern Echo*. His father had been a train driver and his mother a machinist in the local Stockport cotton mill. In the spring of 1962 Harry had been 'taking the air' with his wife Enid, a biology teacher, and their newly arrived baby Kate on the village green of Hurworth-on-Tees, four miles from Darlington, when a mist swirled in, blotting out the bright sky. It was not, he explained, 'a mist of mellow fruitfulness' but instead an all-pervasive stink, reminiscent of decomposing fish and rotten eggs, so powerful it made Harry gag.[4] Heading straight home, Harry tried to console Enid. 'They'll do something about it,' he told her, in what he suspected was a hopeless effort to cheer up not only his wife but himself. He knew as he spoke that he actually had no idea who 'they' were and even if he had he was pretty certain 'they' wouldn't do anything at all.

Hugely popular with his writers, photographers, subeditors, copy boys and inky-fingered, shirtsleeved printers, Harry Evans never failed to praise those who landed a good story or an arresting photograph. His bow tie was adopted by several of the staff, mirroring Harry's enviable jauntiness of mood, his infectious energy and his likeability. But Harry had a private reason for being troubled by the dark skies and thick smoke of Darlington. Not only was he the father of two young children but he was also concerned about the health of his own father Frederick, who had spent long days shovelling coal on the footplates of steam engines. During the war, the sound of Frederick's debilitating cough had punctuated Harry's nights. The cough had never disappeared and Harry, conscious of its cause, was adamant that he would fight the pollution in the spirit that 'something *could* be done and something *should* be done and we weren't just the detritus of the war'.

He was not the only one who felt frustrated by a way of life that was 'all stuck' in an out-of-date world. And he was not the only one who felt the 1960s should be the decade to condemn 'capital punishment, unemployment, the ubiquitous lung-clogging coal slags, prejudice against sexual choice, against people whose skin was a different colour and above all against women'. Harry was increasingly conscious of 'the huge ferment brewing' within like-minded members of his generation. In his position as the editor of a local Northern newspaper, far from the green benches of Westminster, he pledged to himself and for the sake of his father and his wife and children that nothing was going to stand in the way of his campaign for change. Filling the columns of the *Echo* with articles about the poisonous fumes that belched from the exhaust of lorries and roared through northern town centres, he also wrote about the clouds of chemicals that billowed unchecked from dozens of surrounding factories. He printed highly personal stories, such as that of an exasperated housewife who arrived at a Teesside council meeting in the spring of 1962 carrying her polluted laundry as evidence of her case. In the morning she had hung her best white sheets out to dry; by mid afternoon they were black. He spoke to the men who cleaned out the tanks in the chemical factories all round Stockton and Durham. They confided that their wives wouldn't touch them, wouldn't go anywhere near them, let alone go to bed with them; the smell was so bad. The workforce had claimed 'marital rights compensation' but had not been awarded a penny.

For a while, despite Harry's determination, nothing changed. The factories ignored him. The economists dismissed him as a 'fancy writer with fancy ideas'. 'Forget it,' they said. 'It is part of the PROGRESS of industry,' they said. But Harry was not to be rebuffed. What on earth did the 'economists know about black smoke while sitting in their comfortable offices down south'? Suspecting that the Imperial Chemical Industries' (ICI) plant at Billingham was the chief culprit for the 'Teesside smell', Harry had tried to bottle the mist in a test tube to send to London so that the Prime Minister could sniff the evidence. But the fragile glass tube broke before Harry could pack it off to Downing Street. And then the smell went away and Harry thought he had imagined the whole thing. But in December 1962, as the cities of Britain were cloaked in smog, the smell came back and this time it was worse than ever.

At lunch with Rowland Wright, the chairman of the local ICI office, Harry raised the stinking issue. 'But we don't have any pollution,' Wright told him. Any irregularities were caused by a fret coming off the North Sea, a national phenomenon that Harry should interpret as 'God's work'.[5] Harry assured Wright he had '*seen*' this smell. 'It exists,' he insisted. Back in the office Harry gathered his staff. He wanted one of the photographers to record the smell. 'He's gone off his bloody head again,' they said, as all but one of them laughed. That one, Ossie Stanford, came to see Harry a day later to tell him he had got the evidence. Ossie was holding two photographs. One showed a clear blue sky two miles outside Stockton-on-Tees; the other, taken fifteen minutes later in the city, showed how it was impossible to see a hand in front of your face. 'There's your smell,' Stanford announced.

Harry ran the two photographs facing each other as a double-page spread. The telephone rang. Rowland Wright, 'an extremely decent man', was on the other end. 'Yes, you've got us.'

Wright had discovered a small leak from a plant containing ammonia combined with methylamine. The mixture had produced a murky, fetid cloud capable of drifting up to a thousand miles. The mood in the *Northern Echo* was triumphant. ICI pledged to halt any leakage and replace the faulty worn-out plants. A new mobile laboratory ensured the smell was minimised and the workers were given a pay rise of 6d an hour to mitigate any lingering loss of satisfaction in the bedroom.

During the same week that the smog was causing such havoc in Britain, a major conference about pollution was taking place in Washington, DC.

A new book, *Silent Spring*, by American scientist Rachel Carson, was already one of the city's main talking points. In the book Carson described the unrestrained use of pesticides sweeping over rural America's fields, woods and farmlands, and how the presence of a 'grim spectre has crept upon us almost unnoticed'. She spoke of how 'The most alarming of all man's assaults upon the environment is the contamination of air, earth, rivers and sea with dangerous and even lethal materials'. Of particular concern were eight million hectares across nine Southern states, an area fifty times the size of Greater London, which had been sprayed by the American Department of the Environment with one of these chemicals. Pesticides were thought to be the culprits behind the alarming drop in numbers of the bald eagle, America's national bird.

Pesticides were indiscriminate in their destruction and Carson warned that the consequences of their continued use would be to 'still the song of the birds and the leaping of fish in the streams, to coat the leaves with a deadly film and to linger on in the soil'. To some this seemed far-fetched in the extreme, but millions of Americans were traumatised by Carson's cry for action and by her warning that if the rate of chemical contamination of the planet continued, insect and birdsong, animal life, even the quieting of humanity, would result in a silent world. The male-run chemical industry was furious with Carson and contemptuous of her outspokenness. They tried to sue her publisher and publicly discredit her authority. They launched a campaign to attack her for over-reacting, for being unscientific and above all for being a single woman. A letter published in the *New Yorker* magazine said 'we can live without birds and animals but as the current market slump shows, we cannot live without business. As for insects, isn't it just like a woman to be scared to death of a few little bugs?! As long as we have the H-bomb everything will be OK.' And a former Secretary of Agriculture, Ezra Taft Benson, wrote to Former President Eisenhower with the most deflating accusation he could think of when he charged Carson of being a likely communist. Nonetheless, the book became a bestseller. And a movement had begun.[6]

# Chapter Two

*A television set can be as lethal as a gun*

The persistence of the December smog kept people off the streets, out of the parks and away from the pubs. Television offered an alternative form of companionship for the entire family. Children like me were on close terms with Andy Pandy in his voluminous pyjamas, who lived in a picnic basket with his friend the ragdoll Looby Loo. We all knew Bill and Ben, the terracotta men who lived in flower pots and spoke in a satisfying adult-excluding code, and the bumptious conjurer-bear Sooty and his weedy little doggy companion Sweep. All these characters held a significant place in my early imaginative life. The programming on adult television was less sophisticated. The BBC's 1948 censorship guidelines had remained unaltered and unchallenged. They included an absolute ban on 'jokes about lavatories, effeminacy in men and immorality of any kind'. There was a ruling against suggestive material including honeymoon couples, fig leaves, ladies' underwear (e.g. 'winter draws on') and animal habits (e.g. 'rabbits'). And there was a total embargo on 'anything that can be construed as personal abuse of Government Ministers, Party Leaders or MPs'. But by November 1962 it had become clear that the nation's broadcaster needed to catch up with a new movement infiltrating every part of the media.

In 1960 a small group of like-minded undergraduates had set out to use satire to knock the complacency of the British establishment for six. Their influence was already licensing a growing exasperation with the unchallenged deference shown towards stuffy institutions like the Church, the monarchy and Westminster itself. And when satire emerged on television in the winter of 1962 it seemed to give voice to what so many had already been privately thinking.

*Beyond the Fringe*, an amateur theatrical review, had first appeared at the Edinburgh Fringe Festival in August 1960, written by and starring four young wags: Peter Cook and Jonathan Miller (friends from Cambridge University) and Dudley Moore and Alan Bennett (friends from Oxford).

In early 1961, Richard Ingrams and Willie Rushton, who had both been at Shrewsbury School, joined forces with Christopher Booker, a contemporary of Peter Cook's at Cambridge, and cartoonists Gerald Scarfe and Ralph Steadman to launch *Private Eye.* The first issue of the fortnightly satirical magazine resembled a student publication, printed on cheap, yellow, absorbent paper such as one might find in a lavatory.

Although Alan Bennett and Dudley Moore both came from working-class backgrounds, some of the other satirists had grown up firmly rooted in the privileged world that they aimed to dismantle. No venerable or prejudiced institution or viewpoint was exempt from their merciless scrutiny. Their chief target was 'The Establishment', a term first used in 1955 by journalist Henry Fairlie to describe the golden circle of protection that surrounded the two spies Guy Burgess and Donald Maclean. Peter Cook had also adopted the term to christen the club that he had opened in Soho's Greek Street in October 1961, where a medley of music, monologue and irreverence erupted from The Establishment's tiny stage. A beautifully framed, full-colour portrait of Harold Macmillan, the Prime Minister, complete with wartime medals and old Etonian tie, was the tongue-in-cheek bonus gift for all those who signed up for a lifetime's membership.

Barry Humphries, a young Australian comedian recently arrived in London, explained how the 'character' of the club was dictated by its 'early Brutalist' design, the architectural style that was a reaction against artificiality and instead conveyed a look that was raw and unadorned.[1] Sean Kenny, the stage designer of the moment, created the club's interior, where performers would lounge against the long wooden bar at the front, chatting up what Humphries calls the 'satire groupies'. Most of these 'enthusiasts' were friends of Dudley Moore, 'pale-faced girls with fringes' who hung about with their 'pearlised lips and eyes like black darns'.[2] A typical evening at the club consisted of an hour-long show involving a varying cast of entertainers followed by dinner and then jazz. Some of the skits had attracted a favourable press. The *Sunday Pictorial* was a particular admirer and loved the parody on the Crucifixion in which the two thieves complained that Jesus Christ was getting preferential treatment because he had been given a taller cross. The newspaper praised The Establishment for 'serving some of the meatiest jokes in the business'.

But not everyone was amused. Many of the performers, including Barry Humphries, were Peter Cook's personal try-outs. Peter had first made friends with Barry in the Lamb and Flag pub in Covent Garden, where the cast of *Oliver*, in which Humphries was playing Mr Sowerberry the undertaker, would meet between matinees and evening performances. Although Barry found Cook to be 'languid to the point of undulation', he 'never diffused an aura of vanity'. But Cook was intrigued by Barry Humphries, who was perfecting his own dual stage persona. The shrill Mrs Everage (not yet a Dame), whose monologues revolved around her discovery of London, was inspired by the kind of socially ambitious, self-deluded Melbourne housewife that Barry had known since childhood. His second character, Sandy Stone, also Australian, was 'a desiccated old man of the suburbs'. Since his arrival in England in 1959, Barry had been living in straitened circumstances in Elgin Crescent, round the corner from the stalls of Portobello Road Market, where he had learned to rummage for lost threepences in the upholstery of ancient armchairs in order to afford the bus fare to theatrical auditions. Recently he had moved to the superior environment of Highgate and, after leaving a sticky job in the raspberry ripple department of an Acton ice-cream factory, had landed his part in *Oliver*. But the job at The Establishment offered him a chance to try out his own acts on a new and potentially lucrative market.

Ned Sherrin was watching when Edna, Barry's 'slightly pathetic matron clad in a homespun dress', first took to The Establishment stage. John Betjeman, self-described 'poet and hack', was also among the handful of people in the audience. Onstage, Barry plugged on with what in retrospect he felt to be a 'woeful act', delivering the somewhat poignant monologue of Sandy Stone, all too aware of the critics 'crawling out halfway through the performance'. But the *Spectator* critic Bamber Gascoigne forced himself to stay, and his review grudgingly admired 'the care and accuracy of each tiny detail' of the monologue, although he found the overall effect 'distinctly soporific'. The *Daily Mail* described Barry, with his 'lank dirt-coloured lady hair', as like 'an emu in moult'. But that night, after Barry had wept, drunk some sherry and kicked himself for not including a single crowd-pleasing mention of Harold Macmillan, he cheered up when John Betjeman emerged from the shadows and pronounced his act to be 'sheer genius'. In Sandy, Betjeman had found echoes of Mr Pooter, George and Weedon Grossmith's classic comic character, but with Mr P. transported to Melbourne. And although Barry regarded the evening as 'a misjudged performance' from which he 'prefers to avert the memory', the wonderful legacy of his early wit was a lifetime friendship with John Betjeman. Peter Cook also remained steadfastly loyal to a grateful Barry, who was 'never reproached for producing The Establishment's only flop'. Instead, Peter encouraged him to join the illustrator Nicholas Garland in creating *Private Eye*'s Barry McKenzie comic strip, while Sandy Stone lived on in different form as the progenitor of Peter Cook's brilliant E. L. Wisty monologues.

The taste for British satire was also crossing the Atlantic. As Barry Humphries made his debut on The Establishment stage, Peter Cook had been in New York promoting a production of *Beyond the Fringe*, which had been a continuous sell-out since the late autumn. The show had opened in Washington to what the London *Sunday Times* critic described as 'constant convulsive laughter', before moving to New York's Broadway. Unsure whether the British humour and irreverence would travel successfully, the cast was surprised and delighted when *Beyond the Fringe* was greeted with delirious reviews; such a reception meant that the President himself was expected in the audience imminently. Peter Cook was also in the city to launch the American branch of his Greek Street club. Veteran Establishment Club performer John Fortune was in New York preparing for the New Year's opening night when he was asked by the club manager whether he had an 'understandable' objection to working with Theodore Wilson, a black pianist who had been chosen for reasons of economy. Wilson, known as Teddy, who had recorded sessions with all the greats including Billie Holiday, Ella Fitzgerald and Louis Armstrong, was one of the outstanding musicians of the day. Fortune felt he might as well have been asked if he 'minded whether the interior decorator is going to be someone called Picasso'.[3] Early on in the run, John Bird, another member of the cast, hit a nerve with an off-colour joke about sexual performance and how 'there are things you can't do when you've got a bad back'. President Kennedy's office rang the following day warning that 'if that joke is repeated the club will be closed down'. While the President's problems with his health, and specifically his back, were known to journalists if not always to the wider public, the President's prodigious love life was strictly off-limits. But it was impossible to stem Kennedy gossip and Bird did not, of course, heed any injunction to stay away from 'sensitive' topics: subjects like these were the satirist's life-blood.

A little late in catching the satirical wind, Grace Wyndham-Goldie, Head of BBC Current Affairs, and Hugh Greene, the new Director-General, set about creating a live, late-night television programme that would 'prick the pomposity of public figures'. Greene's plans for a shake-up show had in part been inspired by the German political cabaret of the Weimar Republic. But it was the enthusiasm of Ned Sherrin, producer of the BBC's live *Tonight* programme, that finally convinced the high-ups to make the radical move. Attempts to televise journalist Michael Frayn's satirical *Guardian* columns had not come off, but on 24 November 1962 the first episode of *That Was the Week That Was* had attracted an audience of four million. The programme was fronted and produced not by angry young men, but by 'Exasperated Young Men', their exasperation fuelled by 'Britain's recurring failures, by hypocrisy and the shabbiness of its politics'.[4]

*TW3*, as it quickly became known, had picked up with pinpoint antennae the emergent mood of 'ferment' that Harry Evans had also detected. The programme was fronted by David Frost, the son of a Methodist preacher from Kent, who dressed in an ill-fitting grey suit, his forward-brushed hairline arranged with precision. The appointment of the twenty-three-year-old former occasional cabaret artist who had performed in Cambridge University's Footlights was greeted with some uncertainty by his colleagues. Peter Cook accused him of being a 'bubonic plagiarist' for stealing Cook's own imitation of Harold Macmillan. Old Etonian actor Jonathan Cecil congratulated Frost on 'that wonderfully silly voice', only to discover that his distinctive nasal tone was not a put-on. But the presenter's name, as well as suiting the chilly season, carried with it the hint of cynicism associated with self-confident, well-informed, sharp-as-an-icicle youthfulness, and Ned Sherrin knew that in Frost he had found the best front man for the show.

In a television interview years later, Frost explained how the intention had been 'to be as free late on a Saturday night as people are in conversation and to be funny about important things rather than about mothers-in-law with frying pans on their heads'. *TW3* targeted, teased, mocked, exposed and satirised every twitch and blink and dearly held, privileged and bigoted idiosyncrasy of Britain's upper-class and professional institutions and because the programme came under 'current affairs' it could get away with a lot more than if it had been classified as 'entertainment'. No topic was taboo, even the monarchy, although when the live audience was invited to propose a 'subject' for coverage the ever-quick Frost reminded them that 'the Queen was not *a subject*'.[5]

In 'The Consumers' Guide to Religion' David Frost discussed whether the best all-round deal was to be found in Judaism, Catholicism, Protestantism, Islam, Buddhism or the only non-secular religion, Communism, 'whose chief prophet appears to have no background in the industry at all'. The programme concluded that the best buy was the C of E, 'a jolly good little faith for a very moderate outlay'. The Bishop of Swansea and Brecon condemned the show as 'in deplorably bad taste'. But vicars picked up on the debate for their Sunday sermons while John Robinson, Bishop of Woolwich, was preparing to go further with the imminent publication of his book *Honest to God*, in which he questioned the age-old concept of an elderly bearded man looking down from heaven on his flock in church. Robinson argued that God is all around us, mainly to be found in love and not just buried in impenetrable religious texts or floating about on an equally inaccessible snow-white cloud.

As well as the Church, *TW3* seized any chance to attack the law, the police force, scientists and above all politicians. The out-of-touch Tory Chancellor of the Exchequer, Reginald Maudling, was a favourite butt of jokes. The weekly Maudling item saw a *TW3* spoof character ending meetings with the unemployed with a cheery, 'I don't know about you but I've got work to do.' And no week went by without a good riff on the Tory Prime Minister and his formidable wife 'Dot'. The lyrics of *TW3*'s theme song, sung by twenty-eight-year-old actress and comedian Millicent Martin, changed every week to reflect current events. Martin was one of only two women on an otherwise all-male show (the other was Eleanor Bron, Cambridge graduate and yet another friend of Peter Cook). Donald Zec in the *Sunday Pictorial* could not get enough of Martin: 'Though she emits a sound like a circular saw gnashing through tree trunks she is as devastating as Cleopatra.' Each week, as the viewing figures soared, Martin, with her Zec-approved 'red hair, smoky blue eyes, soft peachy lips', and proud of her 'cyanide wouldn't melt in my mouth' technique, was joined by a variety of well-known funny men, from Bernard Levin and Lance Percival to Willie Rushton and Roy Kinnear.

Guest performers of the week included the innuendo-driven, but slightly past-it at the age of forty-five, comedian Frankie Howerd. He had been working as a stand-up in The Establishment when he bumped into Frost having his famous quiff expensively serviced under the dryer at the hairdresser and was invited to join the television show. Flattered to be included in the Oxbridge line-up, Howerd jumped at the chance as he recognised that 'to be filthy these days you've got to have been to university'.[6] Howerd's position at the heart of this liberal, audacious group was personally gratifying because his manager Dennis Heymer, a former wine waiter at the Dorchester Hotel, was also Howerd's secret lover. Scriptwriter Christopher Booker welcomed 'the freedom with which *TW3* addressed politics and morality and the way it showed on screen the audience, lights and cameras in a darkened studio, to create an air of gritty informality'.[7] There had never been a television programme like it. Members of the live audience, which often included famous faces, were encouraged to relax in their seats with a tumbler of what co-presenter Willie Rushton divulged to be 'the most appalling mulled wine'. While those watching in the studio revelled in being picked on for merciless lampooning, a motherly woman called Mrs Reynolds dispensed liberal quantities of refreshments to the presenters from her drinks trolley. Positive reactions to a show that Sherrin had feared would be 'ghetto television' came from unlikely places. The *Daily Telegraph* judged it to be 'brilliant' and 'a demonstration that a television set can be as lethal as a gun'. The *Guardian* said that 'although satire has always been scarce on television this programme shows that wit and mockery can be successful. Uneven wit and mockery, but excellent at its best.' But by the time the third show aired in early December, a satisfactory number of complaints were mounting. The *Daily Mail* summed up the material that had aroused most public objections: 'A small harmony group of Cardinals sang "Arrivederci Roma" – the Prime Minister was insulted – one of his TV recordings was distorted – Bernard Levin was rude to Mr Charles Forte (who was in the live audience) and a sketch about fly buttons brought the house down.' But the viewing figures continued to rise each week as the very subjects of the attacks and jokes cancelled their Saturday-night dinner parties in order to watch. Just as copies of *Private Eye* were mysteriously snapped up from a stand outside the swanky Ritz Hotel, so the gilded elite gathered round their television sets with as much eagerness as their persecutors. By Christmas, twelve million people were hooked.

Among those who condemned the programme was Mary Whitehouse. The forty-two-year-old Shropshire school teacher who heard some of the pupils she taught in a pioneering sex education class discussing a television programme that was playing 'merry hell' with a long list of what Mary held as the tenets of civilised society, including 'the monarchy, moral values, law and order and religion'. With the programme's portrayal of sex as 'nothing more than an obsession with orgasm',[8] Mrs Whitehouse wondered what the world was coming to.

Harold Macmillan himself had no time for what he had called the 'hot, pitiless probing eye' of television,[9] spending every spare minute reading books, devouring at least a hundred a year. The only television at Birch Grove, his home in Sussex, was in the servants' hall. Macmillan felt that 'aggressive interviewing' of politicians risked associating entertainment with people being 'as rude as possible'. But even if Macmillan did not encourage the televising of his own profession's business or indeed watch *TW3*, he understood the programme's value. The publicity must at least mean he was still relevant. On hearing of the intention of Reginald Bevins, the Postmaster General and the BBC's licenser, to cancel *TW3*, Macmillan's response was unambiguous: 'Oh no you won't. It is better to be mocked than to be ignored.' But finding the right balance between relevance and the media's growing desire to enquire into the private lives of public figures was proving less straightforward. And Macmillan knew that the popularity of the satirists had accelerated a nascent public desire to enquire more rigorously into the goings-on of those who ran the country.

# Chapter Three

## *Huntley and Palmers*

When Wilfred Brambell, the fifty-year-old star of the BBC TV drama *Steptoe and Son*, arrived at West London Magistrates Court on 6 December, the smog was still thickening the air. *Steptoe* had aired first in January 1962 and by December Brambell had become a household name. But the actor was in trouble. He had been accused of 'smiling' at another man through the window of a public urinal. Usually it was the behaviour of Brambell's fictional character Albert Steptoe, a curmudgeonly, unwashed, unshaven, lecherous, sweary, prejudiced-about-everything rag-and-bone man, that came under scrutiny. The drama had been inspired by the almost vanished Romany street-traders who lived in Notting Dale, the network of back lanes and alleys that bordered the London districts of Shepherd's Bush and Notting Hill. A few of them worked the Chelsea streets too, and the clatter and clank of the rusty, rubble-laden carts outside my own bedroom window in London was as familiar as the chime of the ice-cream van in the summer. *Steptoe and Son*'s fictional scrapyard was in Oil Drum Lane and Albert Steptoe, the geriatric character at its centre, was based on Arthur Arnold, a real life 'totter', Notting Dale slang for a bone collector. With his beaky nose, wicked leer and half-rotten, half-missing teeth, Albert Steptoe was regularly spotted rummaging in the suet topping of his steak and kidney pudding for his lost falsies and eating pickled onions in the bath. And he had a real aversion to anything 'poofy' or remotely effeminate.

Comedy programmes in the early 1960s had become a surreptitious excuse for airing every sort of prejudice, and every reprehensible side of human fallibility, both moral and physical, despite the criticism of those who privately found such content unacceptable. But there was nothing funny about the prejudice that Brambell would attract off-screen if the secrets of his personal life were to be revealed. He had been arrested outside the public lavatories in Shepherd's Bush Green for, as *The Times* explained, 'persistently importuning for an immoral purpose'. 'Importuning' had become a verb highly familiar to those who followed the reports of such scandals. Making his way slowly in his lawyer's car through the foggy streets from court to the scene of the alleged crime, Brambell was accompanied by Mr Seymour Collins, the magistrate who wished to inspect for himself the place where the 'act' was said to have taken place. Brambell had described to the court how in November he had left a particularly riotous pre-Christmas cocktail party at the nearby BBC headquarters and realised he was 'absolutely sloshed' and 'extremely fuddled'. As a result, he had gone into the nearest lavatory for the exclusive purpose for which lavatories are provided. When questioned he claimed to have no recollection of either peering in through the windows of the lavatory or having any communication, spoken or otherwise, with anyone when he was inside the lavatory. But as he was emerging into the street a couple of policemen stopped him and put him under arrest. At first he thought the whole thing was a joke but the expression on the policemen's faces was serious and Brambell became frightened. He did not reveal to the court that the source of his real fear was neither being arrested nor being sent to prison. What Brambell feared most was the terrible damage the revelation of his homosexuality would do to his professional life.

Despite the publication of the Wolfenden Report in 1957, and the hope that prejudice was dissipating, homosexuality remained illegal and the merest whiff of a rumour could still end careers. Such stigma was attached to the very mention of the 'condition' that during the committee's discussions the Chairman, Sir John Wolfenden, protected the delicacy of the women present by using the coded phrase 'Huntley and Palmers'— the biscuit manufacturers – Huntleys for homosexuals, Palmers for prostitutes. The report had recommended that consenting sex between men over the age of twenty-one should be decriminalised but by 1962 it had still not become law. While Rab Butler, the former Home Secretary, knew the bill would not be passed as long as people viewed sex between men as 'a great social evil', the *Daily Mail* had greeted the report's leniency with horror. 'If the law were to tolerate homosexual acts,' it said, 'a great barrier against depravity would be swept aside.' The campaign to change hearts and minds and establish a societal acceptance of gay people and 'homosexual acts' still seeemed insuperable.

The persecution of queer men was buttressed not only by the newspapers who used innuendo and outright condemnation to demolish reputations but also by undercover police officers posing as gay men on the pick-up. In order to mitigate distress, the homosexual community boosted morale with a series of larkily alliterative nicknames for the police. 'Watch out for Hilda Handcuffs,' they would warn, and, 'Here comes Betty Bracelets.'

The acting profession had long been a popular target for police keen on exposing illegal sex. Almost a decade earlier, in October 1953, the actor John Gielgud had been arrested and accused of 'persistently importuning male persons for immoral purposes' in a King's Road lavatory. Although Gielgud was fined under another name by the Chelsea magistrate, an undercover reporter for the *Evening Standard* recognised the famous actor's voice and blew the story open. That night a photograph of Gielgud filled the front page. But Sybil Thorndike, his co-star in an upcoming play, set the pace for all 'Johnny G's' loyal friends when she greeted him at rehearsals with a hug, exclaiming, 'Oh John, you have been a silly bugger.' A few weeks later she invited a supportive opening-night audience to stand and cheer him.

The establishment was at odds with audiences and friends. A long-expected knighthood was withheld and Gielgud was warned by the British Embassy in Washington that he would not be granted a visa to travel to America for work. The *Sunday*

*Express* commented how the homosexual 'rot has flourished behind a protective veil until it is now a widespread disease'. Gielgud later admitted that he had considered suicide to be his only remaining option.

Dirk Bogarde was another well-known actor driven to disguise his sexual preferences. The reviews of the 1961 thriller *Victim*, a chilling movie starring the handsome Bogarde as Melville Farr, a married lawyer hemmed in by blackmailers threatening to reveal his unconsummated sexual desire for men, had been riddled with euphemism and coyly concealed prejudice. It was filmed partly in the Salisbury Pub in St Martin's Lane in Covent Garden, one of many real-life homosexual meeting places in the capital, and critics used phrases like 'the abnormality', 'the condition' and 'the invert' to describe Farr's illegal practice. Even though Bogarde was often photographed with desirable female co-stars like Sylvia Syms, the whispers that he had much in common with his fictional counterpart grew alongside speculation about the exact nature of his relationship with his business manager Anthony Forwood.

Wilfred Brambell managed to survive his ordeal. After Judge Collins had inspected the window in the Shepherd's Bush convenience, Brambell's trial resumed on 12 December. Although Brambell was found guilty of the crime of 'smiling' at another man, Mr Collins gave him a conditional discharge for a year and fined him court costs of twenty-five guineas, providing a glimmer of hope that such an implicit show of tolerance might one day be shared by other magistrates. But the experience had been shattering for Brambell. Already known for his reclusive ways, he withdrew even further from everything except the television cameras and the role he played that disguised his true self.

Top advocates were employed to help with such cases, including politicians, who were not exempt from the threat of sexual persecution. Civil servant Mortimer Wilmot Bennitt, an under-secretary at the Ministry of Public Buildings and Works, had been charged that winter for 'Making Advances Towards Men In A Public Lavatory'. When the case finally came to the Old Street Magistrates Court in London,[1] the magistrate was unprepared for the perfectly logical explanation given by Bennitt's barrister Jeremy Hutchinson QC, one of the greatest advocates of his generation. Bennitt's defence as laid out by Hutchinson rested on a sumptuous dinner and accompanying drinks that Bennitt had thoroughly enjoyed at the Institute of Builders' dinner at Guildhall on the evening in question. Hutchinson outlined the alcoholic inventory to the court in vividly contextual detail. There had been 'sherry in the ante room, sherry with the soup, hock with the fish, burgundy with the meat, champagne with the sweet at which there was also port and finally brandy'. Such generous libation had left Mr Bennitt with a pressing need for relief. However, as Jeremy Hutchinson informed the jury, the unfortunate Mr Bennitt suffered from a 'physical difficulty passing water' when overlooked by any other person who might also be using the convenience. On entering the lavatory in Islington in which the 'importuning' was alleged to have taken place, Mr Bennitt had needed to make sure he was all alone. His acknowledgement of other men in the lavatory was merely a polite recognition of their presence as he waited for them to leave. This explanation did not convince the magistrate, who fined Mr Bennitt £25 with £10 costs.[2] And there were others, similarly targeted.

Foreign Office minister Ian Harvey had been caught in 1958 with a guardsman in St James's Park and in 1961 Home Office Minister Charles Fletcher-Cooke was found living with a one-time borstal boy, forcing his resignation. And then there was the recent 'Vassall affair'. In October 1962 John Vassall, a British Foreign Office clerk who had previously worked in the British Embassy in Moscow, had been tried and sentenced to prison for eighteen years for spilling classified beans after being blackmailed with compromising photographs that showed him spinning a pair of men's underpants on one finger as he lay in bed with a man. Vassall, also defended by Jeremy Hutchinson, claimed that he had been drugged, but the publicity the case attracted saw a spike in the media's if not the public's homosexual prejudice. Six months after the case had come to an end the *Sunday Mirror* published tips on 'How to spot a homo', highlighting those with 'a consuming interest in youths' and 'an unnaturally strong affection for his mother'. Homosexual men might 'wear silk shirts and sit up at chichi bars with full-bosomed ladies'. They might wrestle, play golf, ski and lift weights. They would go to any lengths to conceal their true nature, including giving 'their wives a black eye when they get back from the working men's clubs'. The newspaper cautioned that 'you can and will meet them in London's Bond Street', and warned they had also been found in 'Tokyo's Ginza, Rome's Via Veneto, Glasgow's Sauchiehall Street, the Road to Mandalay and the street where you live'. But those on the alert need not worry as 'anyone with a gram of sense can *smell* the homos'.

There were some GPs who offered a 'cure' for homosexuality. Aversion therapy, in which deliberately induced pain was associated with undesirable behaviour, had been used to cure thumb sucking, over-eating and paedophilia, but in the 1960s it was a solution of last resort for men like nineteen-year-old Colin Fox from Manchester. Colin had been working in the rag trade, concealing his homosexuality from his family and preventing their discovery that he was not 'the nice Jewish boy' they wished him to be. Meanwhile, he lived 'in fear of going to gaol'. Colin sought help at a Manchester psychiatric hospital where a cable protruding from a 12-volt car battery was wound around his leg. Colin received an electric jolt every time he was shown a photograph of a man. A photograph of a woman was produced whenever the current was switched off. Speaking in a BBC television documentary over thirty years later, Colin remembered how 'the pain terrified me', describing the sensation as 'excruciating'. The process 'was much worse than touching a live electric cable. I knew it was coming and would tense up in anticipation.' Colin persisted with the sessions because he knew homosexual feelings were 'wrong'. But he also knew the treatment would not work.[3]

The further homosexuality was pushed underground, the more resourceful men became about finding places to meet. Decades earlier the poets Christopher Isherwood and W. H. Auden used to meet at the Turkish baths in London's Jermyn Street and Bermondsey. More recently some theatre and cinema managers turned a blind eye to what went on in the stalls. Public lavatories such as the one visited by Wilfred Brambell were riskier venues for assignations. In the 1950s Brian Epstein, a young Liverpudlian clerk in the Royal Army Service Corps, had been caught in the Army and Navy Club in Piccadilly dressed up in the fake uniform of an officer. Sent to a sympathetic army psychiatrist, Brian had felt able to confess his homosexuality but was nonetheless thrown out of the army, explaining to family and friends back in Liverpool that he had been let go 'on medical grounds'. In 1956, aged twenty-two, he had enrolled at RADA, the prestigious London acting school, where he'd found himself increasingly drawn to the margins of risk. A year later he had been arrested for 'persistent importuning' in the Swiss Cottage public conveniences. His written defence was passionate: 'I feel deeply because I have always felt deeply for the persecuted, the Jews, the coloured people, for the old and society's misfits. The damage, the lying criminal methods of the police in importuning me and consequently capturing me leaves me cold, stunned and finished.'[4] He was spared prison but his career as an actor was over.

On returning home to Liverpool, Brian started work in the family furniture store where his efficiency, impeccable record-keeping and popularity with the staff impressed his father. He was promoted to be the manager of the family's North End Music Stores, known locally as NEMS, a successful music and record shop in Whitechapel in the centre of Liverpool, while his family remained unaware of his double life. He would seek 'escape in the cool and cultivated dusk of the front stalls of the Liverpool Playhouse', enjoying the company of men like himself at The Basnett Bar, The Magic Clock and The Old Stork, which welcomed a happily queer and bohemian artsy crowd. Introduced to these sanctuaries by his friend Joe Flannery, a former waiter at the Adelphi Hotel and now a manager of a couple of pop bands in the city, Brian joined a group he could trust. Here he found 'a genuine honest vibrant community' that revelled in friendship, in the pleasure of sharing conversation and as safe a sexual camaraderie as was possible in Liverpool in 1962.

But Brian, described by Joe as 'very fragile but rather elegant . . . a rather exquisite piece of porcelain', was looking for more excitement.[5] During a night-time encounter down at the docks, Brian's wallet was stolen and he arrived at Joe's flat with his shirt ripped open to the waist, blood pouring from his nose on to his white shirt, his lip cut, his cheekbone bruised, and grateful to be mopped up and comforted by his friend. Conscious that Brian's position within a prominent rich Jewish family made him all the more vulnerable to threats, Joe warned Brian to avoid the 'queer-bashing' gangs who blackmailed and beat their victims into submission. He also tried to persuade Brian to tell his parents that he was homosexual, a risk Joe felt he must take if Brian was to lance the potential poison of blackmail. Eventually, after Brian found the courage to confide to 'them at home' about 'who I am', to his surprise and relief they were 'wonderful about it' and he felt encouraged to move on with his life.

Number 19 Gambier Terrace offered another safe haven. The top floor was advertised discreetly in the *Liverpool Echo* as providing a drop-in for all those 'in need of a confidential chat'.[6] Some men risked the journey only to find themselves unable to walk up the flight of Georgian steps to the front door, paralysed by the terrifying prospect of confiding their illegal secret. Watching from the upper windows, Dave, who ran the drop-in with his partner, would see the young lads standing below, rigid with apprehension and sometimes in tears. He would run downstairs to rescue them, give them a cup of coffee and encourage them to speak openly. Pockets of acceptance were unusual, but open-mindedness and compassion or perhaps even better, indifference, marked the response of those individuals for whom prejudice held no place. When he lived on the Isle of Wight, writer Philip Norman remembered how the passengers on the local Southern Vectis bus loved John Thomas, their regular conductor, who carried out his work with efficiency and flair. Dispensing tickets on the green and cream bus, wearing bell-bottom trousers, fluorescent socks and strappy high heels, John sashayed up and down the aisle. In the early days of his unashamed exhibitionism he was derided with cat calls of 'pansy' and 'fairy'. But he faced down the opposition and gradually the name-calling subsided, was replaced with respect and affection. Sustained by his audience, John Thomas thrived on the passengers' applause.

Although female homosexuality was not illegal, it often carried with it a similar antipathy and the consequent secrecy, shame and anxiety. Officially the lesbian 'condition' was regarded as a 'sexual deviation' and because of the legality, or at least the absence of illegality, women were not coerced into aversion treatment in the same way as men. However, some women voluntarily sought a 'cure'. Helen Spandler and Sarah Carr's fascinating research published in the *Lancet* in April 2019 uncovered the cases of several women who received electric shock treatment in Crumpsall Hospital in Manchester in 1962–3. But instead of feeling a new attraction for men, these women simply reported feeling 'terrible'. Several women in Newcastle, London and Leicester were given LSD and shown pictures of men as they went through the hallucinogenic experience in the expectation that they would transfer their sexual preferences from women to men. The experiment was equally unsuccessful. A few doctors were sympathetic. A psychiatrist at the Tavistock Hospital in London told one woman who had tried to kill herself that her condition was merely as idiosyncratic as writing with a left hand. This woman's sexual choice was simply a natural part of her individuality. 'You are sexually left-handed,' she was told, an opinion that offered considerable comfort.

Some psychiatrists actively encouraged lesbians to seek out like-minded women. In London, not far from where our family lived, a green door at the side of a house in Bramerton Street just off the King's Road opened on to a staircase that led to a sparsely lit nightclub. Unlisted in the London telephone directory, Gateways had been founded in 1931 and in the 1960s was run by Gina Ware, friendly and glamorous in her full red lipstick, the daughter of Italian parents.[7] Gina's clientele was distinctively dressed. The 'butches' with their cropped hair wore drainpipe trousers, shirts with bow ties and cufflinks and V-necked sweaters that were 'shed when dancing', according to Lesley, one of the regulars. Winkle-pickers were the favoured shoes because the turn-up at the end 'made it easier to do the twist'. Bosoms were bandaged tight, 'panties' were stuffed with a strategically placed sock. In contrast the 'femmes' wore high heels, starchy skirts, full make-up and always carried a handbag. Couples took to the dance floor without inhibition, where they 'clung to each other, kissed each other, fondled each other, stroked each other as they danced,' and 'throbbed erotically' as they moved.[8]

Esme Langley, Gateways member and single mother of three, was planning to set up a newsletter called *Arena Three.* Having suffered discrimination herself for her unmarried status, Langley wanted to give lesbians a published voice and 'to collaborate in research into the homosexual condition, especially as it concerns women; and to disseminate information to those genuinely in the quest of enlightenment'. There were plans to start a women's club called The Minorities Research Group early in January 1963. But married women who wanted to join the MRG learned that existing 'Limited Company' rules required them to first obtain their husbands' permission to do so in writing. Men also fought to keep women from encroaching on their own gender-exclusive sanctuaries. In a letter to *The Times,* Mr Nathaniel Gubbins expressed his view about the lax implementation of men's club rules. 'Most men join clubs to avoid women,' he argued. 'After all, you can meet women anywhere without paying a subscription for the privilege. Members regard their clubs as male sanctuaries not because they hate women, but because women are never happy on mixed social occasions unless a man is dancing attendance on them.' He continued to expand his thesis on female frailty. 'They are too tired to light their own cigarettes (if they have any), too weak to open doors and too fragile to stand if there is a man to offer his chair or bar stool.'[9]

On 20 December 1962 Norman Josiffe, a twenty-two-year-old horse trainer from Devon, with thick curly hair and an elastically expressive mouth, arrived with a battered suitcase and in an agitated state at the front desk of Chelsea's police station in London. A few tatty Christmas decorations hung above the reception desk as Josiffe announced to Detective Inspector Robert Huntley that he would like to make a statement about 'my homosexual relations with Jeremy Thorpe MP'.[10] He explained that he had been having a 'horrible' affair for more than a year with the charismatic old Etonian, and Liberal Member of Parliament. Josiffe's Roman Catholic conscience had recently been tweaked by a priest in nearby Westminster Cathedral who, on hearing Josiffe's confession, refused to let him off the hook unless he promised never to sin again with a man. Denied the absolution he craved, by bringing his story to the police, despite having to admit his own participation in homosexual acts, Josiffe was now seeking both sympathy and revenge. Speaking to Detective Huntley in a tone of urgency, Josiffe said that he did not wish anyone else to be abused in the manner he had recently experienced. He claimed that Thorpe had made him sleep on a camp bed after sex, that Thorpe was being unfaithful to Josiffe with any old pick-up and that after carrying out his plan to assassinate Thorpe, Josiffe would kill himself. He did not hold back on details of hotel-room encounters or Thorpe's practised and efficient use of Vaseline and other lubricants. Pulling out several letters from the suitcase, letters written to him by the MP who 'has caused me so much purgatory', Josiffe also handed over a postcard sent by Thorpe to Brecht Van de Vater, the owner of the Cotswold stables where Josiffe had been employed and where he had met Thorpe in 1961. The postcard was dated February 1960, shortly after the announcement of the photographer Tony Armstrong-Jones's engagement to Princess Margaret. 'What a pity,' Thorpe had written. 'I rather hoped to marry the one and seduce the other.' Josiffe insisted these papers provided evidence of Thorpe's homosexuality. As well as the postcard (which Josiffe had stolen from Vater when he left his employment), two particularly incriminating letters from Thorpe to Josiffe included the sentences 'my angel all I want to do is to share a Devon farm with you' and, using Thorpe's playful nickname for them both, 'Bunnies can and will go to France.'[11]

After Josiffe completed his lengthy statement he agreed to be subjected to an 'intimate' medical examination which confirmed that Josiffe was indeed a 'passive' homosexual. Detective Huntley contacted the Barnstaple police asking if they could find any corroborating evidence suggesting the Liberal MP, tipped by many to go all the way to the political top, was indeed a practising homosexual. No evidence was found. As Josiffe left the police station feeling calmer and planning to return to Thorpe's flat for Christmas, the Chelsea police expected to hear no more from him on the matter. The letters were forwarded to the Assistant Commissioner at Scotland Yard, who locked them away in the office safe along with other uncomfortable documents concerning leading figures of the establishment. And there they stayed, out of sight and, for the moment, out of mind.

In December 1962 cover-ups were simply part and parcel of how things were done. The police force would not have contemplated taking action that might have demolished the reputation of a leading politician, even if the evidence against him (and it was invariably a 'him') was unarguable: better to keep it hidden under lock and key. Several more years would elapse before the recommendations of the Wolfenden Report became law. But the myriad examples of secrecy and the intolerable stress that this secrecy placed on the homosexual community had begun to infiltrate a national conversation about gay rights. Whether it was held in a doctor's surgery, on a bus on the Isle of Wight or in a new magazine for gay women, this was a conversation conducted at a volume higher than a whisper.

# Chapter Four

## *White people only*

Prejudice was levelled not only at those whose sexual orientation was not shared by the majority. A government report titled 'The Colour Problem' published in 1955 had estimated that two-thirds of Britain's white population held a 'low opinion of black people or disapproved of them'. A third resisted any contact with non-whites, would not acknowledge mixed-race marriages and refused to work with black people or even permit them to come into their houses, feeling they 'should not be allowed in Britain at all'. And just as the recommendations of the Wolfenden Report continued to remain ineffective, the concerns voiced by Labour politicians, including leader Hugh Gaitskell, about racial injustice had not yet led to any significant change beyond the asking of questions.

In the winter of 1962 'Colour' remained a source of prejudice and even entertainment. That winter *The Black and White*

*Minstrel Show* was one of television's most popular programmes as well as being a hit musical at London's Victoria Palace Theatre. Faces of white male dancers and singers were boot-polish blackened and their lips and eyes circled in white pan-stick make-up as they sang songs from the American Deep South, including 'Mammy', 'The Swanee River' and 'Old Black Joe'.

The complex Commonwealth Immigrants Act had come into operation on 1 June 1962. It sought, through new, far-reaching and bureaucratic powers and regulations, to restrict the entry of black migrants from Commonwealth countries and only permitted those with government-issued employment vouchers to settle in Britain. The Act was condemned by Hugh Gaitskell, Leader of the Labour Party, as 'cruel and brutal anti-colour legislation', and the day after the Act became law a test case proved how the legislation could be stretched to prejudicial extremes. On 2 June 1962 Carmen Bryan,[1] a twenty-two-year-old Jamaican who had been living and working legally in England since 1960, pleaded guilty at Paddington Magistrates Court to petty larceny having been caught shoplifting goods worth £2. Carmen had been working in the same welding factory as her fiancé but illness had landed her in hospital and after her recovery she found herself out of a job. The theft had been the result of a single moment of desperation. But the court decided Carmen must be deported to Jamaica, despite being engaged to be married. She was detained in Holloway Prison for six weeks with no access to legal advice, no opportunity to meet representatives from the Jamaican High Commission and no permission to see her fiancé or any of her friends. She had no family of her own in Britain. The case reached the desk of

Henry Brooke the Home Secretary, who insisted that shoplifting was no 'trivial' offence and that Carmen must still be deported. But the Opposition did not find the treatment of Carmen to be 'trivial' and her circumstances reached the debating chamber of the House of Commons where Eric Fletcher, Labour MP for Islington East was her chief defender. He asked Brooke whether it was the Government's intention to treat Commonwealth immigrants 'worse than aliens and to use their powers in respect of trivial offences of this kind – on a first offence?'[2] Carmen was left with the impossible choice of leaving the country and her fiancé or remaining in a British prison indefinitely. With MPs calling across the floor of the House so loudly for Brooke's resignation, the Speaker had to call them to order. Eventually Brooke gave way under Labour's pressure and in July Carmen was released. She was married within a month. Although Eric Fletcher was not convinced that all these cases would find such 'leniency', it was some consolation that the matter had been aired at the highest political level. Tolerance of racial prejudice as condoned by law had been flagged as no longer acceptable.

And even if you were black and 'lucky' enough to have found a home in Britain, the struggle for acceptance could centre around the smallest details of life. Terri Quaye, a twenty-two-year-old jazz singer, knew Christmas in London had begun when the postman delivered a leaky package of mangoes, pawpaw and breadfruit sent by her grandfather from the Caribbean together with 'black, black Christmas cake dripping with rum'.[3] But in order to fit into life as a black woman in London, Terri would subject her hair to a burning solution that made her scalp flame so fiercely that she had to grip the arms of the hairdresser's chair, a process she had endured since the age of eleven. Her maternal grandmother was a white woman who had been victimised by her East End neighbours for marrying first a Barbadian and then a Jamaican. She was Terri's first line of defence when Terri's father, also a jazz singer, resenting his daughter's success, hit her with such force that he almost blinded her in one eye. Avoiding clubs where her father played, Terri chose to sing in the Mandrake just off Wardour Street and the Flamingo round the corner where, in the winter of 1962, she joined Georgie Fame and the Blue Flames and where prejudice knew no place.

Being black in Britain meant being forever on guard. Signs on front doors in Notting Hill displayed cards outlining what was referred to as 'The Colour Bar' and declaring there should be 'No blacks, no Irish, Europeans only' or 'White People Only' or 'English only' or 'No Dogs' and sometimes even 'No Children'. Notting Hill was a magnet for West Indians, many of whom had arrived in England by boat in the 1950s. The Jamaican government's main advice for those embarking on a new life (because 'to go abroad was to say goodbye') was to 'Dress for the Cold' and unfamiliar socks, sweaters, scarves and coats were bought at ill-afforded expense in preparation for their new homeland. But instead of finding roads paved with pay packets, these hopefuls had been confronted with bureaucratic employment restrictions, drab, colourless streets, the unusual sight of fires burning inside houses for warmth as opposed to fires burning outside for cooking, and racial suspicion and obstruction on every street corner. Brothels lined the streets around Notting Hill's Powys Square and the sound of jazz spilled into the night air from the adjacent Blues Club. Memories of the Notting Hill Race Riots in the summer of 1958 had not faded and the campaign against racist attacks was as determined as ever. Colin Prescod, a long-term Notting Hill resident, led a brave crusade to ensure 'whiteness would have to adjust its attitude to blackness'. But frequent police raids were still carried out on the Blues Club as well as on other nearby music venues, including Fiesta One and the Calypso. Persecution was relentless.

The most iniquitous area of discrimination lay in the cost of rent, which was outside police jurisdiction. The extortionate price for accommodation was hiked ever higher by the huge demand caused by the mass influx of immigrants and the shortage of available places to live. In the mid 1950s dozens of still-untouched bombed-out streets had attracted a band of callous opportunists who bought up houses in deplorable conditions offering them at the cheapest rents to the innocent and the desperate. Once-decent neighbourhoods had become slums, and whole streets had been ruined by landlords of whom Peter Rachman was the most ruthless.

A Jewish soldier from the Ukraine, Peter Rachman had arrived in Britain after his parents died in a concentration camp in 1940. Never forgetting the deprivation and persecution of his youth, he kept loaves of bread and rolls of cash beneath his mattress. Nor had he forgotten the miasma of anti-Semitic loathing that engulfed him during childhood. Between his demobilisation in 1948 and 1957 Rachman had bought up 150 houses largely in Notting Hill, raising the roof for rents to tenants who could barely afford to eat. Initially regarded as something of a saviour by the Jamaicans who he 'helped' find places to live when they disembarked at Britain's ports, his own henchmen, often immigrants themselves, became so notorious that by 1960 'Rachmanism' had become a noun denoting brutal behaviour. Charming enough to win the romantic attention of women, Rachman billed himself as an 'entrepreneur'. The truth was that he ran an empire based on prostitution and 'business' ventures involving the leading lights of London's criminal underworld.

Rachman was the inspiration and role model for other unsavoury individuals, including fellow Notting Hill property king Herbert Mortiboy. 'Naughty Morty', as he was known locally, had the doleful air of an undertaker and walked with an apologetic hunch. When interviewed for the *Sunday Times* in the 1970s by journalist and writer James Fox, Morty still spoke with the 'metallic and piercing' accent distinctive to the Portobello Road. He had been in the real estate business since after the war. In his dark funereal suit and heavy rimmed glasses, his eyes lowered to the ground, Naughty Morty stalked an empire that stretched from Notting Hill over the border into Paddington. Publicly he distanced himself from Rachman, who he considered 'lived and played too fast'. Mortiboy on the other hand claimed that he dealt with his tenants 'on a comparatively friendly basis'. But despite all his self-declared principles, Morty had 'embellished' his life with an 'interest' in a yacht in Monte Carlo, his own boxes at Epsom and Ascot racecourses, and a handsome country house in West Sussex. He was crazy about horse racing and one of his favourite boasts was his friendship with a distinguished Old Bailey judge who would often join him at the track and who only recognised two calendars: racing and nude. In addition to two houses in Powys Square, Mortiboy and his wife Marcine had also bought the private garden at its centre into which none of the surrounding inhabitants were permitted. The garden provided a home for Marcine's menagerie, including a goat, one of her husband's retired racehorses, several boxer dogs and a snuffle of pugs that she had bred herself. Wealthy in her own right, Marcine owned a popular nightclub in Soho where she was meticulous in ensuring that all her gentleman customers received her personal attention.

Jamaica had celebrated its highly publicised independence in August 1962. In December, Britain's cinema screens were filled with the taut and muscled macho figure of Sean Connery. Playing the debonair agent James Bond in *Dr No*, the first movie adaptation of an Ian Fleming thriller, Connery was perfectly complemented by his seductive co-star Ursula Andress. Bathed in Jamaican sunshine and spattered in golden sand, her long hair wet from the waves, a dagger tucked into her white bikini bottoms, she emerged dripping and triumphant from the turquoise sea. In the cold British winter Jamaica was undeniably hot. And so the modish fascination with Jamaican culture established itself right across London. But the appeal of its quixotic lifestyle, the beat of its music, the elegance of its fashion failed to acknowledge the rigours of life that lay beneath the steaming plates of curried goat and rice 'n' peas sold in Notting

Hill's back street and basement bars. Disreputable drinking rooms known as 'shebeens' sold Red Stripe beer, bootleg whisky and a dizzying selection of stimulants, including cocaine, purple hearts, Benzedrine and liquid methedrine.[4] The Baby Doll, the Number 9, Bonas, Seventy-Seven, the American and the Mangrove were among the most popular of these crime-funded clubs. Trinidadian Frank Crichlow's restaurant El Rio, populated by a stylishly skinny-suited and pork-pie-hatted crowd and where bargain-priced marijuana was for sale, attracted waves of newly arrived immigrants as well as indigenous Londoners. Crichlow was under no illusions that hanging out with the Caribbean kids was 'a very cool thing for a white boy' as well as a white girl to do. El Rio became an epicentre for streetwise refugees from the King's Road. Beautiful models, the occasional Member of Parliament and society osteopath Stephen Ward all mingled with the drug hustlers and pimps. According to Crichlow, it was a place for 'people who were rebellious and a bit smart, those with street intelligence'.

Two of the regulars at El Rio were twenty-year-old model Christine Keeler and Mandy Rice-Davies. Christine had at one time been Peter Rachman's girlfriend, but when she introduced him to her friend, Mandy had in turn fallen for his 'dark glasses, expensive silk suit, diamond cufflinks, crocodile shoes . . .'[5] More recently, Christine had been dating a couple of El Rio's customers. It was an electrifying environment for a strikingly sexy, chestnut-haired model who blushed easily and whose eyes, accentuated and black-winged with kohl, were made even more dramatic by the long, thick false eyelashes without which she would not leave her house. Three years earlier Christine had escaped to the capital from her turbulent and abusive childhood home in Berkshire. The thrilling, welcoming hubbub of Notting Hill felt like a home-coming. She had at last found men who, despite their extreme possessiveness, truly seemed to care for her.

# Chapter Five

## *Beneath the palm trees*

On Tuesday 18 December, after refuelling in the Azores and Bermuda, Harold Macmillan's Comet IV touched down between swaying palm trees at Nassau's Windsor Field airport in the Bahamas. Shortly afterwards the Prime Minister and his Foreign Secretary, Lord Home (otherwise known as Alec Douglas–Home), were waiting on the steamy tarmac as President Kennedy's jet came in to land. The warmth not only of the air but of the greeting between the two leaders was evident to every onlooker. Celebrating their sixth official encounter over two years – one in Florida, two in Washington, and one each in London and in Bermuda – both men understood the personal value of these face-to-face encounters. 'I am not sure that the world is better off after our previous five meetings,' the President said with a smile as they stood together at the airport in front of a crisp, white and gold military-jacketed local guard of honour and a soggy gaggle of perspiring journalists, 'but I feel that as President *I* have been better off and have benefited greatly from the counsel and friendship you have shown me, Prime Minister.'

For the next three days Macmillan and Kennedy would negotiate their way around the tricky announcement that the USA intended to cancel Britain's order for Skybolt, America's air-launched missile. Because Britain had been intending to rely on Skybolt alone to sustain its nuclear arsenal, the news of the cancellation threatened to leave Britain without any nuclear defence at a time when Russian aggression was at its most dangerous. The British government was well aware that Britain's air force would not be powerful enough to attack Russia's newest, impregnable, air-based defences. Therefore the exclusive purpose of the Nassau summit was to persuade Kennedy to supply Britain with the more advanced Polaris submarine-launched ballistic missile weapons instead of Skybolt. Kennedy had so far resisted this suggestion, arguing that he would only supply Polaris as part of a multilateral arms force ordered from within NATO. Much was riding on a successful summit.

Macmillan welcomed the chance to leave behind the coldness of the London December for the warmth of the West Indies and to spend time with a man he held in high regard. But as he left for the Caribbean he was apprehensive, still smarting from the after-effects of a speech made by Dean Acheson at the beginning of December at the Military Academy at West Point. The former Secretary of State to President Truman and consultant, advisor and guide to John Kennedy had commented that 'Great Britain has lost an Empire and has not yet found a role'. Fogbound in Admiralty House Macmillan admitted to his diary that he had worked himself 'into a splendid anger'. Acheson's judgement, Macmillan snapped, was an error made 'by quite a lot of people in the last 400 years, including Philip of Spain, Louis XIV, Napoleon, the Kaiser and Hitler'. In the margin of his diary Macmillan had added 'conceited ass'.[1]

Macmillan was also preoccupied with the 'hysterical' coverage in the press, and on the radio and television of the problems facing him and his Government at the end of the year, especially de Gaulle's increasingly discouraging opposition to Britain joining the European Economic Community (known as the EEC). And then there was Barbara Fell, a civil servant recently convicted of a breach of the Official Secrets Act after being caught slipping secret documents to her Yugoslavian press attaché lover. Even though no threat to national security had been detected, spying and sex were nonetheless a dangerous mix. 'I do not recall a time', Macmillan had written in his diary on 9 December, 'when there (were) so many difficult problems to resolve and awkward decisions to be made.' The meeting in Nassau would be critical not only to re-establishing Britain's standing in the world but also to shoring up the Prime Minister's confidence in his ability to negotiate. He was relying on the exceptional diplomatic skill of Sir David Ormsby-Gore, the British Ambassador to the United States. Ormsby-Gore had become close friends with John Kennedy during his father Jo Kennedy's foreign posting to London before the Second World War and John Kennedy believed Ormsby-Gore to be 'the wisest man I ever knew'. Harold Macmillan in turn entrusted his Ambassador with views that he knew would be passed on with exquisitely correct etiquette to Kennedy. A first-class, first-hand conduit and interpreter of the American position on nuclear weapons, Ormsby-Gore had played a fundamental part in Britain's response to America's handling of October's Cuban Missile Crisis when Kennedy's two-year presidency had been tested to the limits. In the third week of October 1962 the Russian First Secretary Khrushchev, distrusting and fearing the global ambitions of the United States, had begun to assemble an arsenal of nuclear weapons on the communist island of Cuba. When Kennedy discovered the secret installation of weapons on an island so geographically close to the United States he reacted by putting a ring around the island, preventing Russian ships from stocking their new nuclear base. At the same time Kennedy negotiated a secret conciliatory deal with Russia to dismantle the US missile base in Turkey in the spring of 1963. Macmillan had followed Ormsby-Gore's advice and encouraged Kennedy to proceed with extreme caution before taking any military action against Russia. The crisis was defused with remarkable speed. Khrushchev, it turned out, was, at least for now, as unenthusiastic about nuclear war as the rest of the world. The British encouragement to follow diplomacy rather than aggression, inspired by Ormsby-Gore's perspicacious counsel, meant that the President arrived in the Bahamas well disposed to listening to Britain's nuclear agenda.

In our house, as in millions of others, adult conversation often turned to the prospect of the third catastrophic conflict in one century. War had come along roughly every two decades and by that reckoning we were almost due another. During the

Cuban Missile Crisis, American schoolchildren had become used to television dramas depicting mushroom clouds, nuclear winds, scorched hair and melted eyeballs. Photographs of the giant flower, the monstrous, rippling petal-edged bloom taken in the moments just after the Americans had dropped their bombs on the Japanese cities of Hiroshima and Nagasaki, were familiar to everyone. In American schools the 'Duck and Cover' technique was regularly rehearsed in classrooms as children fell at the given signal to seek dubious safety beneath their wooden desks. And fear had affected children on the other side of the Atlantic. Martin Seeley lived in a bungalow in Portchester near the Portsmouth naval base where his father, a teacher, was also a member of the Royal Naval Reserve. That winter Martin's mother would light the coal fire in the sitting room and his father would warm Martin and his five-year-old sister's uniform over the fireguard before the children dressed for school. This ritual calmed Martin as he tried to blot out the sound of aeroplanes that came and went above the naval base, leading him to suspect that military planes were flexing their engines in preparation for war.[2]

Martin was only eight but as I myself knew eight was old enough to feel frightened. My brother Adam and I had made sure that enough potatoes were kept buried in the earth in our den in the old Second World War air-raid shelter in the garden. My spare comb was also hidden there. And a small trowel. Just in case. At home on the way to bed Adam and I would pass an old tapestry hanging on the stairs, which I would hold briefly to my nose. This ancient piece of fabric was always warm, bolstered by heat rising from the fireplace. I would bite into this cloth that smelled and tasted of permanence even as the ancient wood burning in the fireplace below was turning to dust.

Although the camaraderie between the two world leaders was undeniable, in many ways the relationship was surprising. In contrast to the sixty-eight-year-old British Prime Minister, the seventy-two-year-old French President and the sixty-eight-year-old premier of the Soviet Union, the forty-five-year-old American President felt like youth politicised.

The physical contrast between the two men stood out in every photograph. The young, dynamic, pin-up American in his preppy, natty suits with his full head of shiny, dark hair appeared to fizz with energy and sex appeal. Harold Macmillan, in his old school tie, walrussy Edwardian moustache and tweedy shooting clothes that smacked of an elegance long outmoded, often appeared exhausted. An old Etonian graduate of Balliol College, Oxford, he had been severely wounded while serving in the Grenadier Guards in the First War and had been a senior politician under Churchill in the Second. Macmillan had been brought up by a powerful nanny famous for her emphatic habit of 'speaking in capital letters'.[3] Macmillan gave speeches with references that would have been familiar to Prime Ministers Gladstone and Disraeli. Queen Alexandra, Thomas Hardy and Rudyard Kipling had all attended his 1920 wedding to the daughter of the 9th Duke of Devonshire. Macmillan and his wife Dorothy were often invited to spend weekends at Chatsworth, the Devonshires' Derbyshire home, said to be even grander than Balmoral and where Macmillan's unashamed enthusiasm for the grouse shoot made him seem even less in touch with an electorate whose minds were not on such sports. In 1959 Aneurin Bevan, Labour's Shadow Foreign Secretary, had watched Macmillan at the Durham Miners' Gala Ball 'posing like an incandescent aspidistra'. Three years later Macmillan appeared even more creaky, albeit stubbornly tenacious. His diary of 1962 reveals a persistent fatigue he found almost impossible to overcome.[4] He also suffered from nerves. Sometimes he sank so low that even the prospect of a prize-giving at a school made him incapable of eating before the event. During the late summer of that year Macmillan's eyesight had begun to deteriorate but his resilience remained steady. As he grew older, historian Anthony Sampson noticed, his personal tics became exaggerated, including 'the shake of the head, the dropping of the mouth, the baring of the teeth, the pulling-in of the cheeks, the wobbling of the hand'.[5] The public did not know that the Prime Minister was battling the jumping of a right knee, a give-away of extreme tiredness. They did not know that he often spent entire weekend mornings working in bed. They were also unaware of his deliberate suppression of sentiments no longer appropriate for voicing in public. At a state banquet for President Tubman of Liberia he privately considered himself 'lucky' to be seated between 'two white ladies', the Duchess of Beaufort and 'Mrs Archbishop of Canterbury'. However, he continued to provide *TW3* with the sort of copy they relished. Whenever the Prime Minister appeared on television he 'exuded a flavour of mothballs', so out of date, 'with his decomposing visage and somehow seedy attire', that to acerbic journalist Malcolm Muggeridge 'he seemed in his very person to embody the national decay he supposed himself to be confronting'.[6]

Having lost several important by-elections by huge majorities to the Liberal Party, in the heat of July 1962 Macmillan had sacked a third of his Cabinet overnight. The following morning as the waxy bodies of seven former ministers were carried out horizontally through the back door of Madame Tussauds, the most obvious casualty was Macmillan's chief supporter Selwyn Lloyd. Unpopular with some for his 1962 Budget tax on children's sweets and ice cream, he had been a loyal Chancellor of the Exchequer and was shattered by his unexpected and ruthless dismissal. Former colleagues were publicly appalled by the Prime Minister's act of indiscriminate self-preservation. 'Greater love hath no man than this,' said Liberal MP Jeremy Thorpe with bitter irony, 'that he lay down his friends for his life.' The scale of the sacking backfired. If so many members of his public-school-educated, male Cabinet were unfit for government, was Macmillan himself still a suitable leader?

John Kennedy, a graduate of Harvard, his sun-bronzed face reflecting a lifetime of holidays at the family home by the sea in Cape Cod, came from a wealthy and distinguished political family with strong ties to the United Kingdom. His father Joseph had been the American Ambassador to Britain from 1938 to 1940 and his sister Kathleen had married William, the elder son of the Duke of Devonshire, making John Kennedy and Harold Macmillan related through the former's sister and the latter's wife. Doubly tragically after William had been killed in the war in 1944, Kathleen had died in an aeroplane crash in 1948, but the connection between the two families continued uninterrupted. In 1953 Jack (as John was popularly known) married the beautiful Jacqueline Bouvier, the pleasing synchronicity of the pairing of Jack with Jackie delighting newspaper headline compositors, who never missed a chance to feature the photogenic couple and their two charming children.

Neither Kennedy nor Macmillan were quite what they seemed to the electorate, their stability in office dependent at times on concealment and subterfuge. The youthful vigour of the President was in some part a sham. Kennedy suffered from a series of debilitating conditions.[7] An existing weakness caused by steroids taken for osteoporosis during his teens had been exacerbated by injuries he suffered during the Second World War when his navy patrol boat had been sunk. Several operations had left him with such acute pain in his back that at times he was incapable of putting on his socks and shoes. A difference in length between right and left legs put extra strain on his already fragile body. Dr Janet Travell, the White House physician, had made heel lifts for all his left shoes and would inject penicillin into the muscles of his lower back, a numbing procedure that was temporarily effective but so agonising to receive that the President could not help yelling. Muscle relaxants were prescribed for irritable bowel syndrome, antibiotics for urinary-tract infections and antihistamines for allergies. As much discretion as possible around these weaknesses was key to instilling political confidence in the public. Every day Kennedy strapped himself into a brace that kept his spine aligned and allowed him to sit very upright with the advantage that his distinctive posture meant he could be seen clearly by the crowds whenever he rode in an open motorcade. His most troubling ailment was Addison's disease, a condition that affects the adrenal function and made Kennedy tired, irritable and depressed. Occasionally he had been put on a course of anti-psychotic drugs to control violent and terrifying mood swings.

During the week when the outcome of the Cuban threat felt at its most precarious, the President had been dependent more than ever on medical assistance to get him through the day, sometimes the hour. In addition to the painkillers, steroids, hydrocortisone and testosterone, he also took sleeping pills. And rude good health was not his only deceit.

On the day that Macmillan's plane landed in the Bahamas, another flight from America also touched down carrying nineteen-year-old White House intern Mimi Beardsley for whom a villa had been rented conveniently near Bali Hai, the President's own temporary residence. Jackie Kennedy was not unaware of her husband's infidelities. But she loved her husband and was complicit in maintaining the intact, happy-family image – the First Family's idyllic 'Camelot' existence. So she did not accompany Jack to the Bahamas. Nor had she been in the audience with Jack at New York's Madison Square Garden for Marilyn Monroe's outrageous televised forty-fifth birthday tribute to the President in May 1962. The sexiest and the most fancied movie star on the planet had tiptoed on to the stage, removed her gleaming white fur stole, and tapped the microphone with one extended finger. And there for a moment she stood. She was liquid, languid, wearing a flesh-coloured, rhinestone-spattered, sheer tulle, zipless, buttonless, sheathed gown. Smoothing down the seemingly painted-on dress (said to have cost $12,000, it sold in 2016 for just under $5 million), her hands ran very slowly over every curve of her body. Beneath the dress she was naked. Beginning her tribute in a breathy whisper, Marilyn sang 'Thanks for the Memory' and then as a huge birthday cake was wheeled on stage, she invited the audiences both in Madison Square Garden and watching on television to join her in a final verse of 'Happy Birthday'. The performance was nothing less, according to New York journalist Dorothy Kilgallen, than 'making love to the President in front of forty million Americans'.[8]

Barbara Gamarekian, who worked in the White House office, found the underlying atmosphere of sexual tension around the pin-up President 'sort of thrilling. You were on the inside and you knew.'[9] Two of her colleagues, Priscilla Wear and Jill Cowen, known by the security department as 'Fiddle and Faddle', were not renowned for their enthusiasm for clerical work. But they made up for it by their attentiveness to their boss, especially in the exotic White House swimming pool which was decorated with murals to resemble a tropical island and where the water was kept at Caribbean temperatures. Every day at 12.30 p.m. when Kennedy went for a swim as therapy for his back Fiddle and Faddle would disappear from their desks, returning an hour later with wet hair. None of the other White House secretaries considered the wet hair worthy of speculation and, like Gamarekian, 'figured it was more pleasant for the President if he were doing a swim with people to chat with as he swam'. Gamarekian believed that Kennedy viewed women as 'all part of the package. They were girls, friends to play with, be pals with. If they were in the workplace they would do his bidding and serve him.'

Mimi Beardsley was one of the pretty White House interns kept busy in the President's office answering telephones, handing out press releases and filing. In June 1962, on her fourth day in the White House when Mrs Kennedy was out of town, Mimi had been invited to a small staff party complete with ice-cold daiquiris. She was then treated to a solo tour of the private quarters by the president himself, including a visit to Jackie's empty bedroom from which Mimi emerged without her virginity. She was soon in thrall to this man twice her age. In fact, she felt herself to be in love. He was 'sweet and thoughtful and generous'.[10] She would have done anything for him. And she did. To be singled out in this way was an honour. Barbara Gamarekian thought that 'most women found that if he smiled in their direction or said something that even indicated that he was personally aware of the fact that they had a name and they were an individual, it set you up for the next week or two'.[11] Their loosely secret affair was well established when one day in the White House swimming pool, Kennedy had suggested that she might 'take care' of Dave Powers, the President's closest and most indispensable aide, who was sitting on the side of the pool, his legs dangling in the water, looking a little 'tense'. Mimi complied. From within the pool, the President watched what Mimi herself felt to be this 'pathetic sordid scene' without comment. And when Mimi, not yet old enough to vote, suspected she might be pregnant Dave Powers gave her the name of a back-street abortionist.

Kennedy did little to disguise these liaisons from those close to him. During the Kennedys' visit to England in the summer of 1961 the charismatic energy of the President and the glamour of his young wife had been on full display and a special relationship between the two families had developed. 'I feel at home with Macmillan,' Kennedy had told the London *Sunday Times*, 'because I can share my loneliness with him. The others are all foreigners to me.' Since then birthday cards, Christmas cards and handwritten notes exchanged between the pair were top and tailed 'Jack' and 'Mac', their longer correspondence beginning with 'Dear Friend'.

Taking the discreet and old-school British Prime Minister into his confidence, he explained that he suffered from dreadful headaches if he did not have sex every day, the intensity of orgasm eclipsing the pain, at least momentarily. Macmillan was both amazed and embarrassed by the confession. Although the American President's philandering was talked about in political circles, it was not something Macmillan cared to discuss, his own sexual reticence a source of private distress to him. Macmillan had been celibate for twenty-nine years, living with the arrangement his wife had maintained with Bob Boothby for three decades. Macmillan had long refused to give his wife Dorothy the divorce she craved because such a scandal would have compromised the position of all three. There was much talk in the gentlemen's clubs about the liaison between the well-built, twin-setted, jolly-hockey-sticks 'Dot' and Bob, the charming but unpredictable MP who had been Parliamentary Private Secretary to Churchill's Chancellor of the Exchequer in the 1920s and who also had very close friendships with men. Out of respect to the office of Prime Minister, the press continued to keep the Dot and Bob story out of their pages. Newspapers continued to close ranks in league with and in protection of the ruling Establishment, just as they had done nearly thirty years earlier when the new King's affair with Wallis Simpson was supressed by all of Fleet Street. Only a very great scandal such as the Abdication would have forced them to disregard the Establishment's propensity, whether royal or political, to do as it pleased.

During the Nassau talks both world leaders stayed in the grounds of the exclusive Lyford Cay Club, taking informal walks together along the sand, pink with coral dust, and beneath the waving palm trees. One evening a special entertainment had been arranged for the press corps from both countries. While a glamorous soirée around the Lyford Cay swimming pool was being enjoyed by the American journalists who had been joined by the President himself, the British event took the form of a rather more humdrum barbecue in the Emerald Beach, the hotel housing the British press and where the wind whipped up the sand and Macmillan tussled with the shell of a gritty crayfish and a barrage of questions from Britain's newspapermen. Contributing to Kennedy's sunny mood was the discreet presence of Mimi. Hidden away during the daytime in her own villa, she would be driven over to Bali Hai by Dave every evening after the President's official work was done.

After three days of talks the Nassau summit proved to be successful. An alternative solution to the cancelled Skybolt programme had been agreed. America would supply Britain with the submarine missile Polaris. In most circumstances it would only be fired under the governing authority of NATO, but it could be used independently if 'supreme national interests' intervened. The Royal Navy rather than the Royal Air

Force would now hold responsibility for Britain's nuclear missiles. Relieved and grateful at the outcome, Macmillan took the flight back to London, thankful to the President for his flexibility and to Ormsby-Gore for his steadying hand during the negotiations. Macmillan now looked forward to tackling de Gaulle about the EEC with a reinvigorated determination in the New Year and to spending Christmas with his family. And the President left Lyford Cay to take the aeroplane first to Washington before boarding another headed for Palm Beach, Jackie and the children. As his motorcade passed the press corps, photographers spotted a tousled head just visible in the passenger well of Dave Power's car. Puzzled, they thought the passenger must be a child. But although Mimi Beardsley, who was five foot nine inches, had done her best 'to fit under the dashboard' she had found it impossible to disappear completely, no matter how low she crouched.[12]

# Chapter Six

## *On top of a painted ladder*

We were going to spend our first Christmas with my grandfather at Sissinghurst, our new home in Kent. That December was so cold, the coldest month we had ever known. In the mornings the sharp outlines of the naked trees in my grandmother Vita's beautiful garden were smudged with mist and the lawns glittered with frost in the sunshine. During the week before Christmas Mrs Staples, Vita's old cook, had taken to warming herself up with a generous nip of cooking sherry.

'Which day had you been thinking of celebrating Christmas this year, Mrs Nicolson?' she enquired of my mother, her lower lip jutting in and out, and wobbling slightly on her feet as she spoke.

'I understand my mother-in-law generally favoured December the twenty-fifth,' my mother replied after an appropriate pause, 'so perhaps we should continue with the tradition?'

'An excellent suggestion, I must say, Mrs Nicolson.'

We had been living at Sissinghurst for six months, since my grandmother's death. Vita Sackville-West had left the house to her younger son, my father Nigel, in her will. More of a ruin than a house, Sissinghurst had once been a grand Elizabethan mansion, and then in the eighteenth century a prison camp for French sailors, but by the time Vita and her husband Harold Nicolson bought it in 1930 the place had fallen into a state of total neglect and was virtually uninhabitable. Together they had cleared away the wreckage and rubble of centuries and eventually made what became known as one of the loveliest gardens in England.

My brother Adam and I were both at school in London but Sissinghurst became our real home as each weekend we would swerve and skid our bikes along the narrow grass paths, let the pigs run loose from their styes, make ourselves a camp in the defunct air-raid shelter in the orchard and fling ourselves into hiding in the haystacks in the barn. That summer my thirty-three-year-old mother Philippa had been away in the South of France, staying in the fishing village of St Tropez with American friends in their glamorous seaside villa. Philippa had been particularly taken with another houseguest, a young grandson of Harold Macmillan, and years later I found a photograph of them that suggested they had been shopping together in the port for matching striped T-shirts. Here she found an escape from a marriage in which she felt herself to be under critical scrutiny from her husband for her lack of interest in literature, politics and history. It was a seductive sort of a place where she could feel free and un-judged.

Back in Kent, even though an unusually chilly August had followed an unusually chilly July and a disappointingly chilly June, the hedgerows had thickened with a profusion of honeysuckle and wild roses, nettles and long grasses. My father, twelve years older than my mother, took us children on 'nature walks', when we were encouraged to pay attention to growing things including the ripening blackcurrant bushes. At tea my brother Adam asked for jam. 'You can have some if you tell me how blackcurrants grow,' my father told him. My father described the scene in a letter to our mother in France.

> 'Well Adam, do they grow on the tops of tall trees?' Head shake. 'Do they grow creepy crawly like strawberries in the ground itself?' No. 'Well do they grow under the ground like potatoes?' Immense relief flooded Adam's face. 'Yes Dadda.' No jam. Really your children have not inherited their mother's gift of observation nor their grandmother's feeling for the way of nature.

But *he* had inherited the *joie de vivre* of his own father, taking us not only on nature walks but into the woods for 'boat races' as we would each choose a piece of wood to float down the stream. Sometimes we would set out after lunch on history expeditions to Bodiam Castle with its lovely medieval moat and four round towers, and to the nearby battlefield of Hastings to relive the moment Harold was hit in the eye with the arrow. Nigel was at his funniest, infectiously enthusiastic best when teaching his children about those things that mattered to him, the things he had also loved as a boy. He told my mother that my laughter had 'the quality of a flute', and it was true that I could not conceal how much I loved being with him.

Whenever my parents were apart my father wrote Philippa deeply affectionate, even sentimental letters. And we knew he loved her hair, often mentioning 'Mumma's curls', which were cut short and suited her. But it was all a bit of an act. He was irritated and frequently disappointed by her. She had left school aged fourteen and was not interested in the literary recommendations of an Oxford graduate who spoke Greek and quoted Shelley to make a point. A copy of *The Passion Flower Hotel* by Rosalind Erskine,[1] the story of a brothel set up by a bunch of posh boarding-school girls, sat on her bedside table. Our mother was so pretty. She always smelled delicious, lovable, huggable. She often wore a sparkly brooch in the shape of a dolphin, a wedding gift from her city-slicker father who had been the Warden of the Fishmongers' Company in London. She was the more properly music-loving of our parents. She liked Chubby Checker and Herb Alpert and the instrumental sound of Tijuana Brass; we teased her about the way she used a special accent to over-pronounce Tea-you-hana. Nigel presented himself as –, even believed himself to be – a musical romantic. He loved every song from *My Fair Lady* and in particular the sentimentality of 'On the Street Where You Live', and anything from *Oklahoma* especially 'The Surrey with the Fringe on Top' and 'Oh, What a Beautiful Morning'. The source, or part of the source, of Nigel's irritability with his wife lay in his own private shame at not being able to 'perform' and the self-loathing that went with his view, confided only to his unpublished memoir, that sex was still 'nasty', something one was 'obliged to do occasionally'. His 'distaste for the ultimate act' stoppered up his ability to be a tender, loving husband and contributed to his collapsing marriage. My mother was lonely, her self-confidence faltering as she tried to find her way through unmarked territory, neither young enough to join the youth fest going on in London nor old enough to cling to the conventions of the past. She was not sure where she belonged.

That December the BBC's Reith Lectures were given by a professor of psychological medicine at Edinburgh University.[2] Professor Morris Carstairs discussed how attitudes to sex within marriage were changing. Women were beginning to recognise their marriage was incomplete if it did not give them physical as well as emotional satisfaction. 'A new concept is emerging, of sexual relationships as a source of pleasure, but also as a mutual encountering of personalities in which each explores the other and at the same time discovers new depths in himself or herself.' Carstairs continued, 'This concept of sex as a rewarding relationship is after all not so remote from the experience of our maligned teenagers.' His outspoken remarks were reported as headline news in *The Times*. He condemned the way attitudes to sex handed down from mother to daughter endorsed the myth that the enjoyment of sexual intercourse was confined to 'men and beasts'. But none of this theorising got an airing in our household.

Money was a source of underlying anxiety for my father. As former Conservative MP for Bournemouth, his support for both the legalisation of homosexuality and the abolition of hanging, as well as his role as the publisher of Vladimir

Nabokov's scandalous novel *Lolita* in 1959, had never sat well with his small-'c' conservative-minded constituents. And after his unequivocal disagreement with the imperialistic behaviour of the Conservative Prime Minister Anthony Eden during the Suez Crisis and the invasion of Egypt in 1956, Nigel had resigned his seat. Although his principled action had earned him much admiration among other MPs, it had left him out of a job and, at the age of forty-six, with little idea how he was going to meet his financial responsibilities. His dependants included his wife, children and dog as well as his father and, absurdly, Vita's cook, Vita's chauffeur and Vita's five gardeners, who had all continued to work at Sissinghurst in the immediate period after her death. He had returned to the publishing company he had co-founded with George Weidenfeld in 1949, concentrating on producing extravagantly illustrated books. And he had accepted the position of Chairman of the United Nations Association, an organisation that met in places from Huddersfield to New York to Delhi, bolstering the flagging support for its parent, the United Nations itself. But cash remained short.

One financial hurdle concerned him more than the rest. The privilege of being left Sissinghurst had also come with a huge inheritance tax bill. At first it seemed that the only way Nigel would be able to pay the bill would be to sell the place. But then another option occurred to him. He could try to persuade the National Trust to take over the whole estate in lieu of tax. The Trust did not take gardens because gardens, unlike bricks and mortar, are living things and unlikely to survive. But Nigel had risen to the challenge. He loved the place. Saving Sissinghurst was, as my brother Adam has written, 'an act of intense filial duty'.[3] Nigel felt the National Trust to be his <u>only</u> option.[4]

After we moved to Sissinghurst in June 1962 there was little alteration in a way of life established when Vita and Harold had moved there in the 1930s. There were ghosts everywhere, prompting our dog to bark at an empty fireplace or at a mysterious dusk-time gathering of people in a foreign uniform on the far side of the moat, speaking French. I grew accustomed to the unexplained closing of a door or opening of a window, and to the brief, enigmatic scent of pot-pourri caught in the still air of a shuttered room. To me the presence of these spirits felt not only benign but welcome. We lived happily in the various buildings dotted about the garden just as they had, sleeping in one cottage, eating in another, and establishing playrooms and workrooms in yet another. The stamps and the pens and engagement diary for 1962, empty of entries for the second half of the year, remained untouched on Vita's large oak desk in her writing room on the first floor of the Elizabethan Tower. A sheen of dust had begun to coat the wood, extending an invitation to a small finger to practise a signature or play a game of noughts and crosses. Vita's gardening forks, trowels, spades, hoes and small weeding stool still hung on rusty nails tacked into the wall of the potting shed. Vita's wholly unaffordable butler and cook remained in residence in their flats in the gatehouse. Neither of my parents felt able to sack them. For a while loyalty trumped bank balance. Adam and I loved the portly chauffeur/odd-job man, Jack Copper, his braces stretched taut over his substantial stomach and just about holding up his too-short grey trousers. We inhaled his peculiar combined smell of carbolic soap, petrol, beer and a hint of some surprisingly exotic aftershave. We bounced about on the well-sprung back seat of Vita's black Ford Zephyr as Copper drove us up to the village to buy us sparkly spangles and pretend cigarettes with red-painted tips. Fluorescent-pink sugar shrimps were added to our haul, together with crisps with tiny screws of blue paper containing salt hidden deep inside the packet and which you had to be careful not to bite into. Best of all were the four-for-a-penny fruit chews that stuck to the top of your mouth and had to be hoiked free with a finger.

In his youth Copper, whose father had been Rudyard Kipling's gardener in Sussex in the 1930s, had often been 'up to no good' with the local girls. Marjorie was one of three such girls who became pregnant by Jack Copper in the summer of 1936. Their son was christened Gordon but was always known as Dinky for his slightness of figure. The whispers about Dinky intensified during the winter of 1962, as rumours of new scandals crossed the Atlantic and had the village at Sissinghurst agog. Dinky believed the midwife had misidentified his gender at birth. Born with 'a clitoris so swollen that the startled woman did not know whether I was a boy or a girl', the baby was designated as male although in her memoirs Gordon confirmed she had always known she was a woman.[5] Terrified by the arrival at puberty of what Dinky called her 'irregular bleeds', she was ordered by her Aunt Gertrude in a 'church organ' voice, to treat her period 'like an insane relative that you never talk about' and to 'think of the disgrace you would be to all of us if anyone found out'. At the age of sixteen, leaving the wagging fingers of the Kentish Weald behind her, Gordon sailed from Liverpool and arrived in America where she thought she would feel safe from judgement. She found a job with *General Features*, a local New York newspaper syndicate.

Frequently hospitalised by the severity of these intermittent 'bleeds', Gordon was amazed when a remote cousin 'looking somewhat like Queen Mary' with blue-grey hair piled high and dangling ruby earrings, swept into her hospital room. Isobel Whitney, who preferred to be known for her beautifully executed fresco paintings rather than as the heir to a vast fortune derived from clever investments in the silk industry, was a distant cousin of Gordon's mother and warmed to this fragile, intelligent young person in the hospital bed. When Gordon confessed her secret, Isabel was deeply sympathetic and invited Gordon to live with her in her huge house in Greenwich Village. In the spring of 1962 Isabel Whitney died of leukaemia, leaving her fortune to her newly discovered relation. In Isobel's memory Gordon bought a splendid Georgian house in Charleston, South Carolina, where she fell in love with John Paul, the black butler she had rescued from his job as a mechanic at a local garage. Soon Gordon wanted nothing more than to become John Paul's wife. She presented herself at Johns Hopkins University in Baltimore as one of the first to undergo a pioneering operation for gender reassignment. When some of the residents of Charleston heard about what was taking place at the very heart of their rarefied, dignified community they were horrified. Gordon, who had changed her name to Dawn Pepita, and John Paul became the victims of a relentless campaign of physical and verbal abuse that almost destroyed them both. We children knew that Copper's son Dinky had turned into a girl and the story of how the quiet unobtrusive Gordon had escaped to America and turned into the flamboyant Dawn sounded magical. Only the grown-ups knew the real version.

As the soft gold light of the autumn gave way to the harder grey of a leafless sky, and a few unpicked blackberries, inky and sour-tasting, clung to the hedgerows, the hours of light began to decrease. At the slightest gust of wind starlings, like charred scraps of paper floating up from a bonfire, filled the wintry sky, swooping and dipping before settling on the treetops. And so the mood at Sissinghurst dimmed and the vigour with which Harold had held on to living weakened, the waning of a busy, networky social life hard for him to accept. The preceding February Vita had been diagnosed with cancer. Overnight the quotidian props of Harold's life seemed alien. 'My pipe, my sponge, the book I have been reading all seem like voices from the past. Last time I handled you all was sunlit.'[6] On 1 March 1962 a Grenadier Guard in full uniform had appeared at the door of Harold's London flat and handed him a letter of sympathy and encouragement from the Queen, bestowing the mysterious balm of royalty. 'This makes me feel better,' Harold wrote in his diary, ever the monarchist. His official biography of George V, the Queen's grandfather, had gone down well with the Royal family and even earned Harold a knighthood. But a few months later on the morning of the first day of June, when an overnight wind had flattened the overgrown grass in the orchard, Harold emerged into the pale sunshine from his cottage 'haunted by demons' and 'feeling smashed and knocked'. Vita died the following afternoon. She was seventy years old. At first the anaesthetic of shock provided Harold with a temporary reprieve. There were even a few days of euphoria, the strange, deceptive adrenalin surge that can follow the worst sort of news. Edwin Smith, a distinguished photographer, had been invited by Vita to take some photographs of the garden that week. Inexplicably his appointment was not postponed and on that warm June day we posed for the genial Mr Smith in the garden. He placed us all on a bench that looked down the moat walk, the long grass path that led down to the stretch of water and the statue of Dionysus on the opposite bank. Three generations of us posed for Mr Smith that day – children, parents and grandfather – a distant expression on Harold's face, a toy car in Adam's hand. I felt the warmth of the bench beneath me. The intoxicating, lily-like scent of the azaleas drifted up the path towards us. It felt lovely to be sitting there with Harold, lovely to be part of this place, lovely to belong there.

But the temporary happiness of those days when we had all moved in to be a comfort soon evaporated for Harold when the home he and Vita had occupied alone for thirty years felt invaded. How would he live without her? How would he live with us? On 12 June he had written in his diary, 'I am terrified by my unhappiness.' He alternated between numbness and unquenchable tears as he recorded how they continued to 'ooze and splash'. In the week after his mother's death Nigel was more aware than ever of what the rupture to his father's life meant. He had found a journal containing Vita's long and vivid, pencil-written confession of a tumultuous love affair of four decades earlier, a love affair that had nearly ended his parents' marriage, a love affair with a woman. Harold was also homosexual but his 'muddles' were less intense than Vita's and their idiosyncratic marriage had survived, thrived even, and their love for each other had remained the backbone of existence for them both.

During meals the uneasy presence of Harold's hunched, uncommunicative, unreachable figure in the big wooden chair, the only one with arms, travelled up the table from his end to ours, where my mother sat looking anguished. Although we tried to chat around him his silence was the context in which we spoke, frightened that if we too fell silent his grief would swamp us. Wailing was something to be done behind closed doors. So we tried to chatter to one another and when silence threatened, my father filled the void quickly with a well-worn story. I kicked Adam beneath the table. Alone in his cottage across the lawn and uninhibited by anxious eyes upon him, Harold could choose how to grieve. At times his sadness was inaudible, at others, even at a distance, it was full of noise. 'My heart feels like a dead toad,' he had written in his diary on 12 August. As the winter months arrived he remained nattily and inappropriately youthfully attired in his summer uniform of tennis shoes and cream trousers, as if playing a part in a Noël Coward play or taking a promenade round the deck of a cruise ship. We saw mud on the bottom of the turn-ups as he warmed his white rubber-soled shoes perilously close to an electric fire that was missing a couple of coils and from which he ignited his cigarettes. In 'The Love Song of J. Alfred Prufrock' T. S. Eliot addresses ageing, the losing of hair, impotence, the paralysing indecision of the very old when self-confidence is eroded, even though old age licenses one to roll up one's trousers. For Harold the debonair style of youth had become Prufrockian: stained with age.

*

Harold's latest book, a history of the institution of monarchy, had been published on 6 December. It received more than respectable reviews with *The Times* saying 'he shows himself at the top of his form as remembrancer of things past', but his mood did not lift. As a diplomat, an MP, a journalist, a biographer, historian and diarist, Harold had been one of the most popular and gregarious members of his circle of friends. An obsessive observer and participant in national events for most of his life, he had felt himself to be a man at the centre of things. But now he faced his future with an unaccustomed sense of redundancy, an awareness that he must give way to a new political generation, a new way of doing things, deferring to children, deferring to grandchildren. He began to recognise his own irrelevance, to experience change at the most profound depths of his existence. Getting old and getting old alone made him feel like a stranger in his own world. His father had died in 1928 but he was still mourning the death just over ten years earlier of his adored mother. He had never become used to being an orphan. Bereft now not only of both parents but of a wife, he felt 'untidy inside as if someone had upset a chest of drawers leaving the contents rearranged', as he told his friend James Lees-Milne.[7] As the ending of the year approached we would find him on top of his collapsible ladder, an ingenious contraption the colour of red earth, which he would climb to reach books on the top shelves of his work room and to weep out of sight. Or we would come across him sitting at his desk in tears, as he looked through the window at the fading vitality of the garden.

But it was the chatter, the vibrancy of children, the essential affirmation of a whole life still to live that flushed light and colour into Harold's darkness that winter. His long past had something to offer to our future. We were the exclusive audience for the tales he had to tell. We took to calling him Hadji, the name Vita had always used for him. He would read to us about how the camel had acquired his hump. We learned how a crocodile once pulled so hard on an elephant's nose that it became stretched to absurd lengths. He had met Rudyard Kipling and had noted that his eyebrows 'curl up black and furious like the moustache of a Neapolitan tenor'.[8] And there were true stories from Hadji's own childhood. When he had been my age he had met a very old man with a long white beard from Holland, the country where they grow tulips and ride bicycles and eat cheese with holes in it. The man told him that a long, long time ago when he had been the same age as Hadji the man had loved horses. The man (who had once been a child too, don't forget, Dearly Beloved) had been given the job of leading a horse into a battle. The person riding the horse was Napoleon, the Emperor of France. With one hand the old white-bearded man, who had once been a child, had held the reins of the horse, and with the other the Emperor Bonaparte's flag.

He indulged our own exhibitionism. Inspired by the live audience on the television show *Thank your Lucky Stars*, Adam and I had perfected our twist technique. We had performed the dance for Vita at Sissinghurst in the last few days of her life, as she sat there wrapped in a mothy, once-exotic llama-skin rug, wearing a pearl necklace that softened her otherwise androgynous dress code. Mastering the opening steps by mimicking the extinguishing of a cigarette on the floor with the ball of our right foot we felt very 'with it' showing off to a woman who, at the same age as us, had been learning to dance the quadrille and the polka. That winter we continued to show the dance off to Hadji. Any excuse. But when we left his cottage the sound of Hadji's voice from deep within continued to reach us as, believing himself to be out of earshot, we could hear him shouting 'Viti, Viti' into the empty rooms.

On Christmas morning we went to church in the village because Christmas did not feel like Christmas unless we followed the rituals, observed the long-established structure of the day, ate mince pies and sang 'Hark the Herald'. My father did not really believe in God except at Christmas and during funerals in beautiful buildings. He would have preferred to sing carols in the nearby town of Cranbrook in the lovely fifteenth-century St Dunstan's Church, known as the Cathedral of the Weald. A plaque there commemorated the Baker family who had built Sissinghurst at the same time as the church. The architecture was gratifyingly splendid and centuries of incense and song had been absorbed into the grey stone walls. But Nigel did not want to appear 'grand', so Adam and I sat between our parents in the more modest, less beautiful Victorian church in our village wearing our best blue coats with white collars, passing chocolate coins behind the cover of the prayer book and longing for it all to be over so we could go home and have presents.

Hadji's Christmas present to me that year was an academic history of the County of Kent illustrated with unintelligible maps and charts in black and white. My name had been scrawled across the flyleaf and his own, written in full, almost illegible and with all the anonymity of a stranger, had been written below it and below that he had put 'Xmas 1962'. Even the day of Jesus's birth had been shrunk. No love from. No Hadji. He had no energy left for shopping or for observing the conventions of gift-giving, even for an eight-year-old granddaughter. He must have pulled an old book off his shelf on Christmas Eve and put it beneath the tree. I was cheered up by my two best presents that year. The Frank Ifield record from my father was an addition to the small record collection I shared with Adam. It mostly comprised nursery rhymes, but our favourite LP was Prokofiev's *Peter and the Wolf*, which was satisfyingly scary (the wolf), funny (the quacking duck) and reassuring (the happy ending) in equal parts. My other best present was a scarlet leather manicure set from my London godmother, which came complete with a pair of gold scissors, a nail file (that set my teeth on edge) and other mysterious instruments slotted into little inner pockets. After lunch we all watched the Queen deliver her Christmas message on the small television set that stood on four spindly wooden legs in a corner of the dining room and was only switched on for special occasions. There was no space for sofas so we would pull the dining-room chairs round to face the set or simply stand up in front of the flickering screen.

Wearing a black boat-necked dress, a double string of pearls and her grandmother's favourite 'True Lovers' knot brooch, the Queen spoke of how pleased she was that Jamaica, Trinidad & Tobago and Uganda had all joined the British Commonwealth that year. She wished us all 'a merry Christmas and a heppy New Yar', using what she defined as 'these old familiar warm-hearted words of the traditional Christmas message'. In her summary of the year she spoke about Telstar, the science-fiction-sounding

Presenters of *That Was the Week That Was*, the BBC's new monster-hit weekly satirical TV show: Willie Rushton, Lance Percival, Millicent Martin, David Frost and David Kernan

The impending threat of World War Three hung over Christmas 1962 which, despite *Private Eye*'s jokey cover, was no laughing matter

The *Private Eye* editorial team, which included Peter Cook, John Wells and Richard Ingrams

Public conveniences provided unreliable refuges for (at the time) illegal homosexual encounters

Juliet, Philippa, Adam, Nigel and Harold Nicolson at home at Sissinghurst in 1962, a week after the death of Vita Sackville-West

Frozen waves in the sea at
Herne Bay in Kent, December 1962

The tower at
Sissinghurst as the
snow began to fall

The River Thames iced over at Hampton Court, January 1963

Townscape-snowscape: Cardiff in January 1963

The Lady Falls in Wales no longer falling in January 1963

A milkman in London's Earl's Court delivering his round on skis, his cigarette ice-glued to his lips, January 1963

Pigeons balancing on the ice in Trafalgar Square, January 1963

The little-known American folk singer 'Bobby' Dylan in London's Singers Club, December 1962, on his first visit to the city

Harold Macmillan and John F. Kennedy synchronise watches during their nuclear missile summit in the Bahamas, December 1962

Mick Jagger hanging out with his girlfriend Chrissie Shrimpton in February 1963

The Rolling Stones playing at the Crawdaddy Club, Richmond, July 1963

Penelope Fitzgerald, the as-yet unpublished novelist who in 1963 was Juliet's despairing English teacher

Vanessa, monkey, Adam and Juliet Nicolson (in their best coats) at the cousins' outing to the circus, January 1963

Shirley Punnett, no-nonsense and much-loved nanny

Harold Wilson (left) succeeded Hugh Gaitskell as leader of the Labour Party after Gaitskell died in January 1963

Irton Hall in Cumbria, one of the few homes in the country for children with cerebral palsy

Ettie Evans at the counter of her haberdashery shop The Sewing Centre in Carshalton

satellite that had been launched into space in July, enabling television pictures to travel from America through the air and arrive in our dining room at exactly the same time as they were actually happening across the Atlantic. She finished by cautioning us to be mindful of how we are always looking for new worlds to conquer 'before we have put our own house in order'. My parents and grandfather said how young the Queen looked. Without a crown she reminded me a bit of my mother in her shyness. They were almost the same age.

As Christmas Day came to an end, unknown to us, a very cold wind was moving towards us from Russia, sweeping across Europe. In the seas around the coast of Denmark the water had began to ice over. As the sun set at teatime and the pink glow faded, dusk deepened and thickened into darkness.

On Boxing Day we gave a party for the neighbours in the old Elizabethan stable we called the Big Room. The rarely used, lugubrious space was lined with books and furnished with saggy, damp old sofas and did not inspire a party mood, but the guests had been invited and a struggling fire had been lit in the huge fireplace. Hadji rallied enough to join in as we children raced around the fir tree decorated in skeins of coloured light bulbs and tinsel, offering, as he recorded in his diary, a combination of 'nuts, charm and respect'. There had been reports of snow cutting off thirty villages in the Abruzzi Mountains in Italy and temperatures dipping overnight in Portugal to -15 °C. Snowfall in Germany was breaking all records and wintry conditions in Greece had put the country on a state of national alert. Ten deaths from cold had been reported in France on Christmas

Day. However, in Manchester a fog that had stopped aeroplanes from taking off had lifted by Christmas Eve and there was no cause for concern in Kent. But at the end of the party as the huge oak door to the Big Room was closed and the thick wooden bolts were pushed across to make it secure, the air outside appeared to fill with small white butterflies as the first fragile flakes of snow began to flutter down from the sky.

# Chapter Seven

## *When midnight's all a glimmer*

We had often heard the story of a morning long ago when Vita had woken beneath the not-quite-leak-proof ceiling of her bedroom to find she was lying under a thick counterpane of snow. But that night, the night of the Boxing Day party, even in the darkness, this was the most snow, the snowiest snow, we had ever seen. The greyness of winter had been whitewashed, the decaying, clogging residue of autumn cleared clean away. Where there had been ugliness, suddenly there was beauty, all imperfections wiped smooth, Christmassy stars blinking above us in air that felt clearer, purer, brighter, a Yeatsian moment when 'midnight's all a glimmer'.

That night as we made our way to our bedrooms in the cottage across the garden, the wide lawn outside the Big Room sparkled. We stuck out our tongues, catching the falling flakes as they landed and melted, tingling like Sherbet Dips from the village sweet shop. Once inside we wrote our names on the frosty glass in the old apple storage rooms where we slept. Later that night a barely there moon rose in the sky, the bulk of it still just visible if you looked for it, the soft, pitted shadowiness standing out against the darker sky. The muted glow reached my tiny bedroom, slanting in across the garden and throwing a curved gleam on to the flowery eiderdown, as the fragile, new-born crescent became framed by the window.

The following morning we woke to the peculiar blue-bright light of reflected snow filtering through the closed curtains. Instead of disappearing during the night as we had feared it would, the snow was still there, turning the landmarks of the garden – the walls, lawns, statues, urns – into something unrecognisable but unified. The sight was beautiful, its very transience on this familiar landscape making it even more precious. Snow muffled all sound and the silence felt dream-deep. Outside freezing snowballs melted the second they hit the nape of our necks and we tipped backwards on to the lawn, arms outstretched like acrobats, trusting that the mattress of snow would break our fall. Unlike a sandcastle on a beach, absorbed so soon by the waves, our imprints remained, hollows into which we could flop again and again. Down by the moat, where the naked statue of Dionysus was now clothed in a perfectly fitted white furry coat, we tested the water with the toe of a wellington boot. Disappointingly the surface, glinting under a weak sun, still moved beneath our feet and the ducks still swam, not yet impeded by ice. But the cold felt as if it was getting colder by the minute. Tying a rope to an old abandoned wooden lavatory seat that we found in the back of a barn, we set about persuading any passing grown-up to swirl us around the lawn as we sat wedged into the oval hole, giddy with the novelty of it all. Out in the fields the muddy furrows made by the plough in late summer had hardened into a pattern of miniature mountain ranges. The water in each tiny valley had frozen over, forming a sequence of minute, iced-over ponds, delicious to jump on and crack.

By the end of the Bank Holiday in parts of the south of the country snowfall already measured two and a half feet. Families and friends who either hoped to get together or longed for the annual enforced sociability to be over faced disaster. With some unable to get to the holiday sanctuaries they had intended to visit, others were trapped in family prisons from which they longed to escape.

In Liverpool, where the Boxing Day sky had become as ominously dark as a throng of black-feathered crows, schoolboy Stephen Guy had spent the evening at his Auntie May's in Childwall, three miles from his home in Liverpool's West Derby district. When Stephen and his parents emerged into the night air they discovered that buses had suddenly stopped running. After walking all the way home, Stephen was excited to find that 'Jack Frost had decorated all the windows.'[1] Thirty miles further south the blizzard continued to blow and the railway points at Crewe station had begun to freeze. The *Mid-Day Scot*, the express train from Glasgow to London, taking 500 people in thirteen coaches home after Christmas, had stopped at a red light at the Coppenhall Junction in Cheshire. The driver, John Russell, tried to telephone ahead to the signal box to check all was clear on the line but the telephone was out of order. Proceeding cautiously, Russell first reduced his speed to 20 mph and then with the red light still instructing him to stop, he took things into his own hands and accelerated. The official report published afterwards concluded the train was travelling at 'a speed much in excess of that demanded by the circumstances'. As the steam billowed and lengthened along the passenger carriages, it condensed and froze. Russell was unaware that the Liverpool-to-Birmingham express, carrying three hundred passengers in eight coaches, had stopped at a signal just ahead and was almost invisible in the darkness.

Corporal Dennis Osborn, travelling with his wife and two children on the Birmingham train, had spent Christmas with relations in Liverpool. Suddenly he felt the carriage 'bounce' just before 'the lights went out, and all the luggage shot on top of us'.[2] The colossal noise made by the impact between the two trains was loud enough to snap the snow-laden branches of nearby trees, the sound of splintering glass and telescoping metal thunderous, as the first carriage was half stripped off its chassis. Smashing his way out of the train by throwing a table through the window, one plucky passenger ran through the dark to the nearest farm to call for help. Finding the telephone lines were down in the freezing weather he ran another mile through the snowy fields before reaching a working telephone to call the fire brigade. The nearest farm cleared its animals from outbuildings and a loose box to act as a temporary morgue. A full hour and a half after the crash sixty firemen from fifteen fire engines braved the 25,000-voltage wires that overhung the wreckage as they tried to reach the trapped passengers in the dark. Inside the carriages they were confronted by a hellish scene, a nightmarish confusion of injured passengers lying at all angles, limbs torn and broken, sharing the chaos with shiny new Christmas toys, dolls and teddy bears scattered throughout the tumble of broken compartments. Photographs taken the following morning showed how little of the carriages remained. It was as if a giant scrap-metal yard had been put through a crushing machine.

Eventually a dozen doctors and twenty ambulances reached the scene. A few passing cars stopped to shine their headlights on the wreckage, as medics tried to give first aid on the barren frozen earth that bordered the railway track. Thirty-three people had been injured and were taken to hospital. But for others it was too late. A baby whose neck was broken, a man who had lost both his legs and a young soldier who was found hanging from the roof concertinaed between two upended carriages were among the six children and twelve adults who lost their lives that terrible evening. But even more chilling than all the horrifying sights that faced the emergency workers that night was the sound of the children's screams.

On 27 December *The Times* reported that every single county in England had been affected in some way by snow or ice, with Dorset, Devon, West Kent, Surrey and East Sussex the worst hit. In Kent the cold had been creeping up through the sea at Herne Bay since before Christmas and it had become possible to walk a full mile on ice from the beach out into the open sea. Mini icebergs were seen floating in the River Medway and the navy used an icebreaker to keep Chatham dockyard functioning. In Sussex the runway at Gatwick was layered with almost a foot of new snow and flights to the Channel Islands were cancelled. While Guernsey was celebrating its first white Christmas in forty years, the sea in Poole Harbour froze over for the second time in a quarter of a century, with giant floes floating in the freezing water. The wings of trapped seagulls could be seen pointing up at the sky like miniature sails. In the plummeting temperatures of South Devon the keepers of the four wild apes at Paignton Zoo were on twenty-four-hour patrol in case the animals made a dash for freedom and skated across the frozen moat that separated them from the public. The zoo's elephants shivered a little less after being given a morning tot of warm rum with their breakfast. The RAC had put out a warning on the wireless saying that cars were 'skipping about like learners on ice skates'. The weather continued to leave its imprint as snowfall swept across the country, main roads became blocked, vehicles were abandoned and grown-ups quickly became disenchanted as the RAC issued another image-laden warning to say that vehicles were sliding off roads 'like spinning tops'. Traffic jams ten miles long were reported in Kent. Roads over the Mendips were closed and all horse-racing meetings were cancelled. In Dublin a young man out for a walk with his girlfriend was pinned against railings by a skidding car. Two swans froze to death in the River Stour in Suffolk.

In East Sussex the wind had whipped up the massive falls in the village of Broad Oak into drifts twenty-three and a half feet high. And as the Cuckmere River froze, winter sports came to the south coast near Seaford. Twenty-five-year-old Michael Ann and his younger brother Christopher ran Drusillas, the popular tea garden at the foot of the Sussex Downs with its small adjoining 'Zoo' made up mainly of domestic animals plus a few 'exotics'. With roads virtually impassable and recreational jaunts out to the countryside an impossibility, the decision was taken to close Drusillas until the weather improved, giving the staff an unexpected holiday. In the attic at home, Christopher Ann found the dusty, hickory skis that his late father had worn in the Alps before the war. Strapping on the old leather bindings, the brothers, accompanied by a dozen or more friends, launched themselves down the Sussex tracks.[3] A fabulous run had materialised at the top of Wilmington Hill and would have been watched over by the Long Man, had the vast figure, chalk-etched into the hillside, not already vanished under the snow. Those who had no skis brought sheets of corrugated iron bent up at the front and thundered down the slope, crossing the lower iced-up road that had become inaccessible to cars and arriving where the Royal Oak pub at Milton Street served drinks for the après-ski get-together. Down at Drusillas they used walking sticks to play ice hockey on the large pond until the great expanse of water at the top of the looping meanders of the Cuckmere River provided an alternative frozen sports ground large enough to host a Winter Olympic Games.

Most of the zoo's animals were housed in the large Drusillas barn where plentiful beds of straw kept the rabbits and the guinea pigs warm. They shared their accommodation with the zoo's chatter of budgerigars, two parrots, a fruit bat called Batty and the resident monkeys, including Pedro the notorious spectacle-grabbing Drill monkey. The pigsty was home to Ratty, a coypu rat native to South America who was the size of a beaver. In order for his digestive system to function daily, Ratty required full immersion in water and the zoo's staff's first task of the morning was to crack the ice on his private pool. There was no room in the barn for Big Joey, Drusillas' kangaroo, even though the local vet insisted Joey must be kept inside during the cold. So the Drusillas live-in staff agreed that as they rarely used their large sitting room Joey had the greater need. The furniture was moved out, leaving only the huge sofa. For two months of the Big Chill the large kangaroo lived indoors, luxuriating in great upholstered comfort and in no hurry to return to his former zoo home even if the snow was ever to melt.

As the New Year approached the snow kept on falling. Ten inches lay on the tarmac at Gatwick: six thousand tons of the stuff had been cleared from the runways but not in time to avoid the cancellation of fifty outgoing flights. A helicopter ferried a nurse carrying life-saving insulin to her diabetic patient stuck in Edburton Sands near Shoreham-by-Sea. On the higher ground in Ashdown Forest, where Christopher Robin and Winnie the Pooh had often spent balmy summer days together, seventy cars and lorries were released from huge drifts by the RAC. The transport network had begun to buckle. *The Times* asked why more was not being done 'to prevent the chaos that year after year is caused on British railways and airports by relatively mild drops in temperature and snow'.

Although the southern counties had borne the brunt of the weather at first, the destruction soon moved further north. In Leeds Bernard Ingham, northern correspondent for the

*Guardian*, discovered the washers on his taps had burst but as the pipes were frozen he had plenty of time to mend them before water would flood his house. In Leicester freezing tin lids glued themselves to the fingers of dustbin men. In the country villages of Ashton and Stalybridge outside Manchester they experienced what was referred to locally as 'a night of terror'. Between 7 and 7.30 p.m. a massive gale tore roofs off houses, collapsed chimneys and devastated the stands at the local football clubs. On 31 December, according to the *New Scientist*, the wind-chill factor in Tynemouth, a few miles north of Newcastle, had been equivalent to that recorded during the coldest months in Omsk in Siberia. At that level 80 per cent of body heat is lost and the temperature is low enough to freeze human flesh.

Hampshire residents were warned that New Forest ponies were turning feral and might attack anybody they saw or smelled carrying food. In Westcliff-on-Sea, near Southend, the pipes burst in the swanky Parmadour Hair Salon and customers had to make their way home in their curlers.[4] All over the country delivery lorries were unable to distribute food and rationing returned as queues formed outside village shops. Milkmen reported a critical shortage of milk bottles, the empties that were left outside front doors lost somewhere in the huge drifts. In Leigh in Essex William Starkey was found frozen to death at the steering wheel of his milk float. The snow in Earl's Court in London was particularly heavy as the local milkman, cigarette iced to his lower lip, the ember still glowing, carried out his round on skis. Even the Prime Minister's journey back to London after Christmas was hit by the terrible conditions. His official car and its police escort, both equipped with snow shovels, slipped and stalled their way from Birch Grove in the Sussex Weald up to London. In the subdued quiet of the capital the silence in residential streets was broken by resourceful Londoners scraping doorways and paths with fireside shovels and dustpans.

The atrocious weather continued to hit the West Country during the final few days of the year. Two thousand Dartmoor ponies were buried underneath the snow. Farmers reported coming across sheep in the blood-spattered fields still twitching with the final moments of life, abandoned by ravenous foxes suddenly scared off in the middle of eating the creatures alive. Seventy-one passengers who were trapped in two buses on the Yeovil–Dorchester road spent the night in the Clay Pigeon café at Wardon Hill. The month-old baby on board was given a bed in a blanket-lined cardboard box while a local resident arrived on skis with some baby food. A farmer on horseback came across a family of five who had been caught in a queue of a dozen stranded vehicles at Osmington Hill near Weymouth. While the daughter, son-in-law and seven-year-old grandson all survived, they had been trapped for hours in the car with the grandparents, Arthur and Daisy Barber, who had not made it through the night.

The Tamar Bridge, opened by the Queen Mother just eight months earlier, was now the only link between Devon and Cornwall. Every other road that joined the two counties was closed. In the cold vast emptiness of Dartmoor, solitary ramblers suddenly knew their insignificance and vulnerability. Landmarks had been completely covered over. The imposing granite mass of Haytor was unrecognisable, its giant's thumbs washed white as they rose to meet the grey sky. On the final afternoon of the year the wind had whipped up drifts fifteen feet high and helicopters were heard overhead, although barely seen through the snow clouds, as supplies were dropped to those who could not reach any shops. Branches of tall leafless trees, weighted with snow, bent across the sky to form cathedral-like arches. The picked-over carcasses of dead sheep, sustenance for scavenging animals, even in some cases a desperate cannibalistic fellow sheep, looked like the upturned hulls of miniature rowing boats. Foot and claw prints marked snowy paths, a lesson in identification for every schoolchild looking for evidence of badger or fox, stoat or sparrow.

Families living on the edge of the moor were more aware than ever of their proximity to Britain's most notorious prison. Long before the snow began to fall, convicts managed to escape from the huge moorland penitentiary with ingenious regularity. In November two prisoners had made a bid for freedom. Local resident and poet Sylvia Plath was so alarmed at the notion of violence running unchecked on black winter nights that she kept an apple parer at the ready and made sure the door was bolted. Now two more convicts, Colin David Baldwin and Robert Sydney Ross, were on the loose. They had slithered out of their cells on 21 December, the stolen keys to the padlocks clanking in their pockets as they ran. But after eight days a local Tiverton farmer spotted footprints, the seasonal giveaway, not far from some empty dairy churns. The two men were found cowering, milk-sated, behind a hedge.

The prison's most notorious occupant was known as The Mad Axeman, a nickname bestowed by the press on thirty-three-year-old

Londoner Frank Mitchell after he broke into a house and threatened a married couple by holding an axe over their heads. A hugely built Eastender, strong enough to hold a grand piano above his head with one hand, Frank's chief residence since the age of seventeen had been a borstal, where he routinely attacked prison warders and inmates alike. He had been relocated to Dartmoor in the summer of 1962, after escaping from Broadmoor, and appeared to be responding to his new environment well. A burgeoning passion for budgerigars and an interest in wildlife seemed to have calmed his terrifying temper to such an extent that he had not only been allowed on to the moors to feed the wild ponies but his recent behaviour had been so exemplary that he was given permission to visit the Okehampton pet shop. One snowy day he went missing. Inhabitants of the small, whitewashed Devon villages quaked. The Devon police force were out searching, having taken to wearing pyjamas beneath their uniform for extra insulation. In the nearby village of Sticklepath children did not sleep well in their beds until they heard that Mitchell had been found somewhere in a snowdrift and returned to his cell.[5]

Even in the war milk shortages had been rare, but by January 1963 collection points at 500 Dorset farms had become inaccessible and 250,000 gallons were thrown away, dyeing huge patches of the whitened earth the colour of primroses. At the other end of the country 10,000 gallons of milk were waiting without hope for tankers to collect them from the side of the road at the Wadhurst junction with Mark Cross.[6] Farmers caring for their animals were themselves confronted with life-threatening temperatures they had never experienced before and did not know how to deal with. No one had time for remarking on the beauty of a frozen stream in which reeds and leaves were visible below the ice, stilled as if in a child's game of musical statues. Instead, inside the leafless woods the air clattered and echoed with the sound of shepherds' hammers chipping at ice to make drinking holes for thirsty animals while beneath the frozen ground, the energy of a new season prepared for the day when the snow would stop falling and freezing, the temperatures would stop dropping and it would be safe to emerge.

# Chapter Eight

## *Preserving the pattern on the plate*

Three days after the snow had begun to fall the Foreign Secretary Earl Home observed wistfully over the telephone to John Kennedy, 'I wish we were still in the Bahamas.' He was not the only one longing for warmth. Depths of two and a half feet of snow had been recorded in Kent when a twenty-seven-year-old woman pulled her bike out of the garden shed at her parents' house in Sissinghurst's Mill Lane before swerving and skidding her way down the deserted village street. Shirley Punnett was on her way to a job interview wearing her smartest uniform beneath her raincoat. The jacket was a little tight and she could feel the buttons straining as she cycled. By the time Shirley reached the long lane down to our house the ice had made biking impossible so she got off to push. She was pleased she had decided to put on her rubber-soled boots, which stopped her from slipping and that her sensible black lace-up interview shoes were still dry in a bag in the front basket. My mother was waiting for her upstairs in the Priest's House in the warmest room in the place, sitting in the faded pink velvet armchair beside the fire. She was six months pregnant and wearing the green woollen cape, edged in black ribbon, like Victorian mourning stationery, in which, all through that winter, she wrapped herself. There was a no-nonsense, authoritative feeling about Shirley that was instantly reassuring. She had a surprisingly exotic professional hinterland, including a term of employment with a Greek family who were related by marriage to the famous English actress Susan Hampshire. They had taken Shirley with them on their extensive travels, where she had acquired a sceptical fascination with Fidel Castro in communist Cuba and an unshakeable passion for the Greek singer Nana Mouskouri. My mother was clearly impressed not only by Shirley's confident manner and impeccable references but also, secretly, by the associated whiff of movie-star glamour. Without hesitating, she offered Shirley the job of becoming our nanny and Shirley accepted at once.

A day or two after Shirley's interview, as a vicious blizzard swept right across England and power lines drooped and snapped under the weight of snow, my mother's mother died. Pamela had been weak anyway due to the ravages of tuberculosis, contracted during the war, and which had resulted in the removal of one of her lungs. But the coldness of the weather and, rumour had it, rather too many warming martinis, had finally toppled her. She was only fifty-eight. As I already knew about dead grandmothers I was accustomed to seeing grown-ups in tears. I had no idea that Pamela had been ill and did not mind about her death in the way I had done about Vita and my mother's dog Romeo. I had never enjoyed the weekends we spent in the New Forest with Pamela in her imposing timbered Edwardian house with fireplaces that contained electric heaters instead of real fires, which were thought to be too messy and dirty. In the overheated sitting room next to a built-in counter loaded with glasses and bottles of gin, martini, whisky, vodka and tomato juice, a table was permanently set for four with decks of cards at each place accompanied by little cardboard egg cups full of dice. It looked like the set for an Edwardian play. My maternal grandparents were crazy about card games, but not about Snap and Beggar My Neighbour, the only ones Adam and I wanted to play.

But Pamela's death meant that I would never again have to eat the strange things served up at all times of day in the New Forest: salmon fishcakes for breakfast and fried bits of offal wrapped up in soggy bacon on fried bread for lunch. I was relieved that I would never again knock my teeth accidentally against Pamela's oversized pearl necklace during her lukewarm embrace. Never again would I have to inhale the musty fur of two dead fox cubs draped around her bony neck, their limp tails trailing halfway down her knobbly back.

But we felt sad for our mother, wrapped up in her green woollen cape. For all of the consoling beauty of Sissinghurst, she was not only motherless and struggling in her marriage but she was almost friendless. Leaving London for Sissinghurst at first only for the weekends but then permanently had meant missing Caroline, her schoolgirl chum and greatest confidante. And Philippa was watching the decline of a father-in-law who had adored her. Occasionally I would hear her hushed crying through the crack of her bedroom door. Her voice was quiet but high, as if it was being squeezed through the nozzle of the icing bag Mrs Staples had used for the Christmas cake. And yet despite the inevitable nervousness that flares with each approaching birth, the unconditional love that Philippa would both give and receive from the baby expected in April is what saw her through those snowy days.

Soon after Pamela's death we were sent away, attendance at funerals being considered inappropriate for young children. We went first to some friends of our grandfather's in Guildford and then to the New Forest home of the old family doctor who had overseen the birth of my brother and myself. I had not wanted to go away again. With both parents distracted by endings, and by their evident unhappiness with each other, my own sense of what mattered and who mattered and whether I mattered wove its way in and out of my thoughts throughout that winter. As a reward for not making a fuss at being packed off, I had been given a new sweater from Sidney Smith, the old haberdashers in the King's Road, reinvented as a shop for stylish children. The sweater was Crunchie-bar yellow, loosely knitted in a large honeycomb weave. I kept catching my bitten nails in the holes. I hated it. It was too hot, too bulky and too yellow. I had also been given a pair of stretchy blue jodhpur-like trousers with a stirrup under the foot. The trousers were too big so the stirrup kept slipping off and flapping round my ankle. But the new clothes were an extravagance and I knew not to complain. After arriving for our first night in the New Forest things didn't seem too bad when I found a hot-water bottle waiting for me in my bed, but as I think of it now I can remember a faintly musty quilt from which tiny feathers escaped and tickled my nose not in a good way, and I remember trying not to flinch when the doctor's wife bent down to give me a goodnight kiss. She was as kind and as motherly as she knew how to be, especially to such a resistant child. But I missed the real thing.

I had been glad to return to London where we were to spend the rest of the holidays because it was too cold to stay at Sissinghurst, especially considering our mother's advancing pregnancy. Two years earlier, not long after my father had resigned his Conservative seat, we had moved from Hampshire to a terraced house at the un-smart end of the King's Road where the pungent whiff of fermenting hops drifted at all hours across the terraces all the way from the Fuller's Griffin Brewery in Chiswick. As part of our holiday ritual my mother's father, adjusting bravely to his new widower status, had taken Adam and me out to lunch at the grand Dorchester Hotel. We felt we barely knew him or he us and the expedition had been more of a mutual ordeal than a treat. As we ate chicken cooked in grape sauce we kicked each other in solidarity beneath the damask tablecloth. At the end of this dutiful lunch our grandfather slipped each of us a crisp, unused fiver, as if paying us for our time. Much more enjoyable had been our expedition to Bertram Mills's Circus at Olympia with my Uncle Ben and our six-year-old cousin Vanessa. We even travelled in an extravagant black London taxi because the fuel in the Number 30 bus from Limerston Street had frozen. Adam and I, with our matching blond fringes, shivered in our matching blue linen summer coats with white collars. Our mother thought it best to suffer rather than wear our scruffy duffels for such a special outing. I envied Vanessa her warm-looking embroidered jacket, which felt far more 'with it' than my own old-fashioned outfit. Inside the huge tent, ladies in swimming costumes with jewels and feathers threaded through their pinned-up hair hung upside down from precarious swings at the very top of the Big Top. Horses with white manes carried riders in white suits who sat back to front in the saddles as they tore round the ring, sawdust flying up beneath their hooves. And there was Coco the Clown with his red hair sticking out sideways from his head. He was so funny. The ringmaster in his top hat and red coat with shiny buttons had a whip as long as a rattlesnake. Snap, snap, snap went the wriggling line of leather as it teased the ankles of an Indian elephant wobbling on one leg. There was a chimpanzee staggering on stilts, a sea lion balancing an umbrella on its nose and walking a tightrope, a bear with mournful eyes riding a bike and as a finale a group of three lions, four tigers, two leopards, two black panthers and a Himalayan bear, all perching on tables and being made with the 'encouragement' of the ringmaster's whip to walk on their hind legs. I thought how awful it must be for the animals, some of whom must be so cold, all of whom must be so sad, so many thousands of miles from the sea, the mountains and the open spaces of their countries, so many thousands of miles from their families.

It was usually easy to persuade our mother that, except for special outings to the circus, it was too cold to go outside. Adam and I spent a lot of time on the window seat in our shared bedroom on the top floor, where the coal fire was hemmed in by an old leather fender with a brass railing running around it, a relic from my father's childhood nursery. From the window Adam and I watched the comings and goings in the street below. And then one day the brown curly-headed silhouette of Shirley and her suitcase appeared, outlined against the creamy stuccoed houses opposite. She had arrived, belted into her black nanny-school uniform coat on the Number 19 bus from Charing Cross railway station, having disembarked from one of the few trains to make it through the snow. We watched as she prepared to cross the road, weighted with her luggage, hesitating in case a car should glide noiselessly towards her on the snow-hushed tarmac. Squeezing past my mother's lavender-coloured Triumph Herald, she made her way carefully across the street to Number 79.

One of the perks of Shirley's employment was that she would have her own television. The small set was jammed into her bedroom cupboard on a shelf above a kettle and a toaster. Shirley was a passionate follower of the weekly drama *Coronation Street* that starred a grumpy, hefty-bosomed woman in a hairnet called Ena Sharples, and her slimmer, weedier-looking friend, Minnie Caldwell. This critical baggy-eyed bulldozer appealed to me as much as she did to Shirley, and we waited in league to catch Ena behaving ever more monstrously. We never missed an episode. We would face the set, sitting squashed together in the only armchair, eating toast and Marmite and sometimes a slice of cake from the bakers at the end of the street, while Ena pulled apart her morally depraved neighbours. Haranguing anything that smacked of change, Ena was still devoted to the life she had known before the First War.

The top floor in Limerston Street was a sanctuary. My mother rarely came all the way upstairs except to rummage in the chest of drawers on the landing where she kept her old chequebook stubs and the small pile of ration books that were empty except for a few perforated food coupons, saved for a day when they might once again be needed. In the bottom drawer a mahogany box contained a set of cards for bezique, complete with ivory counters. I had never seen my parents play this mysterious game. The whole chest of drawers felt like a time-capsule of a pre-marriage world with which my mother was apparently loath to part. Shirley also came from a pre-war upbringing. She was full of wise phrases because she hadn't been born yesterday. Some of these phrases were decipherable, others baffled us. We were told to keep our mouths shut in case the wind changed and left us permanently gawping. We were to preserve the pattern on our plates rather than scrape it off together with the very last traces of pudding. Lights left blazing in an unoccupied room reminded her of the Blackpool illuminations, even though she had never actually been there. In a rare sporting analogy we were warned that the consequences of bad behaviour meant we were heading for the high jump.

Shirley was a monarchist and a true-blue Tory. While the Queen always looked 'tidy', Mr Wilson, the Labour MP in his mackintosh and pipe, looked like something the cat had dragged in. She had little time for those who were backwards in coming forwards and no patience at all with anyone who talked the hind leg off a donkey. She tussled with mysterious aches and pains. Sometimes to our consternation she felt like death warmed up. She winced whenever she had a 'bone' in her leg caused by one of the metal wires of her elongated corset working its way loose and poking into her thigh. We had to be careful when running past the ironing board on the tiny landing for fear of toppling the pile of clothes that teetered interminably for Shirley's reluctant attention.

Sharing the confined intimacy of the top floor, we were expected to observe an unspoken agreement not to ask questions about her mysterious, personal arrangements. A red and blue bottle of Eno's Fruit Salts for settling the stomach sat next to the jar of Vicks VapoRub on our shared bathroom windowsill together with a bottle of Epsom salts, an old wives' preferred laxative that Shirley also swore by. We knew not to knock on the door when she was soaking her aching feet in a bucket of warm water and Radox. We knew not to comment on her substantial combinations, which, once washed and rinsed through in the bath, were left to dry on the collapsible wooden clothes horse in front of the fire in mine and Adam's bedroom.

Shirley was a country girl, the daughter of Horace Punnett, Sissinghurst's bricklayer, a man of few words who would vanish into his potting shed at every opportunity. Her mother was Gladys Punnett, pillar of the village WI, master cake baker, in charge of refreshments at the bingo nights held in the village hall, a gutsy, authoritative figure who spoke slowly and clearly with all the time in the world to get to the end of a sentence. Aunt Pun, as we knew her, wore her long hair in a plaited bun and the same forget-me-not sprigged dresses she had owned since her youth. Shirley's handsome brother Michael was cricket-mad and to us children he was a hero of fun and games. Shirley adored her younger brother. And he adored her too. And no wonder. Shirley was a miracle of good sense, dependability and love. We never had any doubt that she considered us to be her family and we never thought of her in any other way either. In careful script, Shirley's birthday was added to those of my parents and my brother in my small leather 'birthday book'. Her wisdom had been absorbed from her own childhood, and the understanding, deep rooted over many generations, that decency and kindness were the tenets of a good life well led. And we children became the beneficiaries of an astuteness that could not be eroded by time or fashion.

Shirley had been brought up to believe that a good dose of fresh air, even freezing air, would blow the cobwebs away. Wrenched from the window seat on the top floor, we were now sent out with an empty kettle and a bucket to fill up at the standpipe that had been erected at the end of our street while the pipes were frozen. Every afternoon, come snow or snow, we would put on our sturdy outdoor shoes and walk through streets lined with pretty Georgian houses, taking the back way to the playground in Battersea Park. Trailing a pencil along the railings to make a satisfying clattery rattle, we peered down at the semi-frozen river through the portholes of the Albert Bridge. To vary things, Shirley would lead us on a different route home. If we were going straight back to Limerston Street, we would walk down Oakley Street past the blue-plaqued house where Oscar Wilde (who wrote the fairy tales we loved) had once lived before turning left. If we had an errand to do – school nametapes to order, a new saucepan to buy – or if Shirley just felt like going up to have a look in the shops, which she often did, we would turn right. On the top floor of Peter Jones, Chelsea's all glass-fronted department store, Shirley had struck up quite a friendship with the patchily bearded man in haberdashery. We often returned home empty handed if the items had proved too 'dear', but the chat with the man in haberdashery seemed to make the expedition worthwhile. We had no idea what lay behind the enticing entranceways that we passed on our way, hurried on by Shirley, who although not yet thirty herself, was wary of us staring at men in their fashionable finery, muttering under her breath how they might 'swing both ways'. Chelsea could be a strange place, with what Shirley saw as this 'newfangled carry-on'.

# Chapter Nine

## *The best legs in the world*

The habitual uniform of the countryside was never accused of being newfangled. Outside the cities, fashion played little role in daily life: a combination of temperature and mud dictated the dress code. In January 1963 garments that had been packed away since the freezing winter of 1947 – long woollen underwear, thick wool trousers and shirts, woollen jumpers, sou'westers, army-issue greatcoats, body warmers and hobnailed boots – were retrieved from attics and dusty suitcases. Railwaymen, postmen and milkmen, who were all facing especially prolonged periods of exposure, were finding 'wet cold', the cold that accumulates either through snow or through sweat in people's clothing, to be especially dangerous. On 4 January the *Guardian* reported that new research into the effects of the 'wind chill scale' showed that the combination of high winds and low temperatures contributed to a more severe form of frostbite, which in turn could develop into hypothermia. Extreme pain in a finger or toe was the first sign of danger, but the absence of that pain signalling the destruction of nerve endings could be even more alarming. Lieutenant-Colonel J. M. Adam, the army's consultant on adapting to different temperatures, described how in excessive cold soldiers wore 'a string vest, loose-knitted woollens' and anoraks on top. Loose pyjama-like trousers were recommended. Women should pack their skirts away with their swimsuits, the Colonel advised, and, if possible, be persuaded to wear trousers because an exposed leg could result in a potentially dangerous even-patterned discolouration known as 'grannie's tartan'. A pair of sunglasses was also suggested to cope with the glare and supplies soon sold out. Lieutenant-Colonel Adam also cautioned people not to be duped into thinking that Eskimo 'blubber' would provide insulation from the cold. People needed to be fit, not fat, to survive.

Up in town it was a different story. Few city dwellers knew how to equip themselves for a harsh winter climate. The *Spectator* offered women some useful retail tips for keeping warm in January. Jaeger had a good line in 'small-clothes', wool and nylon 'unmentionables' in a choice of black, red or royal blue for a guinea with 'a naughty-nineties frill around the leg that adds a touch of "with it" nonsense to an essentially utilitarian garment'. Also recommended was a visit to Richard Shops for 'a bulked cotton lock-knit pyjama (fitting snugly to throat, ankles and wrists) for only 18s. 6d.'. On 14 January the *Daily Mirror* demonstrated with the help of top model Grace Coddington how layering 'a black Shetland sweater edged in mustard and white over a mustard sweater with a polo neck' made good sense in this sort of weather. The *Spectator* suggested a visit to stockists of Brevitt shoes. A pair of 'those shapely leather boots that are all the rage this year can cost as much as an Ascot hat, but they need set you back no more than four guineas if you can track down a pair made by Brevitt'.

In London's King's Road, once the private route for monarchs travelling from Whitehall to Hampton Court and Kew, the contrast between young and old or stuffy and 'with it' was increasingly stark. The generational, even historical, shift was never more evident than in the stretch of pavement that extended from Sloane Square to the World's End. Undeterred by London's freezing temperatures a shoe polisher who had lost a leg in the Great War was a familiar sight behind his portable workshop outside Peter Jones. He could easily be persuaded to lend his blacking to schoolgirls who dipped their mother's discarded mascara wand into his pot of paste to darken their lashes while he spoke about a barely remembered time when the term 'teenagers' had not existed. By the New Year of 1963 it had become cool to have a lover, cool to smoke dope, cool to be clever, cool to be seen with a copy of *Pornografia* by the Polish writer Witold Gombrowicz or anything published in the United States by the Grove Press tucked under your arm. It was cool to be young. Nobody below the age of twenty-five wanted to dance, make love or dress like their mothers any more. Most of the older, long-term residents wore a uniform inherited from *their* parents, comprising formal suits and ties or waisted frocks that reached to the shin, beneath belted mackintoshes, scarves and rain hats.

But the King's Road had long been an environment that attracted the avant-garde, and the new Italian-style coffee shops that had begun to line the street were the new 'in' places to meet. Writer Penelope Fitzgerald wrote in her novel *Offshore* how 'the shining Gaggia dispensed one and a half inches of bitter froth into an earthenware cup and for two shillings lovers could sit for many hours in the dark brown shadows'. Meeting places that punctuated the King's Road included Picasso's at the junction with Shawfield Street, The Temperance Billiard Hall at Flood Street, and the Kenco at Sloane Square. Between them all sat the Cosy Café, where the clientele of painters, hustlers, gamblers, workmen, nice girls and bad boys shared a trestle table for a one-and-sixpence lunch.[1] The Markham Arms, with its popular, table-football machine on which you could win a bob or two, was right next to a sweet shop, a tobacconist and a small clothes shop called Bazaar.

In 1953, the year of the Queen's Coronation, Mary Quant, aged twenty-two, had graduated from Goldsmiths, whose art faculty she described as 'the most provocative and exciting art school of the lot'. While there she had fallen in love with and soon married fellow student Alexander Plunket Greene, a flamboyant, silk-pyjama-wearing charmer.

After Mary's brief apprenticeship with 'Erik', the leading Mayfair 1950s milliner where she made customised hats with the help of her trainee-dentist brother's curved incisor needle, she had begun to design her own practical, often waist-less, androgynous clothes. In 1955, Alexander and Archie McNair, their friend, lawyer and photographer, each invested £5,000 in the boutique they named Bazaar. The shop was the showcase and salesroom for Mary's clothes. There they sold an eclectic bizarre and bazaar-like mix of Mary's own self-taught designs and a seemingly arbitrary collection of jewellery and accessories commissioned from art student friends. Mary's look centred on simplicity. 'I can't bear over-accessorisation,' she wrote in her memoir *Quant by Quant*, appalled by the very idea of 'a white hat worn with white gloves, white shoes and a white umbrella'. She had always believed that 'fashion anticipates a mood', and her predictions became reality as youthful exuberance began to flourish in the winter of 1962–3.

Mary was all about being young and never leaving childhood behind, believing children to be 'free and sane' and grown-ups to be 'hideous'. She had grown up 'not wanting to grow up', avoiding an adulthood that meant 'having candyfloss hair and stiletto heels, girdles and great boobs'.[2] Six years earlier when a 1950s beehive, with hair backcombed and lacquered into a motionless helmet was still de rigueur, Mary had asked Vidal Sassoon, a hairdresser she had come across working in a Bond Street atelier, to transform her shoulder-length hair into a five-point, bat-winged, swingy bob, a fringed hairdo that was too much for some. *Transforming a Beatnik*, a Pathé News promotional film shown in cinemas that winter, hoped to persuade teenagers to ditch 'your leather jacket and unkempt hair' and become more desirably 'ladylike'. The movie showed how, with the help of the protein nourishment of a raw egg, you and your hair could be transformed into 'a gracious lady, a modern Cinderella'.

Forever intolerant of accusations of frivolity, Mary celebrated the cleverness of youth. 'The young intellectual has got to learn that fashion is not frivolous,' she explained. 'It is part of being alive today.' With fabrics traditionally associated with men or with childhood she reinterpreted the conventional uses of gingham for tablecloths, Liberty print for children's dresses and grey flannel and tweed for dreary, unimaginative garments. Using her mother-in-law's Harrods account because the department store gave a year's worth of credit, she bought bolts of men's suit fabric which she combined with lace and frills. And while the contrast of masculine and feminine styles became the foundation of her designs, the physicality and even the fitness of the female form – the legs, the arms – was encouraged to be on unashamedly, full-on-sexy view. Mary's clothes were inspired by the sort of thing she wanted to wear herself. 'Rules are invented for lazy people who don't want to think for themselves,' she said.

But unspoken rules there were. You had to be androgynously thin to wear Mary's clothes. The miniskirt worked because 'the Chelsea girl had the best legs in the world and the courage to wear it'. An unkind cartoon in a pre-Christmas edition of *Private Eye* in 1962 pictured a shop with a question mark over its name: '*Bazaar?*' A tall, skeletal girl wearing a tie and a tiny skirt stood looking sensational in the window beside a drawing of her skinny, naked self. A small, very plump girl wearing a tie and a bulging skirt pictured beside her own overweight, naked figure was looking in at the window, an aspirational longing in her eye. The harsh truth stared back at her. Thinness was not exactly compulsory in order to look good in these clothes but as the cartoon caption advised 'it does help'.

Although Mary's shop had been quietly making its name among the inhabitants of the rangy squares of the King's Road and the pages of the fashion magazines for seven years, in the spring of 1963 it suddenly became the social hub for the 'with it'. While snobbery was, as Mary decreed, 'out of fashion', shopping in Bazaar became an event for everyone. Drinks for customers, who Mary noted included 'dukes' daughters, doctors' daughters and dockers' daughters', enhanced the fun of browsing, as the thump of jazz spilled out of the open door on to the pavement.

Men, too, were mesmerised by Bazaar. The artist (and motorbike rider) Mark Peppe was working on a series of cartoon-strip photographs in a first-floor studio that faced almost directly on to the entrance to Bazaar. One day he went into the shop and bought a hat for his art student wife Tereska to wear to his twin brother's wedding. Working part time for a dentist on Gloucester Road to earn some extra money, Tereska made a habit of gazing in at Bazaar's windows whenever she dropped in at Mark's office.[3] She had been educated in a convent where the restrictions of religion had structured her day, so Bazaar became symbolic of the moment when for Tereska 'life suddenly felt different'. Caring very much about clothes, she loved her hat and in fact all the Quant clothes 'best of anything'. Mark also bought her a 'really lovely, most unusual orangey bangle with other colours blended in'. But Tereska had been ahead of the curve. In 1957, the year before her marriage, she had bought herself a navy blue sailor-suit dress made of beautiful jersey fabric, trimmed in white and with a woollen ribbon that tied down the front. The dress ended in a short skirt that was 'a nice thing to wear on a motorbike with tights'. Worried the white trim would eventually stain, she needed advice. And although a certain amount of cool was required to walk though Bazaar's somewhat intimidatingly groovy door she was surprised and delighted one day to find Mary herself inside the shop, swinging her conker-coloured hair. Explaining her anxiety about the discolouring of the trim, Mary had shown Tereska how to unpick and replace it with red ribbon.

The shop was always open to those looking for employment. Nineteen-year-old Andrew Loog Oldham had finished a part-time job in Carnaby Street and in the evenings worked at Ronnie Scott's and also the unlicensed Flamingo Club where whisky was disguised in Coca Cola bottles. Music was Oldham's first love but he was ready to try anything. When he knocked on the door of Bazaar's office, Alexander, Archie and Mary simultaneously fell for his youth, energy and flamboyance. He was invited to join the team.

Andrew's duties involved dressing windows, driving the delivery van, walking the models' dogs and, when he realised 'liquid can become print',[4] pouring drinks for journalists. On Saturdays the shop was so frenzied that the doors were kept closed as Mary waited for someone to leave before allowing anyone else in. Shirley, Adam and I were among the passers-by who could not help stopping to stare at the eccentric window displays, where mannequins leaned at ungainly angles, shiny, real-life motorbikes serving as their props. One beautifully dressed plastic model was leading a real (dead) lobster on a golden chain like a dog. Another, dressed in tweeds, held a fishing rod attached to a goldfish bowl in which a solitary goldfish (live) swam round and round. Women were in charge.

Suddenly shopping felt enfranchised and sexy. Shirley did not approve of this sort of carry-on, especially the shortest of the short, underwear-hinting skirts. 'You don't want to be looking at tomorrow's washing,' she humphed, sniffing in disapproval.

The tiny matching shorts that accompanied the diminutive skirts in order to make it possible to go upstairs on a double-decker bus without showing knickers, garter or stocking tops did not go far to mollify Shirley. But the look was a huge hit with Mary's customers. In an interview on the BBC's *Woman's Hour* many years later Mary explained how her hemlines had enabled the wearer to 'move, run, catch a bus, dance' – the basics for getting through a day. And stockings were on the way out. During the winter of 1962–3 Bazaar began to sell the black stretch tights Mary had worn since her childhood dancing lessons and which Tereska had also already found useful to wear when riding on the back of Mark's motorbike. They had become invaluable not merely as a fashion item but also for decency and warmth. Commissioning manufacturers to make the tights in every colour, Quant found that in the harsh weather they sold 'like hot cakes', appealing especially to those whose figures did not conform to the ethereal slimness of most Bazaar customers. One 'rather large lady' who had heard that 'good black tights' are 'rather the thing in Chelsea' was reassured about her purchase by the ever-courteous Alexander, who insisted that for him 'bottoms can never look too large'.[5]

Referred to as 'abbreviated' by a disapproving BBC executive when the minis made their way on to a live television show, the skirts were not universally popular with the bowler-hatted residents of the frozen leafless squares of Chelsea. Umbrellas were whipped out to trip up the ill-clad gals and on occasion to give a sharp whack on the shin of the leggy offender. On a December visit to London, David Ormsby-Gore, Britain's Ambassador in Washington, had taken his daughter Victoria to lunch in a smart restaurant.

'I'm sorry, you can't come in,' the maître d' had announced, shaking his head and eyeing Victoria's expanse of leg.

'Why ever not?' her father enquired.

'Madam's dress does not comply.'

After a huge row a diplomatic agreement was reached in which the Ambassador and his daughter were allowed to stay on the condition they were seated behind a pot plant well out of sight of all other sensitive diners.

In the basement of Bazaar's building where Alexander had opened a restaurant there were no such boundaries. Alexander's was the pace-setting restaurant where customers might encounter an avocado pear for the first time and where the in-crowd chose to gather, a mecca for conversation and gossip enjoyed by the clientele that Mary described as 'the bohemian world of painters, photographers, architects, writers, socialites, actors, con-men, and superior tarts'. Added to this list were movie directors, visiting movie stars, including Brigitte Bardot, as well as pop stars and royalty. As they waited for their spaghetti to be served, Prince Rainier and his Princess, the former film star Grace Kelly, were noticed to be forever touching each other and holding hands beneath the tablecloth. At the adjoining table their bodyguards, sensing a certain discretion was required, turned away and ordered caviar on expenses.

# Chapter Ten

*Purple hearts*

Any impression that the glitzy King's Road was a place of innocent glamour was misleading. Nor was its catwalk reserved exclusively for women, as was obvious to us on our way home from visits to Peter Jones's haberdashery department. Men in cowboy boots, men in faded, moulded-to-the-body blue jeans and men in colourful multi-patterned, sometimes collarless shirts previously designed for wear in some far-away corner of Britain's Empire all earned Shirley's sniff of disapproval. Photographers were ubiquitous, certain of bagging a daily saleable image on the glittering tarmac. Four cockney snappers, David Bailey (who had launched the career of Paulene Stone as she posed with the stuffed squirrel), Terence Donovan, Brian Duffy and Terry O'Neill, stole both shots and hearts. Fashion photographers of the 1950s had been, as Terence Donovan described them, 'tall, thin and homosexual' with no interest in going to bed with the models, whereas he and Duffy and Bailey were 'short, fat and heterosexual', and had every interest in sleeping with as many models as they could. Bailey, Donovan, Duffy and O'Neill had an unshaven sex appeal more in common with the grooviest British film stars like the current pin-ups Albert Finney, Tom Courtenay and Alan Bates, and their intention was to 'try and make the model look like a bird we'd want to go out with'. *Harper's Bazaar* and the new *Sunday Times Colour Magazine*, which used a Bailey photograph of Jean Shrimpton, London's number-one model, in a Quant dress on its first cover, were the magazines of the moment and they could not get enough of these cool pictures. Bailey commanded added glamour after hooking up romantically with Shrimpton. Hatless, gloveless and known as the Shrimp, Bailey's 'bird' was slim as a Gitane, with her long tousled hair, very short skirts and naked lips, the smouldering dark circles under her eyes untouched. Hers was the look that eclipsed all other looks. The hairspray and well-groomed old-school elegance of Jackie Kennedy suddenly belonged to a has-been era. Cherry Marshall, 1950s model, doyenne of modelling agencies and upholder of immaculate standards of personal presentation, fell for the new generation with their 'un-brushed hair and chewing gum',[1] and for their 'enthusiasm and lack of bitterness, down to earth common sense, confidence in tackling something new'. Above all, she applauded 'the dwindling away of class divisions epitomised by clothes'.

Debutantes, unleashed from parental codes of behaviour, hit the streets of Chelsea that winter, determined to de-class-ify themselves in their shivery, knee-revealing skirts and shiny new cars. But their nervous vulnerability and gullibility was ill-concealed beneath the cigarette smoke and the pearl earrings left to them in their grannies' wills. Believing themselves to be 'modern' enough to handle their emancipation, they were sitting ducks for another category of men, the smooth-talking predators who stalked the streets of Chelsea.

'Gentleman Adventurers' in their look-at-me cars – scarlet E-Type Jaguars and black Aston Martins – with state-of-the-art sound systems, scouted the King's Road for susceptible and beautiful heiresses. Frequently masquerading as well-bred sons of the aristocracy, or as eccentrics with exotic backgrounds, these dashing debonairs were often fakes. If photographer Antony Armstrong-Jones could nab a rebelling princess then the theory was that maybe one of these chancers was in with a shot.

A brand-new discovery had enabled such behaviour. The contraceptive pill had become available through the National Health Service just a year earlier on 4 December 1961, but for married women only. However, the packet of tiny white tablets costing two shillings a month could also be acquired by the single woman who accessorised her appropriate finger with a brass curtain ring and knew an amenable private doctor. For the majority of those who swallowed the daily magic pill sexual desire became liberated from the risk of conception. The pressure to marry for the sake of giving a child legitimacy was eased, and it became possible to plan a new family around working lives. But with all these advantages there was debate and disagreement between unmarried and married women alike about how much real freedom the liberation from unwanted pregnancy had given them. There was suddenly less of an excuse for women to say no, especially to men on the make.

One of these seductive rascals was Mim Scala, a theatrical agent and variously a Teddy boy, an ice-cream salesman and a self-declared 'scallywag', whose gambling activities had nudged up against the criminal menace of the Kray twins in their matching herringbone suits. Lucky enough to have escaped such encounters with no more than burned fingers and a warning that if the Krays heard rumours that Mim was badmouthing them they would 'probably break both your legs', Scala was one of those self-confessed professional freeloaders whose aim was to get into as many parties as possible and to meet just as many pretty girls.

Mim was born with a love of glamour. His grandparents had left Italy for Britain in the 1890s, selling Italian ice cream from a tricycle in Battersea Park. The business grew and Scala's, a genuine, gleaming Roman chrome and stainless-steel ice-cream parlour, had opened in London in the 1950s in Fulham's North End Road, complete with neon lighting, mirrored tiles and multi-coloured art deco chandeliers. Mim's favourite treat as a child was to drive past Harrods slowly enough for his father to point out the actual building in which God lived. In the spring of 1962, after Mim, with his seductive Italian looks, had won the Associated Rediffusion Twist Competition, broadcast live on television, a career was launched. After dancing with teenage popstar Helen Shapiro in the musical comedy movie *It's Trad, Dad!*, he had landed a part in Cliff Richard's film *The Young Ones*, and in the winter of 1962 he was offered a job as a junior theatrical agent in Soho. Mim shared a top-floor flat in Chelsea's Cadogan Gardens with film-maker Christopher Stamp, the younger brother of Terence, super-starry star of the film *Billy Budd*. The flat was 'outrageous', the quintessence of one-night stands, joints and 'the clap', but the presence of the charismatic Stamp brothers ensured it became a hub of enchantment and sex appeal and played, Mim said, host to 'the most beautiful girls in the world who traipsed through these portals on a daily basis'.

In early 1963 Kim Waterfield, dressed in silken cravats and perfectly tailored camel coat, was the Chelsea runway's thirty-two-year-old Pied Piper.[2] His Bentley Continental was a familiar sight as he made the 'Chelsea Cruise' up and down the King's Road. The car was envied by all his friends for having a telephone connected to the main exchange through a radio link. Nicky Haslam, twenty-three-year-old Etonian designer and socialite, was transfixed by the 'Dandy Kim', who moved 'white polo-necked, caramel-suede jacketed' among his following of 'rich girls and actresses and models fed up with skinny unwashed aristocrats'.[3] Kim's past was as exotic as they come. Having been a gunrunner for Cuban dictator Fulgencio Batista he had been smuggled back to England by the ubiquitous Kray brothers before becoming a dealer in post-war black-market black stockings. He had dated the film 'starlet' Diana Dors, who judged him 'almost beautiful', before he moved on to Pamela Hayward, the ex-wife of Randolph Churchill. Known by a former lover as 'the greatest courtesan of the century', Pamela was in Kim's words 'a true redhead . . . aflame, mop, collar and muffs'. Kim's parties, hydrated with Roederer Cristal champagne, were attended by Peter Sellers and Bob Hope, and invitations required everyone 'to be pretty, rich or wise' and girls to be 'slim, beautiful and over 5 foot 8'. Society osteopath Stephen Ward never missed these occasions and often brought with him the model Christine Keeler, 'dark, beautiful, quiet and composed', and her friend Mandy Rice-Davies, who, according to fellow guest, advertising smoothie Jeremy Scott, gave 'lip as good as she got'.[4] Although Mandy hung out with the millionaires who funded her lifestyle, she knew they bought women 'as casually as they order champagne'.

Second sons of the country's richest landowners were generous hosts, throwing open their Mayfair bachelor apartments, where quantities of liberal trust-funded champagne and methedrine were on offer all night. Jeremy Scott was only momentarily annoyed when he felt the jab of a hypodermic needle in his thigh as he walked through the front door of a flat belonging to the second son of the Lord Lieutenant of Cornwall. 'You'll feel just great in a few minutes,' his ebullient host reassured him. And he did. Confident that the sun would 'sparkle on the greyest day', he also knew from experience that taking another hit would swiftly cure the resulting hangover.[5]

Carola Casson, aged twenty, and her sister Nicky, younger by two years, were both beautiful rebels, girls from the proudly alternative boarding school Cranborne Chase, which had inspired the naughty novel *Passion Flower Hotel* so enjoyed by my mother. Cranborne Chase students wore black stockings, and knew themselves to be different and, as Carola and Nicky cheerfully acknowledged, 'morally superior'. Their father, Sir Hugh Casson, was Professor of Interior Design at the Royal College of Art, often sharing the lift with bubble-gum-pink-haired Textile student Zandra Rhodes. In the convention of the day for ex-public-school girls, even ex-Cranborne Chase girls, the sisters were dragged along to elegant cocktail parties and lavish dances thrown by friends of their parents to meet 'posh, toothy girls and well-born twittish boys'. Although Carola and Nicky did their best to comply, they 'felt like screaming' at the top of their voices 'I *really* don't want to be here,' even when a handful of dishy male art students relieved the atmosphere 'because students were always hungry and there was always free food'.[6]

Nicky was the more reserved of the sisters. Before a party she would get a migraine and be sick. As a bribe, her parents gave her a drop-waisted Mary Quant cocktail dress in purple from Bazaar, which helped to boost her confidence. But Drinamyl, known colloquially as 'Purple Hearts', clinched her self-assurance. The drug, which came in small triangular or heart-shaped pills, was a deceptive lookalike for the Parma violets loved by children. This combination of barbiturates that calmed and amphetamines that stimulated had been prescribed for Sir Hugh, for whom they tamed nerves before giving a lecture. A small quantity of her father's purple hearts together with the purple dress eased Nicky through these social ordeals.

Carola had more sangfroid than her sister. She knew that elements of the King's Road crowd were made up of 'brigands and con artists' and was aware of the fashion for rich girls to be picked up by predatory tricksters. Defiant friends of hers had run away with members of this 'bad lot', their false aristocratic covers sometimes blown when hauled up in front of the courts for small-time misdemeanours. There was talk, too, among the Chelsea Set of unmarried girls who had somehow failed to slip a curtain ring on to the left finger and either were taken to Switzerland for 'a rest' or disappeared from the scene while recuperating from a mysteriously long 'appendectomy'. One of the most flamboyant figures among Carola and Nicky's acquaintance was Tara Browne. Everyone knew Tara. But everyone knew Tara was different. Dressed all in black, his blond hair thick and rumpled, his eyes green, his skin sun-bronzed, his manners impeccable, Tara was the son of an Irish peer and, through his mother Oonagh, heir to the Guinness fortune. He had grown up in Luggala, a fairy-tale house in the lee of the Wicklow Mountains, where weekend guests included Jean Cocteau, Salvador Dalí and Samuel Beckett. Tara, who at the age of eleven had announced to the world that he was giving up cigarettes and drink, was described by the poet Hugo Williams as a combination of 'Little Lord Fauntleroy, Beau Brummell, Peter Pan and Terence Stamp in *Billy Budd*'. Tara had arrived in London's Eaton Square in the spring of 1962 just as Cliff Richard's song 'The Young Ones' hit the top of the charts and just in time for his seventeenth birthday. He was unmistakable in his 'green suits, mauve shirts with amethyst cuff-links, his waves of blond hair, brocade ties and buckled shoes, smoking menthol cigarettes (always Salem)'.[7]

Although he had not yet passed his driving test, Tara proved that the present from his mother of a scarlet Alfa Romeo, one of the most powerful racing cars on the market, was capable of reaching 110 mph in the middle of the night along the straight stretch of Piccadilly. Cars were Tara's obsession, speed his aphrodisiac. His friend Martin Wilkinson, who as a teenager had fancied a career as a bullfighter, would join Tara in his

Mini Cooper as they both rounded Hyde Park Corner at 80 mph, in what Tara described as 'a poetic gesture'.[8]

Tara was not only loved by his closest friends, like the Ambassador to America's daughter Victoria Ormsby-Gore and by the flash set in which he moved, but for his interest in what people thought and said rather than the background they came from. In the summer of 1962 he had met Nicki MacSherry at Battersea Park funfair. With her narrow frame, peroxided and cropped hair, tight denim jeans and heavily kohled eyes, Nicki was the nineteen-year-old daughter of an Irish farmer turned postman. She was working as the coat-check girl at the Marquee Club when she and Tara fell in love, forever photographed leaning their slim bodies into each other, sitting on top of one another, racing the traffic in Tara's car, twisting the night away. With this thunderclap combination of lust and money their friends smelled danger. During the winter of 1962 Tara and Nicki moved in together into a flat not far from the King's Road opposite South Kensington Underground station. As the winter cold took hold, the pair spent most of their time shut away in bed in their freezing bedroom, where, subjected to regular power cuts, they watched their breath turn into clouds from beneath the sheets. Late at night they would lean out of their bedroom window to watch the romantic figure of Rudolf Nureyev on his way home to his flat in Knightsbridge's Ennismore Gardens after a rehearsal at Covent Garden. After his defection from Russia two years earlier during the height of the Cold War, Nureyev had become the Royal Ballet's new sensation, their Principal Dancer. Dressed in costumes designed by Cecil Beaton he had made his first joint performance with

Prima Ballerina Margot Fonteyn in February 1962. By the end of that year Tara and Nicki were not so much awed by Nureyev's fame or taken with his full lips and widely spaced eyes as they were open-mouthed at the sight of his 'extraordinary taut and muscled bottom'.[9]

Chrissie Shrimpton, an old friend of Nicki MacSharry and the younger sister of David Bailey's model girlfriend Jean, often dropped by Tara and Nicki's flat with her student boyfriend Mick Jagger who lived in a flat in Edith Grove in the far reaches of the King's Road. The son of a teacher and a hairdresser, Jagger was studying finance and accountancy at the LSE. He planned to become a foreign correspondent for the *Financial Times*, basing himself between Paris and London. Meanwhile, he maintained his slender androgynous figure or what Andrew Loog Oldam called 'the human form of a puma with a gender of its own' by playing soccer for the LSE's second eleven. But he was hoping that his fledgling rock band would have a lucky break soon.

Tara's friends were right to be alarmed by his recklessness, especially when he was behind the wheel of a car. Four years later Tara was driving his pale blue Lotus Elan through the streets of Chelsea with his new girlfriend, model Suki Potier, when he suddenly lost control. Swerving to avoid a car crossing his path, he managed to wrench the wheel round before hitting a parked van. Some reports estimated he had been driving at a speed of 106 mph. Thanks to Tara's last-minute turning of the vehicle Suki, who was sitting in the passenger seat, avoided the force of the collision and suffered nothing more than bruises as the driver's side took the full impact. A local observer who saw the damage to the almost disintegrated car said, 'the steering wheel was bent like a flower stem'.

Tara was taken to nearby St Stephen's hospital, where he was found to have suffered 'brain lacerations due to fractures of the skull'. He died two hours later. He was twenty-one years old. Singer Marianne Faithfull said, 'It was like a death knell sounding over London . . . it was the end of the sixties for many people.' Paul McCartney (who knew Tara well) and John Lennon were among those horrified to read about the accident in the newspapers. Their haunting song 'A Day in the Life', with the lyric 'I Heard the News Today, Oh Boy', was one of Lennon and McCartney's most moving compositions, and became the forever-boyish Tara's lasting epitaph as the dark underside of the gilded Chelsea glamour was finally laid bare.

# Chapter Eleven

## *If you pretend to be wicked, you'll get rich*

Brian Jones, who shared the Edith Grove flat with Mick Jagger, was a part-time shop assistant at Whiteleys department store in Bayswater. Keith Richard, a third occupant, spent most of his day in bed or taking shots at visiting rats with the revolver they kept in a lavatory where the frozen cistern water made it impossible to pull the chain. Sleeping on mattresses on the floor, the flatmates lived on pork pies and coffee and food parcels sent by Keith's mother from Dartford. They lived within the contemporary philosophy that everything – flats, rooms, beds, spliffs, money, food and girls – must be shared. Bill Wyman had joined the band in December 1962 as bass guitarist and had worked out how to earn a few shillings by collecting the empty beer bottles from the yard behind the Weatherby Arms in the King's Road and selling them back to the landlord. But it was music that bonded them, and that winter the Rolling

Stones had been encouraged by a series of bookings made by local pubs and clubs, including the Weatherby Arms and further afield in Richmond and Twickenham. They also occasionally played at the Marquee in the West End, most recently on 3 January, although the jazz-loving audience remained sceptical about the rhythm and blues sound as well as the dishevelled appearance of Mick in his cardigan and Keith Richard with his spotty teenage face.

But with the bad weather the bookings had become even sparser than usual and the band's intermittent flow of income had dwindled. Even if people had felt like going out in such cold weather, the seizing up of the transport system had made it impossible to reach some of the venues. All the gigs at the Eel Pie Island Hotel in Twickenham had iced to a standstill with the bridge across the Thames closed to the Stones' scattering of fans, the sound of some of London's greatest blues bands that played there also silenced. Diehard enthusiasts who would usually swim across the short stretch of the Thames, their dry clothes balanced on their heads in order to dodge the twopence entrance fee to the famous venue, were forced to look elsewhere for music. One night at a gig in Ealing only two people braved the weather to come and see the Stones play. On another evening in the Marquee the power failed halfway through their second set. But the band remained undaunted, practising with Wyman's invaluable bass amplifier, occasionally splashing out on a beer in the Weatherby Arms, 'hanging places, stealing food and rehearsing', as Keith described in his memoir *Life*, as well as watching the steady accumulation of filthy dishes, 'junked pyramids of foulness that no one could bear to touch', piling up in the sink. After the electricity meter had been fed there was no money left for washing-up liquid. And yet. Despite the struggle to afford to eat and despite the cold, Keith felt there was 'something beautifully friendly and elevating about a bunch of guys playing music together'.

Like so many others who were snowed in that January, the Rolling Stones listened non-stop to the BBC on the huge radiogram that Brian had brought with him as a dowry to the band's marriage. From beneath their grubby blankets it suddenly became impossible to ignore the sound of the group from Liverpool with the pudding-basin haircuts who seemed to be getting an inordinate amount of airtime. On the BBC Light Programme's morning show *Saturday Club*, the Stones listened to the Beatles play copycat versions of Chuck Berry and Bo Diddley songs with the occasional bouncy original composition thrown in. The interviewer asked John how the band had chosen its name. 'It came to us on a flaming pie,' John, ever the sarcey one, told him. 'And the pie spoke these words: "From this day on you are the Beatles with an A."'

But the Stones were not to be outdone, and Brian Jones was pleased when his letter to Brian Matthew at the BBC asking for an audition was accepted. Always immaculately turned out despite the squalor of the flat, he attempted to blow-dry his hair into a Beatles lookalike pouffe for the occasion and emerged looking more like a St Bernard. Soon after the audition a letter arrived turning the band down because Mick Jagger sounded too 'coloured'. But then, on 17 January, the regular band at the Crawdaddy Club, which was based in the back-room venue at the Station Hotel in Richmond, couldn't make it through the snow. The Crawdaddy was as popular as the Eel Pie and when the Rolling Stones were asked to play as stand-ins they jumped at the chance. Because of the weather, 'two for the price of one' tickets went on sale. The band had expanded and that night graphic artist and part-time drummer Charlie Watts joined the Scottish pianist Ian Stewart (also an ICI employee), Brian Jones on the harmonica, Bill Wyman and Keith Richards on bass and Mick Jagger as lead singer.

When the doors opened that night the room was half empty, but word of mouth spread that the Stones might be worth listening to on a boring snowy evening, and by the time they took to the stage the Crawdaddy was full to capacity. Three hundred teenagers, mods, rockers, students and shop assistants defied the snow that night. And as Jagger removed his jacket, pouting, self-conscious, cool, he proved he had no problem working a stage no bigger than a kitchen table. Standing in his drip-dry shirt and loose black string tie, and holding his tambourine and maracas, he whipped his blue-jeaned and sloppy-joe-jersey audience into a frenzy. Andrew Loog Oldham, part-time window dresser and do-everything assistant in Bazaar, was now on the hunt for emergent singers to represent. Making it his business to race around as many clubs in London as he could cram into one night, Oldham was there in the 'dark and sweaty' Crawdaddy as the band kicked off their set. He had never seen or experienced a reaction like it as 'the remaining air left the room from the whoosh of hundreds of waving hands, dancing feet and heaving bodies having sheer, sheer pleasure'.[1] The performance became the creative act through which the musicality and the physicality of the audience themselves were released. A primal sexuality poured off the stage and on to a dance floor that bounced so violently that one woman reportedly fell over and broke a leg. For Oldham it was like experiencing the ultimate orgasm, as the music 'reached out and went inside me'. He was caught up in an audience who were 'as flushed and happy as if they'd had the real thing'. This was a group of musicians and singers that offered an alternative to the clean-cut Beatles image, not really the sort of music that your mother would be happy to listen to. This was the sort of band whose fans asked for autographs to be inscribed not on their programmes like most pop fans, but on their bra straps. 'If you pretend to be wicked, you'll get rich,' was nineteen-year-old Oldham's advice to Mick Jagger, putative foreign correspondent for the *Financial Times*. Jagger decided to take Oldham's advice.

Just before Christmas Bob Dylan, a young folk singer known as Bobby to his friends, had flown into London from New York. Philip Saville, a BBC drama producer, had been on a recce to New York when his friend, the fifty-five-year-old poet W. H. Auden, who lived in Manhattan, gave him a tip-off.[2] Auden urged Saville to visit Tony Pastor's club in the Village. 'Everybody goes there who is anybody,' Auden said. 'It's like going to the place up in Liverpool,' he said, trying to remember the name of the cellar where that up-and-coming Liverpool band was known (by those in the know) to play. Bob Dylan, aged twenty-one, with his fine long nose and uncombed, exuberant, curly hair, had been singing in Tony Pastor's for a year by the time Auden had sauntered in and been captivated by his gravelly, half-speaking singing voice. It was a voice capable of conveying emotion like few others, a voice in soft contrast to the other harsher sounds like those of Bobby Vee and Little Eva and the Coasters that were being played in New York that year. Berry Gordy's Motown label in Detroit was also turning out singles by the Supremes and Stevie Wonder at the same rate as cars on a production line. Dylan's gentler, ballady sound came from someone unimpressed by the fast pace of Manhattan, not interested, Dylan explained, in 'the atomic bathrooms and electronic bedrooms and souped-up can openers' but in 'feeling and watching the people and the dust and the ditches'.[3] Choosing to reject the rock and roll of Elvis and Buddy Holly that he had loved as a teenager, Dylan now favoured folk music, songs 'filled with more despair, more sadness, more triumph, more faith in the supernatural, much deeper feelings', many of which he wrote himself.

His music spoke the language of the concerns of his generation and of war and of love. Saville was struck by the beautiful, prophetic, despairing, apocalyptic, ballad that Dylan had first sung in October just before the Cuban Missile Crisis. *A Hard Rain's Gonna Fall* told of the poet who 'heard the sound of a thunder, it roared out a warnin', heard the roar of a wave that could drown the whole world'. The lyrics belonged to the preceding autumn when everyone thought the Russians might blow up the world. 'I wanted to get the most down that I knew about into one song,' Dylan explained, 'the most that I possibly could.'[4]

Saville was as entranced as Auden had been, thinking, 'This is too good to be true.' He was directing *The Madhouse on Castle Street*, a new BBC television play written by Evan Jones, a white Jamaican playwright, and he urgently needed a character to play the part of Lennie, an anarchic young songwriter who lived in an English boarding house. Although Dylan had released an album and was the talk of the local Manhattan folk club circuit, the album had not done well and his reputation had barely broken the boundaries of the East Village. Dylan had no acting experience at all, but even so Saville offered him the part and agreed to pay him a fee of $500. And Albert Grossman, a New York agent who had been watching Dylan with keen interest, risked standing the cost of Dylan's airfare and accommodation. Dylan accepted. The prospect of such a gig was pretty cool for an unknown-in-Britain twenty-one year old.

With Robin Hood and St George the Dragon Slayer as his indefatigable heroes, Dylan was better prepared than most to tolerate the freezing weather that had met him on arrival in England. 'The thing that most people don't realize is that it's *warmer* to have long hair,' Dylan explained in a later interview to *Playboy* magazine. 'People with short hair freeze easily. Then they try to hide their coldness and they get jealous of everybody that's warm . . . a lot of prison warders have short hair,' he explained. Having checked into the bohemian May Fair Hotel in Berkeley Square, which boasted pianos in every suite and whose famous Beachcomber bar came complete with parrots and a tank containing real caiman crocodiles, Dylan set out in his blue jeans and cap to explore London's pubs and clubs. For the next couple of weeks, before he was needed on set for Saville's play, he discovered how unsophisticated the facilities in London's famous folk-singing cafés were. Many of them had been founded in the 1950s and did not even include stage lights or a microphone. People sat around the small raised platforms drinking their pints and listening to the music. Bobby sank below ground to the 400-year-old wine cellar beneath Bunjie's Coffee House just off the Charing Cross Road. He visited Peter Cook's Establishment in Greek Street. And he turned up at the Pindar of Wakefield for the regular singers' club nights and, twice, accepted an invitation to perform with folk singer Nigel Denver. Initially friendly and supportive of one another, the two men soon clashed. When Denver declared that Dylan 'couldn't sing his way out of a paper bag' and that his playing of any instrument, including the guitar, was nothing short of a disaster, their collaborative appearances came to an end.[5] Another night Dylan went south to the Old Brompton Road where the sweaty, beery Troubadour, the place to go for skiffle, with its ceiling hung with musical instruments, was the high note within London's symphony of musical pubs. The Troubadour was also a hub of political activity. It hosted Ban the Bomb meetings, sold CND pamphlets and was one of the scattering of places where copies of *Private Eye* could be bought. Troubadour's manager Anthea Disney was selling tickets at the door when Dylan appeared; she recognised the young man in a shaggy coat, cowboy boots and jeans from a photograph on the front cover of *Sing Out*, an American folk magazine. She offered to return his entry fee in exchange for a song. But Dylan hugged his sheepskin collar closer to him for warmth, and turned down the invitation, preferring to sit and listen, absorbing and learning the words and the sounds of the British and Irish folk singers as, washboards and tea chests at their feet, the clientele waited their turn at the bar to perform.

Although Dylan had accepted a few invitations to sing at a handful of the London venues, his drug habit had alienated some. 'Fuck off,' came the cry from the floor of the Roundhouse one night when Dylan's performance had drifted into mumbling incoherence while the doorman at the Singers announced that Dylan was barred. The Singers Club did not admit 'shits'. But Dylan was not to be rebuffed. On New Year's Day he joined the crowd at the King and Queen pub in Foley Street when Nigel Denver took to the stage. 'What's all this fucking shit?' jeered Dylan from the back. A day or two later Dylan was back at the King and Queen wearing a thick, wool, tartan shirt. His face was familiar to singer Martin Carthy, who succeeded in getting Bobby to leave his seat and give the customers three songs. He was an instant hit with his impromptu audience, who loved his laid-back way and what Carthy described as 'a great sense of comedy'. Dylan's reputation, good and bad, inevitably reached Andrew Loog Oldham. Turning up at the May Fair Hotel, the would-be agent described in his autobiography how he had been confronted by a young man with 'a grey face, eyes both dead and knowing'. Dylan was dressed in a uniform that Oldham recognised from his own days in New York, 'the Greenwich village clobber' of flat colours and army-surplus gear. Oldham sold himself as Dylan's temporary London 'press representative' for the bargain price of a fiver. He hoped he had found himself a client with potential.

Bob Dylan had smoked his way right through Christmas and into the New Year. The manager of the May Fair Hotel complained. 'Those sorts of cigarettes' were not permitted, even in such a liberal establishment as the May Fair. And there had been objections from other guests about the sound of late-night guitar strumming in the hotel lobby, which had drifted upstairs and kept them awake. When the May Fair announced they had put up with enough of this young disruptive pot smoker, Dylan was rescued by an increasingly apprehensive Philip Saville, who brought Dylan home with him until a more accommodating hotel could be found.

At a loose end much of the time, Dylan wandered into the offices of the hugely influential *Melody Maker* magazine one day and bumped into notorious journalist Bob Dawbarn. The author of a satirical and acerbic gossip column, Dawbarn held in his pen both the ticket to fame and the power to destroy. He had no time for scruffy harmonica players, especially on going-to-press day and threw the folk singer straight out. Dylan spent a lot of time hanging out with Martin Carthy, in his freezing flat. When his impecunious friend seized a handy samurai sword and began to chop up an old piano for firewood, Dylan joined in and Carthy's flat rang with the sound of demolition.

With snow in London settling in at seven inches and drifts of up to six feet, the day of filming Saville's play eventually arrived. As soon as the cameras began to role Saville became the last to realise that Dylan could not act. The putative star of the play was eventually demoted to a small part, playing, in Saville's words, 'a rather uncommunicative American' who had found his voice in song. But one morning before leaving for work Saville had spotted Dylan sitting at the top of the stairs with an audience of two, singing something quite beautiful, a melody Saville did not recognise. One glance at Saville's Spanish au pairs, their faces beatific, 'like two little robins or starlings', told Saville that 'Blowin' in the Wind' was the song with which he must open and close his play.

When *The Madhouse on Castle Street* was broadcast in mid January in the *Sunday Night Play* series, reviewers were not ecstatic about Saville's discovery. The *Listener* said Dylan 'sat around playing and singing attractively if a little incomprehensibly'. But by then Dylan had left London to return to the clubs in New York and to see whether the American critics would be a little more receptive. He would take his chance with the song that had captivated Saville's au pairs. He suspected that the answer to his success lay not in acting, or even in Britain, but back in the clubs of downtown Manhattan.

# Chapter Twelve

## *A murky place*

Throughout January, in factories and coal mines, on land and road, at airports and out at sea, the consequences of the big freeze were being felt. Twenty thousand driving tests had been cancelled during the first week of the New Year and by the end of a third consecutive week of bad weather snow had fallen on Exmoor for thirty-six continuous hours. On 6 January 1,300 sheep, ponies and bullocks had been dug out from drifts on Dartmoor. The pinch-tight, single-car-width lanes that criss-cross the Devon countryside around Okehampton were challenging for drivers even in the cow-parsley froth of summer, but that winter the drifts had reached the six-foot stone-built boundaries before engulfing the hedges that topped the old stone walls. As the wind continued to blow under a ghostly blue-white sky, the soft snow that had blocked the gullies of the narrow roads was cleared by County

Council machinery leaving thrillingly long ice corridors of cleanly cut impacted ice.

At the beginning of January twenty-six power stations had begun to work to rule over the union's dispute about pay and overtime. With up to a third of the country's supply affected at random times of the day, another eleven power stations soon joined the industrial action. Charles Doyle, the union's spokesman, estimated that about a third of the industry was involved in the sporadic walk-outs, making the availability of light and heat unpredictable and coinciding with the widespread freezing of water pipes. In the streets queues of people holding buckets waiting their turn to replenish supplies of drinking, bathing and kettle-boiling water grew ever longer. The strike brought a sense of desperation but also merry havoc. The London Underground was frequently plunged into darkness, but maternity units in the capital's hospitals acquired a biblical glow as babies arrived by candlelight. Mothers were given piles of the latest 'disposable' nappies to take home as the 'terry towelling' version would no longer dry on freezing washing lines. Meanwhile, the Central Electricity Generating Board suggested helpfully that housewives might postpone their ironing until the dispute was resolved. Services in Canterbury Cathedral were conducted in candlelight. At a performance of *The Sleeping Beauty* at Barking Assembly Hall, the lovely Princess Christabel observed to the Prince, 'So this is the underworld. What a murky place,' at the very moment the lights went out. In the pitch darkness the audience cheered and clapped at the serendipitous timing.

Richard Wood, The Minister of Power responsible for the smooth running of Britain's coal, gas and electricity supplies, was a stoic individual. Although he had lost both legs in the Second World War after they were crushed by an unexploded bomb in Libya, he managed his demanding political career with the help of artificial limbs, even though they had reduced his once impressive height of 6 foot 4 by three inches.[1] Wood owed his gutsiness in part to his father, Lord Halifax, who kept his withered left hand concealed in a leather glove. As Lord H. had never spoken about his hand, the family felt there was no need for his youngest son to mention not having legs. In the same spirit and with these sturdy new appendages, nothing stopped Wood from continuing to drive and to shoot game. But at times, despite his tireless negotiations with the unions, even Wood could seem as powerless as a light switch in a power cut. A resolution to the dispute did not seem to be imminent.

Meanwhile, the Minister's equally gutsy wife helped sustain the morale of her husband and the readers of the *Daily Mail*. Diana Wood was the daughter of a distinguished army colonel and had wartime resilience coursing through her veins. She believed that electricity-powered warmth was not the only means of combating cold. Extra layers of clothes were Mrs Wood's answer, and she was happy to be photographed by the press demonstrating the efficacy as well as the appeal of a pair of tight, black Jaeger woollen knee-length trousers worn with fishnet stockings beneath. *Time* magazine also published the story, reporting how 'pretty' Mrs Wood had 'helped raise at least some temperatures by posing for the *Daily Mail* in her cold-weather costume'. As neither the strike nor the snow showed any signs of letting up, Mrs Wood was an example to us all.

The Automobile Association did not demonstrate quite as much optimism. They claimed the weather was 'satanical' and warned that 'the only thing travelling up the M1 is snow', while the RAC, equally pessimistically, said that the 'Peak District looks like the Alps'. To help with the black ice on Britain's roads, five hundred lorries from across Britain converged in a queue at a rock salt mine in Cheshire. Helicopters dropped food on Dorset's fields for stranded villagers to collect as well as hay for hungry animals before lifting up the ill and ferrying them to hospital. An orphanage housing thirty children under the age of seven at East Knoyle in West Wiltshire was isolated from the world for days. Across the county, Stonehenge was photographed from the air looking like upturned, sugar-sprinkled bourbon biscuits.

There were fears that the straits of Dover would ice over and cut Britain off from Europe. In Rottingdean in East Sussex the rare sight of 'frazil' ice had accumulated just off the beach, the tiny particles collecting in moving water and sinking to the seabed. The spray from the breaking waves froze as it speckled the air and fell in ready formed ice patches on to the sand. An Essex fisherman told the *Southend Standard* that their regular catch, including sole, roker and plaice, 'have been driven so far into deep water that it will take a very strong spring to entice them back', as he and his colleagues in Southend and Leigh were forced to sign on at the Employment Exchange.[2]

In Oxford home-owners on the banks of the Thames drove their cars across the frozen river to meet friends living on the opposite side. Estuaries and backwaters were glassy with ice, preventing water birds and wildlife that lived along the river-banks from finding food. Kingfishers, waders and wildfowl died in their hundreds of thousands. Birds caught in freezing air currents and paralysed with a lethal gust of cold air mid-flight fell to the ground like bricks. 'Glazed' ice, a phenomenon in which falling rain is transformed into solid transparent droplets, coated the trees as the feet of birds froze to branches. Pheasants were unable to lift their iced-over wings, failing to become air-borne and leaving themselves ever vulnerable to a farmer's gunshots. Birds of prey, including buzzards and kestrels, as well as starlings, crows and magpies, changed their diets and fed from the corpses of smaller birds. And the Ministry of Agriculture recommended that farmers should shoot the hundreds of house sparrows that had begun foraging for food intended for their animals. Newborn chicks and ducklings abandoned by their mothers and seeking warmth were wrapped in woollen hats and occupied the airing cupboards on many a farm. Bats, hedgehogs and dormice had followed their hiber-nating instincts well before the ground froze and had hidden themselves away deep within the dark womb of the earth.[3]

*Private Eye* took the view that excitable press coverage of the snow story was tending towards over-reaction, teasing that 'the first to be struck down by "The White Terror" was Mrs Enid Thrust, who aged 107 died of pneumonia in the Bedstead County and General Hospital where she had been a patient for 45 years.' The magazine recounted the story of another 'tragic' victim of the weather after Hamish McNurd was hit by a falling bale of hay that tumbled from a helicopter attempting to rescue 'the little highland village of Killiguelish, cut off for the past seven years'. And yet the drama felt justified when Meteorological Office archives showed that such temperatures had not been experienced since 1814, a year before Napoleon Bonaparte's defeat on the battlefields of Waterloo.

# Chapter Thirteen

## *Pink Sorrento lipstick*

All over the country as a new school term was scheduled to begin in January, schools struggled to open. Travel in this fourth week of snow for both pupils and staff was sometimes prohibitive and the cost of heating, even when the electric power was flowing, threatened to break all budgets. A school bus in Southwold in Suffolk found it could not move when the diesel in its tank froze, giving the children a day off to play in the snow. But for those who lived within walking distance of school, the journey became an adventure in itself. At Seaford Head in Sussex a rim of ice along the barbed-wire fence tempted daring seventeen-year-old schoolboy Lionel Pelling to linger as he and his friends showed off their tightroping agility beside the sea.[1] In Prudhoe, Northumberland, eighteen-year-old Christine Hewitt had no choice about going to school. 'You put wellies on and walked. If you could get on a sledge, you went to school.'[2] Lavatories froze over and schoolboys who broke the ice with a stick were told not to hit too hard for fear of cracking the porcelain. Six-year-old Carl Chinn, son of a bookmaker who was trying to keep his business afloat after the cancellation of all horse racing, began his day in Birmingham by making patterns with his finger inside the frozen windows before setting off to school. 'Until you were eleven and at big school you wore short trousers,' Carl explained, which meant you had to pull up your socks 'as far as you could so you only had a little bit of leg showing.'[3]

At posh boys-only boarding schools the mood was transformed from the usual post-Christmas anticlimax into something that felt like a continuation of the holidays as snowball fights replaced the official games curriculum. But at Rugby, where things had always been taken seriously and boys still wore the black ties initially required for mourning the death of Queen Victoria, no concessions were made for the harsh weather. When A-level student Jonathan Chiswell-Jones asked his housemaster for a little more warmth in which to work, he was told to invite others into his tiny study because 'each person is equivalent to a 30-watt heater'.[4] Twelve-year-old Simon Knight shivered at Elms prep school in Herefordshire where there had been no relaxation of the short-trousered uniform rules. Getting ready to toboggan down the foothills of the Herefordshire Beacons, Simon remembered he had a polo-neck sweater in his trunk. Admired and envied by his friends for his ingenuity, Simon would turn his sweater upside down and slip his small icy knees into each sleeve. The remaining bulk of the jersey warmed his waist as he climbed the snowy hill.[5] At his school in Oxfordshire, eleven-year-old Matthew Engle was wishing the summer would arrive. Matthew was cricket mad. The Ashes were being played in Australia that winter and at 6.30 a.m., just before the getting-up bell rang, Matthew would listen under his pillow to the final daily half-hour of live BBC radio commentary. As he heard how the fielders were pulling down their hats to shield their faces from the sun, all Matthew could think about was the prospect of being warm again. Soon his obsession with sunshine and cricket grew into an obsession with Australia. And when he heard rumours that a slightly older new boy named Alex Berstein actually *came* from Australia Matthew could not leave him alone. Kindly playing along with Matthew, Alex secretly consulted atlases and guidebooks in the school library to answer his fan's insatiable questions about Alex's sunny homeland. But eventually the research proved too much and Alex finally confessed that he had never been to Australia because he actually came from Dublin. But the Australian bug had infected Matthew for life. When he grew up he planned to become a first-rate sports journalist and travel to Australia to be warm and to write about cricket.[6]

For older students, including those in their first year at university, the thrill of independence was lost in itchy chilblains and the trudge through the snow to classes in damp socks, unsuitable shoes, unsuitable clothes and the by now universal feeling that the snow would never stop falling. Charles Anson had just completed his first term at Jesus College, Cambridge, and had spent the week after Christmas skiing in Austria. But snow, or snow that had turned into packed ice, was not what he was expecting to find as his train pulled into London's

Victoria station. Stepping out onto the icy platform, Anson slipped. It was a long slow-motion slip but the landing was agony. A ligament had been ripped badly. He spent the following university term negotiating his way through the slippery winter weeks on crutches, his leg encased in a thick inhibiting bandage. But Anson was resourceful and found that despite the icy pavements, he could, with practice, make his way along the path from college to tutorial to lecture to pub. He even managed to limp up the metal fire escape at the back of his lodgings escorting a series of personal visitors whenever the front door was locked, finding that the bandaged leg proved no deterrent to a committed romantic.[7]

Hazel Roscoe was a school teacher who described herself as 'one of those doughty north-westerners'[8] who was 'strong in the arm and quick in the head'. She had recently moved with her scientist husband William and their two children from Cheshire up to Ravenglass where the Roscoes and other families from the surrounding Cumbrian villages were enchanted by this frozen world. With one pair of skates between them, Hazel and Bill took turns to enjoy the icy lakes as Ros aged seven and Gareth aged five tobogganed down the Fells in the snow. There was a timeless beauty in their new surroundings. There was even a local vicar who slid past Hazel in perfect control of his skates, with his arms held behind his back showing off this unexpected skill to his impressed parishioners and reminding Hazel of Henry Raeburn's wonderful 1795 painting of *The Skating Minister*. The Ravenglass community wanted for little. The pipes may have frozen, but buckets were lowered into old village wells that had not been opened for centuries, and gallons of unusually sweet-tasting water were hauled up. Although the snowy roads affected deliveries of food, home-grown potatoes and carrots had been put by from habit during the summer. Dozens of small local farms continued to fill their milk churns and the shortage of bread deliveries called for a run on yeast and for the lighting of ovens at home.

Hazel taught at Irton Hall, a residential school in the neighbouring village of Holmrook that took children aged seven to sixteen. Irton was an ESN or an Educationally Sub-Normal establishment, one of the few special needs schools in the country. A postcard of the ivy-clad hall identified the building as a 'spastic school', where those children whose muscle spasms were a symptom of cerebral palsy were cared for. These children were not only classified as displaying below average intelligence but they were also physically disabled and confined to wheelchairs. Marks remained visible on the foreheads of those as old as twelve, evidence of the forceps used by doctors to persuade reluctant babies from the womb, unwittingly inflicting life-long consequences both mental and physical. Visits from parents were rare, not through lack of love but owing to the long distances many needed to travel. At the beginning of every autumn term Hazel would help the children unpack their suitcases. Knowing they would not see their families for three months, the sight of their end-of-term party outfits that had been neatly and tenderly folded at the bottom of the case, even as the summer weather lingered, always moved Hazel to tears. These proxy parents, including Hazel, made sure the children received all the love and compassion they could give. When the children asked what the initials ESN stood for the teachers told them it mean 'Ever So Nice'. But the early days of the new spring term of 1963 held one compensation for these children whose lives had rarely been touched by magic. The snow-covered fields presented a world suddenly transformed and in that moment Hazel caught a glimpse of enchantment illuminating the faces of these children for whom she had come to care so deeply.

While Irton Hall never closed its doors whatever the weather, some of the younger pupils at Holmhurst St Mary, an Anglican convent for girls near Hastings in East Sussex, felt lucky to be told to stay at home in an extension to their Christmas holidays. Only a handful of shivering exam candidates returned for the spring term. To sixteen-year-old Joanna Lumley, her companionable pet mouse tucked warmly into her blazer pocket, the school felt 'clammy, cold, empty and vast'. The reluctant young academics shared just one dormitory.[9] The nuns, usually very stern about uniform rules, allowed the girls to wear trousers under their pleated skirts. But this concession to warmth looked and felt strange and the sense of unease was enhanced when the familiar, bell-bound routine of the school day was exchanged for an unfamiliar silence. Usually the awakening jangle at 7.15 a.m. would be followed by another indicating the time to be up and dressed. The chapel bell, the breakfast bell and the interminable clanging that marked the beginning and end of every lesson usually punctuated the day into rigidly observed segments. But in January 1963 the bells at St Mary's had become redundant with so few pupils and Joanna missed the noisy routine that made school life reliably familiar. During those long snowy days the A-level girls were expected to study on their own, a solitary activity that prevented Joanna from doing much work at all. Even though languages were her best subjects, she found it impossible to absorb a single word of French, Latin or German while 'sitting in a snow-lit room, that weird unearthly colour, the blue light of snow, and the quietness, the horrifying quietness'.

But at the same time Joanna's sense of the sweetness, goodness and self-sacrifice of the nuns who had no first-hand knowledge of being a parent, and yet who cared for the girls' educational and physical well-being, was intensified during days that held so few distractions. The Holy Sisters' 'enthusiasm and encouragement for learning was boundless', nor was sanctimony the dominant mood. These holy women kept sweets in the hidden pockets of their floor-length grey habits that were, in turn, hitched up in the summer for games of cricket. In the nuns' private quarters leftover portions of the 'rather disgusting' meals served to the pupils augmented the nuns' modest meals of bread and margarine. Eggs left to congeal for an hour in the oven made their way over to the 'nuns' side', appreciated as if they were 'nectar of the gods', by these women who 'had so little and wished for so little'. Even their simple blue bedspreads, the colour of innocence, the colour for the Virgin Mary and for the motherhood these Sisters would never know, would one day cover their coffins – a comfort in life and a shroud in death.

Joanna, who was tall, broad-shouldered, 'smothered in spots, with hair like an army blanket, really rough and frizzly', didn't put much effort into the natural beauty that was quite obvious to her friends. They all 'dreamed of becoming gorgeous later'.

By the age of sixteen a few of the girls had actually kissed a boy, but only on the cheek. No one really knew any boys except those who went to nearby schools and with whom the Convent sometimes shared a dance and occasionally in the summer term an awkward joint picnic outing on the beach at Camber Sands near Rye. But Joanna wasn't interested. 'All the boys wanted to join the army. They behaved like old men, and called the girls "my dear".' None of the boarders had done IT but there was one day girl who apparently had, on the beach, beneath Hastings Pier. Joanna and her friends examined their fallen colleague covertly 'to see if she *looked* any different'. Disappointingly, she didn't. Fashion-conscious sixth-formers at St Mary's were allowed to wear home clothes in the evening but the results of the compulsory dressmaking classes would not have found a place on the rails of Bazaar. Very un-Quantish patterns for drapey skirts with modest tops in a nod of concession to flesh in the form of a shallow V at the back and sleeveless 'because no one knew how to put in sleeves' were all considered 'ghastly'. However, with a deft pocketing of the teatime sugar bowl, the sticky-out-skirt look the students yearned for was within reach. Late at night petticoats were first soaked in sweetened water and then hung on a radiator. By the morning Joanna always felt triumphant when she found the petticoat stood upright on its own hem, 'as sturdy and sticky-out as a lampshade'.

On Saturday afternoons sixth-formers commandeered the Dansette in the gym, piling up their favourite hits ready for the portable record player, dancing themselves crazy and panting between discs as they waited for the clack of the next circle of vinyl to drop down onto the turntable. At night the girls shared one illicit transistor, passing it around the dormitory, smuggling it beneath the bedclothes and listening to the muffled sound of the American Forces Network and Radio Luxembourg. They shared a passion for American singers, especially Elvis, but also Chuck Berry, the Everly Brothers and, less out of passion than patriotism, Cliff Richard. But during the preceding autumn term beneath the screen of sheets, Joanna had encountered a different sound on Luxembourg's late-night *Friday Spectacular*. The band consisted of four lads, three of them old teenage friends from Liverpool. The sound was like nothing Joanna had heard before, with its 'hypnotic harmonies and irresistible invitation to get up and dance'. As Muriel Young the radio presenter began to read aloud the names of John Lennon and Paul McCartney her introduction was drowned out by the live audience erupting into applause. 'Love Me Do' came first, then 'Ask Me Why' was followed by 'Please Please Me'. As John's naughty-sounding invitation to 'C'mon, c'mon' was repeated over and over again, all Joanna's other musical 'beloveds' went out of her mind and her whole way of thinking about music 'had to be reshuffled' so that 'the new world order of music could accommodate these magnetic cheeky boys'.

Suddenly all Joanna wanted to do was to get to Liverpool. 'It was like Nirvana, like Xanadu.' The music contributed to a new feeling that there was more to life than just getting a job. She longed to wear a pink gingham dress like Brigitte Bardot and 'drive round Italy in lipstick called "Pink Sorrento"', the most romantic and also liberating pair of words she could think of. She knew she could have been thrown out of the school for breaking bounds and smoking and listening to Radio Lux. But as the weeks of the final spring term went by the nuns surprised her with their unexpected view of what life might offer. 'They did not want to make the girls into nuns. And people with good jobs did not impress them. They had a sort of higher hope for us: that we would turn into marvellous people.' And they saw, too, that deep down under a 'ghastly spotty cheeky exterior' Joanna 'longed for life'. She wanted 'the nerve to stare dictators in the face'. And she thought that acting would give her that. 'After all, all of life so far had been acting, all of life involved pretending you were marvellous when with hair and with spots, life was actually awful.' There were three other things that made Joanna hopeful for the future: firstly an extreme sense of humour, 'the capacity to laugh till you cried about everything', secondly an idea of how it would be 'bold and fine not to have rules and to run away into the great world and become a sort of Artful Dodger', and finally a love of literature and in particular poetry about travellers and caravans. She was taken by John Keats's 'Meg Merrilies', quite unconcerned at the prospect of existing exclusively on a diet of 'swart blackberries'. During the early snowy months of 1963, schoolgirl Lumley 'somehow knew' she would manage.

I had not been looking forward to going back to my own school much, although I loved the journey. Travelling there alone through the snowy streets on the top of the 33 bus, I felt at my most independent, eight-year-old self, handing over three-pence in exchange for the flimsy paper ticket that rolled out from a machine hanging on a thick band of ribbon around the conductor's neck. Surprisingly sharp ice flakes pricked my skin like belligerent mosquitoes on the short walk from the bus stop, while all around me flurries floated like dust motes, their whiteness sharpened against a grey sky. There was no school uniform and as often as I could I wore my favourite red woollen mini-dress, 'a shirtwaister', with silver buttons down the front. I had mastered a new language copied from the older girls during the school lunch break. 'With it' was the term everyone was using to feel 'with it'. And there were other words too. 'Super' I would say at home instead of 'yes please' when asked if I wanted another helping of potato. 'Groovy' was my casual response to an enquiry about my day at school, each such answer received with either incomprehension or a satisfying wince of adult disapproval. My school reports showed I was struggling, playing the fool to get friends. To my disappointment, I was not impressing the teacher I liked best. 'Her written work is weak and her attitude is defeatist,' reported Mrs Penelope Fitzgerald, who took us for Religion, History and English literature, my three favourite subjects. Her red-inked comments in my autumn term report had already indicated that things were not going well. 'It is very hard for us to help Juliet when she is not willing to try to reach the level of the class.' I was fulfilling my father's taunt that I was a giver-upper, a 'Little Miss Can't', staring out of the window, passing sweets around, hiding my head under the lid of my desk and pulling faces at my neighbour. The headmistress was equally despairing. 'This lack of confidence in Juliet's approach to work may be the reason why she resorts to irresponsible behaviour, in order to boost her morale.' The crimes felt negligible but the feeling of inadequacy didn't. The more hopeless I felt, the more hopeless I became.

But despite her lack of faith in my capabilities, I continued to love Mrs Fitzgerald. Her lessons were my favourite. Her rendering of Charles Dickens's *A Tale of Two Cities*, which she read aloud to us sitting on the teacher's desk, was electrifying. We had begun with the idea that she lived an exotic life on a houseboat on the Thames with her two daughters, who were a little older than we were. But the winter weather eliminated all impressions of glamour. She would dash into the classroom late, arriving at a tilt, belted into a gabardine mackintosh, umbrella dripping melting snow all over the classroom floor, her auburn bun a little more dishevelled than usual and red biro marks all over her hands. Once I saw her put a piece of chalk from the blackboard in her mouth. You would only eat chalk if you were desperate, I thought. She kept her books in a paper bag. One day the damp bag gave way and the books fell through, tumbling in a heap on to the raised dais in front of us. As a puddle began to form around them, the water continued to pool from her sodden woollen stockings and through holes in the soles of her lace-up boots. We did not know that her husband was a barrister and a drinker, and that he had been stealing from his Chambers. His crime had been discovered, a painful court case followed and on 4 December 1962 he had been disbarred from the Inn of the Middle Temple after being found guilty of twenty-six offences. The story had been reported in *The Times* and the humiliation and anxiety for our dignified schoolteacher must have been complete as she became the family's sole breadwinner. We could not have imagined that these stories, which our inspirational teacher was storing away so carefully in her creative mind, would one day emerge in some of the twentieth century's most wonderful novels.

Twice a week our class walked though the snowy streets in crocodile formation to the Chelsea Town Hall. The thrilling smell of chlorine scented the air of the entrance to the Chelsea Baths, where swimming lessons took place in the blue-tiled pool against a deafening echo of screams. On two afternoons a week we were bussed several miles to a sports ground in Richmond Park. The game of lacrosse, with its stick attached to a leather-latticed pocket, slimy and smelly with linseed oil, held little appeal for me. But at half-time, sustained with half a frosty orange, we would huddle en masse in the corner of the field where on the other side of the fence a long, low hut provided a diversion. Vaulting the fence and squashing our noses against the icy windows we would watch a couple of guitarists and a drummer banging out the most amazing sound we had ever heard. We found out from the groundsman that they were called the Metropolitan Blues Quartet but were thinking of changing their name to the Yardbirds. When we returned to the lax pitch for the second half of the game our squashed noses were numb but our hearts were beating a little faster.

# Chapter Fourteen

## *Frost on the eiderdown*

Jo Evans, a ten-year-old London schoolgirl, had once lived not far from us, across the city in Notting Hill, until her family had had enough of the new challenges that had come to their borough. Jo's after-school days in the spring term of 1963 were filled with the sort of rich, hugger-mugger, full-of-laughter family life that I envied. Her family's life had a 'before and after' that encapsulated this pivotal winter. Jo's parents had come from a generation whose experiences and values were intrinsic to a previous age. And yet her mother was now embracing the professional opportunities suddenly available to her as Jo and her sisters encouraged their mother to move with them into a liberated future. Jo was one of four daughters born to Alfred and Ethel Evans. Alf's youthful ambition to join the RAF had been thwarted at the beginning of the war when instead he was taken on as a member of the Reserved Occupation working as a plumber, required to fit out Merchant Navy ships. At first he was employed in the London Docks then moved to Southampton and then back to London. Alf was given no help in finding digs in any of these places and no concessions were made to the disruption and distress involved in leaving his family at a moment's notice. His wife, known as Ettie, was a qualified milliner and tailoress who had always wanted to run her own fabric shop. During wartime rationing she had cadged as much parachute silk from the local factory as she could and had been in considerable demand for her silk nightdresses, silk wedding dresses and all manner of silk garments required for a trousseau. After the war she worked at 'The Men's', the Working Men's Institute, where she taught tailoring to men who had left behind their homes in Jamaica. With Ettie's help they made themselves suits to wear to job interviews. Ettie only had one caveat: she refused to take an inside leg measurement. After the birth of their four daughters and in the heat of the Rachman regime, Ettie and Alfred lived in a cramped flat in Notting Hill for almost ten years, all four sisters sharing one bed as they waited for a house to become available through the council. A male child was the unarguable qualification for being awarded a council house, a criterion the Evans family was unable to meet. Eventually Alf borrowed enough money from his older brother to buy a small two-bedroomed flat in nearby Highlever Road, a few minutes' walk from the Portobello Road market, with a little help from the famous property tycoon Naughty Mortiboy's Building Society and at a bargain price because of the sitting tenants on the ground floor.

But the area had recently begun to worry Alfred. Socialist in principle, and a passionate defender of his large family, Alfred was growing wary of the drug-dealers who had moved into the neighbouring streets. Jo's eldest sister Susan was obsessed with animals and spent every moment outside school hours with her equally pet-crazy friend, Morty's daughter Carol Mortiboy, who lived with her parents Marcine and Herbert in nearby Powys Square. Fearing for the safety of his family, Alf allowed Susan to bring the Mortiboy family's boxer dog home with her. Alf christened the dog Morty the Saint, hoping that the name, let alone the bark, would keep those he loved from any danger. But just as it was becoming impossible to find or fund a decent flat in Notting Hill, Alfred's distrust of his unpredictable neighbours finally convinced him that the family would be better off living out of the city. Even though Jean, the second of the four daughters, was showing considerable promise in her local clarinet lessons and was loath to leave her school, Alf sold the flat in North Kensington. What with her long-held aspirations, Ettie was delighted. She had emerged from the war with nothing and although the amount of money they had borrowed for the move meant that Ettie and Alfred were persecuted by 'the credit squeeze', they were pleased with their large new flat in Ross Parade in Carshalton in the London Borough of Sutton. Even though the place had no inbuilt heating and in the winter of 1963 the paraffin lamp barely took the edge off the bathroom chill, the new home was within commuting distance of London and visits to their old Notting Hill friends remained possible. As the January temperatures continued to plummet, ten-year-old Jo and the rest of the family ran from one room to another hoping to find warmth. The washing froze on the line, Alfred's shirts becoming stiff as a board, his trousers capable of standing up on their own. Jo and her sisters would fight for sitting space on the 'drying cabinet', a white electric box as tall as Jo herself, containing wooden rods on which they would hang their wet clothes. It was the warmest place in the house. Jo slept in a tiny box room with a pane missing from the one small window through which the icy air blew. The stone hot-water bottle that she took to bed with her each night cooled as soon as she tucked it beneath the bedclothes. And even though she began the night with all the family's overcoats piled on top of her eiderdown, they soon slid off and on to the floor. Only as dawn broke, about an hour before she had to get up to go to school, did Jo begin to warm up. Sometimes on waking she found that a layer of frost had formed on top of her eiderdown during the night.

The flat was above their greengrocer's shop, which Ettie now ran with a bookkeeping inefficiency bordering on anarchy. Ettie's interest and all her spare time away from the shop was focused entirely on sewing and quite frankly the flat looked as though a bomb had hit it. Sofas were buried beneath wobbling piles of ironing and half-completed frocks festooned the chairs, pins sticking out of them like sea urchins. Jo's childhood environment was garlanded with female underwear and Ettie's elder daughters would hesitate before bringing their steady boyfriends home, apprehensive about taking the route from the front door to the back bedroom. The yard hosted a thicket of five women's supply of bras, knickers and nylons, frosting in the air as they hung out to dry. At the end of the working day, Ettie would unhook her intricately boned corset and fling it in relief over the sofa. When Susan's romance had looked as if it might be getting somewhere, she used to steel herself to take Geoff into the lounge, praying he would not notice Ettie's impressively big smalls. Occasionally male intolerance for turmoil would surface as Alfred hurled Ettie's chaos out of the window on to the snowy street below.

In the summer of 1962 the Fine Fare Supermarket chain had opened a branch on the site of the now defunct Odeon cinema near Carshalton railway station, just up the road from Ettie's greengrocer. Most of the local shop owners were horrified at the competition and had challenged the supermarket's decision but without success. The footfall for the shops in Ross Parade had dwindled overnight to almost nothing. But Ettie's dreams had come true. Borrowing the money from her kind Aunt Edie who had retired from her job in a chocolate factory with a generous pension, Ettie opened The Sewing Centre, her very own haberdashers. In the freezing January of 1963 with the shop formally established, Jo became her mother's unofficial assistant buyer. Once a week mother and daughter would make the most of Wednesday's early closing of the shop. Instead of lurking on school sports grounds lusting after fledgling popstars through windows misty with ice, at the end of the school day, dressed in home-knitted hats and scarves, Jo would travel into town with Ettie, squashing into the guard's van, the carriage nearest the engine and the warmest part of the train. After calling at MacCulloch & Wallis in Bond Street for zips of every colour, they would go on to Cavendish Textiles in Cavendish Square for bolts of luxurious fabric. The next stop was the East End, where mother and daughter always got a warm welcome.

In Brick Lane the Jewish tailors were ever attentive to Ettie as she sat sipping her cup of tea and rattling off her weekly order for needles, hooks and eyes.

There was now a little extra space inside the flat. One of the Evans sisters had moved on. Despite the hurdles of the boned corset, Susan had managed to bring her courtship of Geoff to a happy conclusion. That first winter of marriage, by which time Susan was expecting her first child, the streets around their new home in Croydon were slabbed with ice and Susan made herself take extra care on her way to her job in the busy RAC offices. But behind the door to their tiny apartment, from which icicles of up to four foot hung, a shimmering giant version of Ettie's knitting needles, the newly-weds had found that the only way to warm themselves up was to have sex as often as possible. In January 1963 Susan's was a future filled with independence of which schoolgirls like me and Jo and Joanna could only dream. She was embarking on her own 'Annus Mirabilis', the living proof of Philip Larkin's poem of that title in which he celebrates how sexual intercourse began between the Lady Chatterley trial of 1960 and the 1963 release of an album that would change pop music for ever.

# Chapter Fifteen

## *Ne pleurez pas Milord*

Schoolchildren were not the only members of the population for whom life had resumed after the Christmas holidays. After five weeks of snow falling and freezing and falling-once-again, Members of the Houses of Commons and Lords had returned to the green and red benches of Westminster. But the business of politics continued to run up against major obstacles abroad as well as at home. The Prime Minister, usually a man of a publicly equable temperament, was not always able to hide the challenges he now faced. He had become pessimistic about the effectiveness of the diplomatic investments he had made on a pre-Christmas visit to France. Just before leaving for Nassau in December Macmillan had accepted an invitation to go shooting with General de Gaulle at the Palace of Rambouillet, the presidential country residence outside Paris. Macmillan had hoped that his presence there would emphasise just how much he valued the Anglo-French relationship as well as helping smooth Britain's application to become a member of the European Economic Community, approval for which lay in de Gaulle's hands.

With members of this post-war alliance so far comprising Germany, Luxembourg, the Netherlands, Italy, Belgium and France, there was no consensus of agreement in Britain about whether our inclusion would strengthen the country's future military and economic security. Labour Leader Hugh Gaitskell opposed Macmillan's view, arguing at the Labour Party conference in October for Britain's continuing independence. In reply Macmillan emphasised the necessity and urgency of joining the EEC. And in his diary the Prime Minister repeated his conviction that 'for Britain to stay out and isolate herself from the mainstream of European strength would, I believe, have very damaging results both for ourselves and for the whole of the Commonwealth. There might be no immediate disaster, but we could not hope to go on exerting the same political influence.' But de Gaulle was becoming increasingly resistant to the application. The combination of what he perceived to be Britain's arrogant pride in its island insularity and its fortunate escape from German occupation had contributed to what Macmillan defined as de Gaulle's 'inherited hatred of England'. Furthermore, de Gaulle made no effort to conceal his scepticism as well as alarm about the 'special relationship' between Britain and the United States and their renewed collaboration over supplies of nuclear weapons. He was fearful that Britain would Americanise the member countries and had been unable to ignore the evident personal closeness between Harold Macmillan and John Kennedy during the President of the United States's visit to London in 1961. The recent Nassau summit had only exacerbated de Gaulle's sense of exclusion.

At Rambouillet Macmillan's practised skill with a gun had failed him and each time he missed his target de Gaulle stood behind muttering, '*Pas de chance.*' Macmillan had flown home with barely a shot in his bag but not before de Gaulle had confided to the British Ambassador, Sir Pierson John Dixon, that he had tried to cheer Macmillan up by singing Edith Piaf's 'Ne pleurez pas Milord'.[1] It was as if de Gaulle was delivering a sign in song that he had already made up his mind to veto Macmillan's most ardent wish. On 14 January de Gaulle held a press conference in which he announced that he had asked Britain to abandon commitments to any country with which it enjoyed a free trade arrangement, citing the incompatibility between British and European economic interests. The underlying message of this unreasonable request was a definitive and uncompromising rejection of Britain's application. '*Non,*' said the Frenchman. '*Non. Non, Non.*' England was an insular place, a maritime set-up. Reinforcing lawyer and commentator Dean Acheson's remarks of the preceding autumn about Britain's impotence and irrelevance, the French President declared that '*l'Angleterre, ce n'est plus grand chose.*' By the end of the month Britain's application was void.

Macmillan was stunned by de Gaulle's 'extraordinary behaviour'. He seemed to have assumed the role of a demagogue, rejecting the idea of a European partnership and supplanting it with 'a Napoleonic or Louis XIV hegemony'. In a further echo of Acheson's remarks, Woodrow Wyatt wrote in the *Sunday Pictorial*,

'Everybody is asking what is Britain's role in the future? Everything seems such a muddle.' Violet Bonham Carter, daughter of the Edwardian Liberal Prime Minister Henry Asquith, lifelong political campaigner and Winston Churchill's oldest friend, was one of those observers to condemn 'the contempt de Gaulle has shown to his five partners'. After a lunch a few weeks later at which she had been seated next to the Prime Minister, she wrote in her diary how he had given her 'the impression of an "exhausted man"', who 'hardly seemed to have the energy to propel the words past his lips'.[2] She had already raised the subject at a previous weekly get-together with Winston Churchill. Despondent at how 'blank' he seemed and drained by 'the effort to reach' him, Violet was buoyed up by a 'sudden spurt of flame from a sinking fire' when at the mention of de Gaulle the old man snapped out two words with real anger: 'Dirty beast.'[3]

Violet had been right. Macmillan's energy was flagging. 'This has been a shattering time ever since Christmas,' he wrote in his diary, continuing with a pessimism that was becoming increasingly frequent. 'All our policies at home and abroad are in ruins. Our defence plans have been radically changed from air to sea. European unity is no more. French domination of Europe is the new and alarming feature. Our popularity as a Government is rapidly declining. We have lost everything except our courage and determination.'[4]

On the same day as de Gaulle's press conference, the leading article in the *Guardian* began with a sentence chilling in its simplicity: 'People are dying in Britain now because of the cold.' We had stopped going to Sissinghurst for the weekends because the roads were so treacherous. And on the few occasions when the trains were able to run on the dangerously icy tracks, the carriages were freezing cold inside. Everyone was waiting anxiously for Dr Richard Beeching, Chairman of the British Railways, to publish his report on the future of the railway. With the increase in car ownership and the arrival of motorways, many railway stations were beginning to feel redundant. The closure of a colossal 55 per cent, or 2,363, of Britain's stations was anticipated, with a loss of 70,000 jobs. But during January 1963 the weather had been doing Beeching's job for him: many of the stations were already empty.

Stuck in London, we could not avoid a visit to our dentist. Mr Dearcon held his practice in a converted Georgian terraced house in Upper Wimpole Street and that January Adam and I froze both with cold and nerves as we waited for our appointment in the huge, downstairs sitting room. Two hard sofas upholstered in frayed pale blue silk had been pushed up against the stuccoed walls, a glass vase of shrivelled chrysanthemums sat gloomily on the marble mantelpiece above an unlit fire. A table bore two-year-old copies of *Country Life* and *Horse and Hound* which remained untouched. We sat in silence, perched on the blue silk beside lipsticked ladies, still in their hats, and men lighting cigarettes from the ends of the ones they were about to stub out. We jiggled our bare knees, our breath forming misty puffs in the unheated air.

Mr Dearcon was not in a good mood. A Conservative voter all his life, he had heard rumours that Harold Wilson was tipped to succeed Labour Leader Mr Gaitskell, whose mysterious illness had been cropping up in newspaper columns since mid

December. Mr Dearcon hoped Gaitskell was not on his last legs. Goodness knows what sort of a 'leftie' might succeed him. He was outraged at the way the electricity unions had been holding us all to ransom. The country was going to the dogs. Bibbed up like a baby, I was encouraged to focus on the little blobs of cotton wool attached to the drill mechanism which spun round and round about a foot from my nose. As the drill dug its way ever deeper into my mouth Mr Dearcon instructed me to 'watch the bunnies' trapped on their mechanical racetrack in front of me. Forgetting all about his small blonde victim he explained to my mother sitting behind us with Adam and wrapped in her green cape, exactly how the world should be run. My cries of distress were drowned out by the clanking and roaring of his instruments. Silent tears wetted my cheeks. Afterwards we went to Harrods where my mother bought me a pair of brown suede mittens lined with rabbit fur. For a long time I could not wear them without thinking of those bunnies swirling in front of me as Mr Dearcon did his worst.

On 17 January Mr Dearcon's gloomy political forecast seemed to have been justified when an eight o'clock wireless bulletin informed listeners that although Hugh Gaitskell had slept a little during the night his infection had spread to his abdomen and kidneys. And on Friday 18 January the hugely popular Leader of the Labour Party succumbed to kidney failure at the age of fifty-six. Despite reports that Gaitskell had been feeling increasingly unwell, no one, not even his closest parliamentary colleagues, was prepared for such a tragic outcome. Only five days earlier there had been encouraging suggestions that Gaitskell's health was improving. His death was a shock to the country as well as to Parliament. Alice Bacon, MP for Gaitskell's neighbouring constituency at Leeds South East, reported to the House that the curtains had been drawn across windows throughout the local areas where Gaitskell's work on housing and social conditions and his visits to working men's clubs had earned him much local respect.

My father Nigel minded this news very much. Gaitskell was 'one of the most agreeable men I have known', he wrote to his father, remembering how once, when dropping by Gaitskell's office in the House of Commons as a junior MP, Nigel had caught the Labour Leader combing back his 'sparse' hair so as to make himself presentable for his visitor. Something in this small gesture, something dignified and respectable in the man, had touched Nigel. Even though he maintained a sort of old-school politesse, and was firmly on the right wing side of socialism, Gaitskell still felt more relevant, more in keeping with this new decade and the contrast with the fusty image of the Conservatives. Yet his appeal also spoke to the very establishment who were part of that passing generation. Violet Bonham Carter wrote of Gaitskell in her diary, 'It is true to say that I loved him. He had pure integrity which is the quality I value above all others.' She was not the only woman in mourning. Ann Fleming, the wife of writer Ian, had been in love with Gaitskell for several years. Knowing of his illness but unaware of its severity, she had flown with Fleming to the warmth of Jamaica. Ann and her husband both deplored the rigours of the winter in England and especially the way people's 'legs are whipped by the wet hems of their macs'.[5] But when Ann heard the news of Gaitskell's death she admitted that she minded 'very much more than I could have imagined'.[6]

The following week Macmillan leaned hard on the despatch box, choosing his words about the former Labour Leader carefully and generously. 'He had a rare power of lucid exposition even of the most complicated and difficult problems,' he said.[7] In a private nod to the questionable security of his own position, Macmillan continued to speak of how Gaitskell was 'a man of quite outstanding parts, clearly destined, had he been spared, to play an ever-increasing role in the world of affairs'. Confiding in his press secretary that in fact he had found Gaitskell 'difficult to warm to', his decision to adjourn the House of Commons in tribute was significant, an acknowledgement of high standing traditionally reserved for the death of a sitting or former Prime Minister. Macmillan knew his decision would please Labour Party MPs as well as voters at a time when he needed all the friends he could get. Anthony Wedgwood Benn MP saw the gesture as 'revolting as he and Macmillan hated each other'.[8] George Brown, Deputy Leader of the Opposition, thanked the Prime Minister for his 'gracious' words while stating how, contrary to the public impression of Gaitskell as a cold man, 'he was in private, the gayest and the warmest of companions and men to spend time with'. *Private Eye* seized the chance to tip the news of Gaitskell's death on its head by paying 'a tribute' to the death of 'The Rt Hon Harold Machiavellian' whose condition 'had been giving rise to considerable anxiety for many years'. The magazine lamented that 'Machiavellian' was 'taken from us' just at the moment when he might have triumphed in becoming Leader of the Opposition'.

As Gaitskell's successors began to line up, journalist Kenneth Rose spoke to the Conservative Minister William Deedes, who compared politics to cycling: 'One either has the wind with one or against one. Until very recently Macmillan has always had it with him. Gaitskell has always had it against him.'[9]And now Gaitskell's death gave the Government's Opposition an unanticipated opportunity to choose a different sort of leader at precisely the time when politics felt in need of something new. The three names standing for the leadership election were James Callaghan, George Brown and Harold Wilson, respectively eighteen, twenty and twenty-two years Macmillan's junior. Comparing the two leading candidates, Violet Bonham Carter considered Brown to be 'a drunken boor – rude, clumsy, devoid of finesse or subtlety but an honest and loyal man', while Wilson was 'a very able, clever, experienced but a universally distrusted one'. Personally popular and seen as the natural follower of Gaitskell's policies, Brown's unpredictability had been confirmed years ago when, voluble with Embassy wine at a reception in South America, he had been heard to invite a magnificently red-coated fellow-guest to dance. Unfortunately Brown was not sober enough to recognise that the band had just struck up an appropriately solemn rendition of the National Anthem and that his scarlet-robed date was His Excellency the Papal Nuncio. *Private Eye* took to regularly describing Brown's mood as 'tired and emotional', leaving readers in no doubt of Brown's affection for the whisky bottle.

My father's money was on James Callaghan, whose socialism veered in the opposite direction to Wilson's and who seemed to him like a safer, more solid bet. But despite the experience in the public eye that he had gained as Shadow Chancellor since 1961, Callaghan lacked the charisma of the other two candidates. Many in the Conservative Party, who felt and feared Harold Wilson leant too far to the left, hoped that his Northern-ness would be considered too extreme for the electorate to accept. Furthermore, Wilson lacked a public-school education, rushed his speeches in the Commons *and* his Gannex raincoat with a plaid lining was considered the epitome of stylelessness. His efforts to show himself to be a man of the people by smoking a pipe in public rang hollow. It was known that behind closed doors he far preferred a cigar. But to the majority of his party he seemed forward thinking. He understood science. He championed the computer. He felt modern.

If Wilson was to be successful in his bid for leadership he would face multiple challenges with Britain's most important industries and the related problem of unemployment. The destructive power of the weather had contributed to these challenges. Eighty of Britain's eighty-six counties reported roads blocked with stranded cars and lorries, and the anxiety caused by not knowing when an end to the great freeze might come was combined with shortages of coal, food, oil and petrol after lorries and trains were unable to complete their deliveries. The *East Anglian Daily Times* carried a dramatic photograph of a Calor Gas lorry crashed on its side at Stradishall as local firemen tried to lift the tanker upright. The newspaper also reported how the Retail Fruit Trade Federation was warning against panic-buying. Despite low stocks of fruit and vegetables, and transport hindered, there is enough for 'immediate needs'.

Coal mining, steel manufacturing and shipbuilding, the industries that made up the backbone of Britain's economy, had already been threatened by long-term unemployment. The demand for coal production had been at risk from the increasing use of oil, while the viability of cargo ships was being jeopardised by a growing dependency on airfreight. And now shipyards both on the Clyde in Scotland and on the Tyne in England were even emptier and more silent, with conditions too cold to work in, even if the demand had been there.

Lord Hailsham, Minister for Science and Technology, held the weather in part responsible for the temporary loss of 100,000 to 200,000 jobs, taking unemployment in line with figures not seen since the end of the Second World War. The Minister wished to encourage those that were suffering by assuring them that the snow and ice would eventually melt and 'that shipbuilding itself would never be regarded as expendable. So long as we can see into the future the world's goods and the world's oil will be carried by sea and not by air; and there is no reason in the world why the ships should not be built on the Clyde, or the Tyne, Wear and Tees, or at Harland and Wolff's at Belfast.'[10] In the final week of January Lord Mancroft led a light-hearted debate in the House of Lords about Sweden, Switzerland and Canada's superior handling of bad weather, especially the way they successfully managed to prevent 'transport and other public services from grinding to a standstill'. Discussions about what to do with a country that was 'knee-deep in cold and dirty water' progressed little, apart from a resolution not to allow the fading wartime 'bomb bores' with their stories of the Blitz to be succeeded with a new species of 'freeze-bores'.[11]Mancroft maintained that the nation's infrastructure would cope equally badly with a heatwave. Lord Shackleton suggested equipping cars with a saw or large knife with which to build an igloo. The debate and its tone both inside and outside the House were felt to be in keeping with the Lords' propensity for schoolboy humour.

The country's morale, which had been eroded by the freezing temperatures, was made worse by the intermittent electrical strikes. Although Richard Wood, Minister for Power, was relieved when towards the end of January the strike neared a settlement with a 4 per cent increase in pay, the demands on the national grid caused by the weather remained huge. As the breakdown in supply continued, Chequers was often without power from midnight on Friday until Saturday teatime. Luckily for Macmillan, the ovens at the PM's official country residence ran on coal and the Elizabethan fireplaces worked as beautifully as they had in Shakespeare's day. But on 27 January a massive power failure in the East Midlands, the worst in thirty-five years, was followed on the same day by a temporary thaw. As a result, 1,473 water mains burst. In Oxford hundreds of books in Trinity College Library were ruined in the deluge. On 28 January ten tons of melting ice swamped the train track in Caerphilly, and at Snake Pass in Derbyshire a perilous 200-foot snowy overhang was detonated by gelignite. On the same day the British Insurance Association estimated it would be liable for claims for snow and ice damage of up to £15 million. Out in the countryside stories of nature behaving strangely were not uncommon. As well as reported sightings of feral ponies and cannibalistic sheep in other parts of the country, Mrs Elizabeth

Shepherd of Winscombe in Somerset wrote to her fellow readers of *Country Life* to ask whether they too had seen 'Great Spotted Woodpeckers emulating tits'.

During the sixth week of snow the weather forced the cancellation of most of the weekend's sporting fixtures, crushing the enjoyment of fans when fifty-five football games failed to kick off. In Brighton an enterprising builder who sat on the local football club's board attempted to defrost his home pitch with his professional tarmac-laying equipment. Unfortunately the pitch did not survive.

Meanwhile, the newly established Pools Panel looked set to last for a good many weeks. Made up of professional players and an alternating set of chairmen, including the Second World War flying ace Group Captain Douglas Bader and the Conservative MP Gerald Nabarro, with his Sergeant-Major moustache, the panel met behind closed doors at the Connaught Rooms in London. In seclusion they guessed at the theoretical results of the matches so that the coupons could go on being filled and the top prize of £75,000 could be won. The 'results' were announced live on BBC television. One of the chairmen, Conservative peer Lord Brabazon, pronounced the forecasting to be a 'farce'. Beyond the world of football, the MCC (the Marylebone Cricket Club that owned Lord's Cricket ground in London) announced on 31 January that it had removed the divisive social distinction between 'amateurs' (traditionally the middle- and upper-class players) and 'professionals' (the working-class players) and was making all first-class cricketers professional. Incrementally the rigidity of the class divide was being weakened.

# Chapter Sixteen

## *Snow on snow*

Life in snowy London did not always offer the same diversions as those to be found in the countryside. We were not skaters and the grubby snow in our street did not suggest snowball fights as temptingly as did the pristine fall in Kent. However, urban weekend outings organised by my father were fun. When Nigel celebrated his forty-sixth birthday in January, Adam and I gave him some braces, my mother a pair of garden shears 'for cutting down brambles' and his Aunt Gwen sent him a postcard. But instead of having a party and to cheer himself up after the news of Gaitskell's death, he had taken us children on the bus to the National Gallery. Trafalgar Square's magisterial lions, grey, stone and sombre, were crowned with snow and the water in the fountain was still and silent. A week earlier the Ministry of Works had stopped the flow to the fountain in an energy-saving exercise and a thousand ice stilettos clung in a shimmering circle around each of the descending stone rims. Only the hardiest of the square's robust pigeons remained under the protective crook of Nelson's marble arm, balancing their delicate feet on the icy puddles, looking in thirsty consternation at the impenetrable glassy surface.

Inside the gallery summer sunshine was framed and waiting for us. To Nigel's astonishment five-year-old Adam greeted the warm hazy glow of Seurat's *Une Baignade* with enthusiastic familiarity. In his school picture book the chapter explaining light and colour carried a reproduction of this vibrant painting of two boys only just a little older than Adam, one in a sunhat, the other bareheaded. One stood up to the waist in the rippling water and the other up to his shoulders. Fathers, uncles and older brothers watched from the riverbank. Asked to pick my own favourite picture I settled on Gainsborough's *Mr and Mrs Andrews* for the covetable, tactile, pale blue taffeta-rustliness of Mrs Andrews' dress. The timelessness of the cornfields that surrounded the young, grumpy-looking, tired-of-sitting-still married couple and the dog at Mr Andrews' feet also seemed to me perfectly summery and lovely. Perhaps I also secretly chose the portrait because I knew it was my father's own favourite and because it was his birthday.

My father bought us each a postcard of our selected painting as a souvenir and when I went to university a decade later he gave me a framed poster of Gainsborough's couple to hang on my walls, a memory shared with him from that snowy January. After the birthday outing we went home on the bus and I ruined the impression of daughterly taste and modesty by reporting that I had overheard a lady in the gallery looking in my direction and saying, 'What a pretty little girl.' My father said she must have been referring to Velazquez's *Infanta*.

One of the chief reasons for braving the journey down to Sissinghurst was missing. The week before our gallery outing my grandfather Harold had sailed across the Atlantic to New York, a plan intended to take him away from the gloom of the ice, the snow and his unhappiness. The journey had not begun well. Nigel realised he was waving his father off from the same platform at Waterloo that Harold and Vita had departed from for their annual winter cruise the year before. This time Harold boarded the *Queen Mary* alone, but fellow passengers Noël Coward and the historian Sir John Wheeler-Bennett both saw a new fragility in their old friend and were as solicitous of him as only good friends can be. On his arrival in Manhattan Harold was presented with a programme of social events arranged in his honour. Throughout his visit he was entertained and cossetted by a luminary group, including W. H. Auden, Ann Lindbergh, Adlai Stevenson and Alistair Cooke. Parties were thrown for him and galleries and museums opened their doors to him. But he felt he was losing his memory, unable to bring to mind the names of the people he had lunched with that very day. At one of these ordeals he was seated next to Mrs Doubleday, the wife of Vita's publisher. In reply to her solicitous enquiry about the progress of Vita's next book Harold explained that his wife was unfortunately 'no more than a handful of dust'.[1]

Two days after Harold's arrival at the Knickerbocker Club three letters written on pale blue airmail paper known by my father as 'flimsy' arrived from England. My mother's letter was full of concern for her father-in-law's welfare, anxious after Harold had confessed to her that his sadness was 'unceasing' and that his legs were feeling 'groggy'. Philippa worried about how he would cross the busy New York streets without a willing arm to guide him. My letter, written in pencil for ease of correcting mistakes, told him that Adam and I had been tobogganing and 'I fell down an awfull [sic] lot'. 'Come back soon please,' I wrote to Hadji, from 'your loving granddaughter'. The third letter was from Nigel and described how he had spent an evening discussing the promotion of a new book with Cecil Beaton. Nigel and Mark Boxer, the editor of the one-year-old *Sunday Times Magazine*, had been invited to Pelham Place, the house of the eminent photographer and artistic polymath, who kept warm in his golden four-poster bed as Nigel and Mark sat beside him sipping cups of Bovril. But the rest of Nigel's letter to his father was a mixture of sternness and concern. It was a letter by a son awed by his father's desolation, of his purposelessness and sense of irrelevance. Nigel found it almost unbearable to see the change that grief had made in the person whom he loved and respected most and on whom he depended. It was a letter from someone who could not bring himself to accept the effect that bereavement had made on a mind that only six months earlier had hummed with agility. And yet it was also a letter packed with constructive psychological insight, surprising from someone who usually found emotional truth-telling so difficult. Cautioning Harold against labelling himself as the 'povero vecchio', the poor old man who 'has no longer anything worthwhile to contribute', Nigel advised him to avoid being with 'strangers and bores'. Instead, he should remember that he still 'thinks the same way, sounds the same way, is the same person' as he was before Vita's death sent his self-confidence tumbling. What Harold must now do is 'write, write, write'. If Harold were to immerse himself in a subject that monopolised all his creative energy he would 'keep senility at bay'. Nigel did not see his father 'settling down to a life of expensive leisure like Winston'.

Harold stayed in New York for three weeks, during which time everyone who loved him hoped that the transatlantic demonstration of appreciation and affection would restore him, rejuvenate him, cheer him up. Just as Harold continued to feel lost and bewildered, longing for the impossible, for the return of Vita and of his previous way of life, my father urged his father to 'stop thinking about dying and start thinking about living'.

Despite Harold's temporary absence, from time to time we managed to persuade our father to take us on one of the erratic trains to spend the weekend at Sissinghurst. Although for grown-ups the first thrill of the beautiful wintry weather had long given way to the practical frustrations that accompanied it, there were still days when sheer enjoyment in snowballing, snowman building, sledging and above all ice skating took over. Whenever possible dusty skates were retrieved from attics: shops had sold out of supplies weeks ago. In Kent, just a mile across the fields from Sissinghurst, the Stearns family were holding skating parties on Goose Pond in front of Bettenham Farm.[2] Stanley Stearns, a skilful Canadian ice hockey player, encouraged his three children to have a go at his native country's favourite sport, even though they invariably ended up spreadeagled on the ice. We had no skates but made do with our wellingtons as we crunched our way down the avenue of frosted poplar trees, still imposing in their winter cut-out silhouettes, and down to the lake. As we crunched we sang our father's favourite carol 'In the Bleak Midwinter' at the top of our voices, slowing down for the refrain, 'snow on snow', which made us laugh; it felt as if those words had been written for this very moment. Testing the strength of the ice with first one boot and then two, my father declared himself confident that if the surface could hold all sixteen stone of a grown man, it could take the weight of a slight eight-year-old girl. Pulling me behind him, we swished out between the spears of frozen reeds that stuck up through the frozen water, water like a stone. From time to time we heard a distant creaking, as if a fishy monster entombed far below was sending up a warning. When we reached the middle of the lake I put both my booted feet on top of my father's booted feet as he walked, foot-printing the snowy surface. Suddenly he lost his balance. Tipping forward, the body of his small daughter softened his fall. As I lay unconscious beneath him on the ice, my father thought the worst thing imaginable had happened. But as soon as I came round his first reaction was to swear me to secrecy about the whole incident. My mother would never have forgiven him.

The frozen lakes and ponds of London provided dozens of new playgrounds as well as show-off venues for experienced skaters. Only the elderly and those who were heavy with the extra weight of an unborn child viewed the deceptively solid surfaces as hazardous. Tereska Peppe, devotee of Mary Quant and dedicated follower of fashion, was seven months pregnant with her and her husband Mark's second child. She managed to keep her balance on the Pen Ponds in Richmond Park by holding on to the pushchair in which their twenty-month-old daughter was warmly wrapped as the skaters cut past her. Sliding, hissing and grinding into the ice with their blades, handfuls of frozen ice pebbles were thrown up above the surface as the sun caught the metal of the skates and flashed up a dazzle of light. Occasionally the twirling figures came to a standstill, an emergency stop, tilting the edge of the skate into the surface to break the momentum, still dizzy from spinning, waiting for their equilibrium to return. But Tereska was full of pluck and as she and the pushchair made their way tentatively across the ice she thought, 'There's water under this. I will swim if I have to,' oblivious to the 'sheer madness' of her daring.[3]

In central London John Nash's nineteenth-century lake in St James's Park had been frozen for weeks. From the slender, blue-painted suspension bridge air bubbles were visible, breath trapped beneath the ice. The lake was covered with a dusting of frost but it was still possible to make out the green leaves below the crust. The pelicans who had been in residence since 1644, a gift from the Russian ambassador to Charles II, remained true to the climate of their distant heritage and skittered about the ice, their feet splayed. The dark bulk of Buckingham Palace was clearly visible to the west, and in the east the turrets of Whitehall and the towering minaret of Big Ben silhouetted the sky. Down at the far end of the park was Duck Island Cottage, the home of the park's birdkeeper, a two-part Victorian red-tiled dwelling linked by a bridge over a small stream. Incongruous in its grand setting, the sloping, snow-covered roofs insulated the rooms below with the efficiency of the Swiss chalet on which it was modelled.

During the Great Frost of 1608, five years into the reign of James I, London's river artery had come to a halt on ice twenty feet thick. A great fair had been set up on the surface with sleigh rides, animal baiting and flaming barbecues selling steaming roast oxen from little wheeled trolleys. Described by Virginia Woolf as 'a carnival of the utmost brilliance' in her magically realised novel *Orlando*, patches of transparent ice revealed 'shoals of motionless eels' lying far below the surface and a cryopreserved fruitseller, 'her lap full of apples'. Only the 'certain blueness about the lips' gave away her chilly demise.

In the February of 1814 an elephant had been sent across the frozen Thames between London Bridge and Blackfriars Bridge. Almost a century and a half after that the river was once again frozen, although not to such depths, thanks to the ever-flowing, warming seepage from the thermal power stations of Battersea and Bankside.

In early February the blurred light of a pale evening sun gradually disappeared from the ice and Thomas Pakenham gave a skating party in the park.[4] His sister Antonia Fraser, who was eight months pregnant with her fourth child, stood on the edge of the lake watching as each guest was given a little lantern housing a burning candle. As if in a scene from Wordsworth's childhood experience in 'The Prelude', 'they 'hissed along the polished ice' as 'through the darkness' they flew 'and not a voice was idle'. Gradually the surface became marked by a tangled scribble as, lit by the flickering flame, the swarm of fur-collared glow worms circled their way round the pond in the dusk and Big Ben bonged above them. From under the ice came the occasional sound of a submarine boom, reminding the skaters of the fragility beneath their feet.

In Devon, as the snow continued to fall, the first week of February should have seen the appearance of snowdrops with their delicate white heads, the customary first flowers of the year. But the hard earth had kept the snowdrops pinned beneath the surface and silver caps popped up on doorstep milk bottles as the frozen liquid expanded. Three-quarters of the ancient oyster beds in Pyefleet in Essex, abundant since the twelfth century, were suddenly wiped out because of the frost. And so the cold deepened and human beings, young and old, whether in cities or in the countryside, grappled with the restrictions. For the lucky ones romantic love offered consolation. At the beginning of the big freeze Beryl Cornford was nineteen years old and lived in Sussex with her mother Ellen Cornford, the postmistress in Berwick village. Each morning Beryl took the train to Eastbourne to her job at the Halifax Building Society, calculating figures all day with her handy Ready Reckoner.[5] Reg Smith was a cabinetmaker who worked in the local town of Lewes and lived in nearby Ripe. Beryl and Reg were engaged to be married. On Boxing Day, Reg and the Cornford family had spent the evening together, playing cards with Beryl's next-door neighbours in Berwick. When they got up to leave at 11 p.m. they were amazed to find that the snow had risen to a depth of three feet. As the icy roads were not safe enough for Reg to ride his motorbike home to Ripe he had stayed the night with the neighbours, unable to tell his parents where he was, as they did not have a telephone.

The following morning as Beryl and Reg walked across the snowy fields to tell his parents what had happened, the drifts on the road between Chalvington and Ripe were so deep that they found themselves walking *above* the red triangular 'School' sign that usually towered above *them*. Beryl's younger brother, eighteen-year-old Andy, was the local milkman. Unable to use his van to complete his round in such atrocious conditions, Andy would wrap the milk bottles in sacking, stack them on his tractor, and deliver them to the local pubs from where customers would come and collect their daily pints. The details of these strange cold days remain vivid in the collective family memory more than sixty years later. But one afternoon at the beginning of February Reg was on his way home from Lewes, braving the blizzard conditions on his bike, when a lorry skidded across the main road at Glynde and collided with Reg's motorbike. The injuries to Reg's knee were serious enough to confine him to bed in the Victoria Hospital in Lewes, where the doctors said he must remain for two weeks. As the snow continued to fall and freeze and melt and freeze and fall, every morning Beryl would check the water in a vase that her mother kept in the hallway at home, the family barometer of the indoor temperature. Every morning the water remained frozen. Every evening, after a long day at work, Beryl would take the train from Eastbourne to Lewes and make the long walk from the station through ice and snow, up the steep hill and along the High Street to the hospital to visit Reg before making the journey back home to her village. The commitment that existed between the engaged pair was absolute, unconditional. No amount of snow or ice would come between them.

Not far from Beryl's village, Sussex's enterprising foxes were seen hunting in pairs. Residents of East Grinstead were advised to keep their cats inside for fear of catnapping by the voracious rust-coloured predators. Nature Conservancy reported that the weather was proving 'calamitous' for some species of birds in watery habitats, especially waders and in particular the redshanks, curlew and snipe. Dorset Muscovy ducks were finding movement on land difficult, especially as their tail feathers lengthened into tapering icicles. One hundred and twenty coots had been found lying lined up, like game in a butcher's shop, motionless on the banks of a reservoir in South Wales. They had not died of hunger: an inspection revealed their stomachs to be full. It was the cold that had killed them.

In the skies high above the frozen waterfalls in the Brecon Beacons, Welsh skylarks had perished in great numbers through lack of water, although at Weir Wood Reservoir in the Ashdown Forest observers were amazed when a snow goose appeared, as none had been seen in the skies since before the war. But casualties within Britain's songbird population were also severe. One Hampshire resident counted 262 dead birds from forty-five species, among them huge numbers of thrushes and blackbirds.

The RAC designated 3 February as Snowplough Sunday when seventy lorry drivers were stuck in drifts on the road between Exeter and Okehampton and were forced to spend the night on the floor of a school in Whiddon Down. Patches of ice formed off the coast of East Anglia, frozen waves stretched 200 feet into the ocean out from Eastbourne harbour, ice choked the Solent and ice stilled the Humber. Blizzards rose in the Irish counties of Wicklow, Wexford, Cork, Waterford, Dublin, Kildare, Meath and Louth, and roared across the choppy Irish Sea at seventy miles an hour, creating snowdrifts in Liverpool of up to fifteen feet. Within the city the steeply rising streets were proving hazardous, especially for the elderly, who avoided broken limbs by crawling up the sloping pavements on their hands and knees to reach the shops and the post box. Ice sheeted the lake at Liverpool's Sefton Park, a Lowry-like landscape populated by figures silhouetted against the white slopes in their dark winter coats moving across the frozen surface. But in the shadows of the dark fog that often shrouded the city, the dreadful weather failed to muffle the sound of music.

# Chapter Seventeen

## *Digging the sound*

For the first time since anyone could remember, icebergs had drifted into the ocean from the River Mersey and were beginning to obstruct vessels in the Irish Sea. Cargo ships struggled to make their way from Liverpool towards the bright lights of the American ports. But Liverpool was a city that set its own pace, a city resilient to hardship, resistant to outsiders enforcing change, robust in bad weather. In the network of streets around St John's old market a group of formidable street vendors wrapped in shawls and known for reasons long lost to memory as 'Mary Ellens' sold local vegetables and smoked haddock from a handcart. They traded in gossip as much as in fish, attracting their Catholic Friday-fish-observing clientele by shouting, 'Finny Addy . . . salt fish!' Inside the vastness of St John's Hall, Mrs Elizabeth Moore lurked beneath her deep pudding-basin hat, still trussing chickens and boxing the eggs at the stall she had been running since 1895. She had become something of a historical curiosity, her commercial expertise stretching back to a time when Queen Victoria was on the throne, when Oscar Wilde was arrested for 'unlawfully committing acts of gross indecency', when Thomas Hardy's *Jude the Obscure* was published and when Tunbridge Wells held Britain's first motor show.

Mrs Moore had seen much death in her lifetime. Almost 4,000 people had been killed in Merseyside during the war and relentless bombing had destroyed some 10,000 houses. Evidence of the damage was everywhere and throughout the 1950s and early 1960s the city had clanged and banged and hammered with the sound of destruction and reconstruction. A concentrated effort at slum clearance had begun in the city centre during the summer of 1962, an identifiable move towards a fresh start. The skyline in the artistic district of Hope Street near the city's main art school was dominated by scaffolding, as two vast ecclesiastical buildings separated by just half a mile were slowly rising. Edward VII and Queen Alexandra had laid the foundation stone of the Anglican Cathedral Church in 1904 and although progress had been interrupted by both world wars, the huge edifice was at last nearing completion. At the other end of Hope Street, after an original design by Edwin Lutyens for a Roman Catholic Cathedral had been abandoned in 1959, the daring circular Metropolitan Catholic Cathedral was taking shape at speed. Even if church attendance was on the wane, a result of post-war cynicism that a mysterious but loving God would not have permitted such scale of death TWICE in one century, perhaps there was a new way of believing in wonder, if only through the beauty and drama of new buildings.

Liverpool's docks swayed, ebbed and flowed to the rhythm of arrivals and departures. Ships packed with passengers coming from Ireland, America and the other side of the world arrived every day carrying merchant seamen, and refugees from African countries, especially Somalia and Sierra Leone. After the war, West Indians in search of employment and a better way of life had brought their families from Jamaica, Martinique, Barbados and Trinidad to Liverpool. Between 1951 and 1961, with increased shipping lines and the building of new airstrips, the number of settlers from the Caribbean had increased tenfold. In 1952 only six citizens of Montserrat had applied for passports to go to Britain; a decade later almost a quarter of the country's population had made Britain their home. New, self-sufficient and segregated Caribbean communities established themselves in the city just as other communities had done over the centuries, including the Chinese and the Somalis. While the indigenous Catholics and Protestants conspired to keep themselves apart from the 'newcomers' – and also from one another – there was, in addition, a tenacious class divide. Brian Epstein, with his private schooling, private wealth and well-known family name, was considered a cut above. The young grandson of Dr Jaffir Rumjahn – a well-known Indian doctor, public school educated and enviably elegant in his turban – bravely put up with the mockery of his posh accent as the boy with a regal plum in his mouth would shout from the practice ground of his local club: 'Cumm Honnn, West Darbeh.' In the rough districts around the Liverpool docks, prostitutes mingled with modish girls wearing jeans that were so tight they appeared to have been painted on. Seafarers known as 'nancy boys' wore full make-up and bouffant hairdos. And there were flashers, policed not by the Bobbies but by local men. One of the most persistent exhibitionists was forced by the vigilantes to lay his penis on a low wall before it received such a walloping with a cricket bat that he never flashed again.[1]

During and after the Second World War, the military GIs from America had come across the Atlantic, settling half an hour outside the city at the Burton Wood Airbase at Warrington, the largest concentration of American serviceman outside the USA. And with them, by air rather than sea, came their guitars and their songs. Music was on the move. In the black-and-white bleakness of a bombed-out outpost, the GIs' music-making had encouraged young Liverpudlians to reach beyond the restrictive perimeters of their city and make the journey across the sea towards New York. Many found work on board Cunard's passenger and cargo ships that criss-crossed the ocean every day. The sleep-averse East Coast city rumbled with the engines of huge cars, buzzed with machines that cleaned dishes and moved with legs encased in blue jeans, swinging along the sidewalks. These 'Cunard Yanks', shuttling, dishwashing, waitering, fetching, carrying between the English and American ports, sauntered down the Liverpool streets between voyages, objects of derision or envy, depending on the age of the observer. Scented with aftershave, they dressed à la mode in white trousers, slip-on shoes, all hot from the New York shops and bought with the cash they made from sales of the clothes, gadgets, tape recorders and cameras brought home on each trip. And as New York thrummed, bopped and shimmied to the sound of Count Basie, Nina Simone, Nat King Cole, Dizzy Gillespie and Elvis Presley, the Cunard Yanks packed their records into their luggage and sold them on the Liverpool streets.

Liverpool's distinctive sound came in part from these bootleg discs and in part from the influence of other first- and second-generation immigrants.[2] As Anglo-Saxon poetry, Gaelic melodies and Irish Sea shanties layered and deepened the African beat, a highly flavoured, long-simmered, idiosyncratic broth had evolved. Just as in New Orleans earlier in the century, when music danced out of southern doorways and alleys, this amalgam of African jazz, of trad, folk, skiffle, of calypso, of rhythm and blues boomed out of Liverpool's basements and jumped out of more than four hundred clubs, pubs and cellars. There was so much music in Liverpool that it was impossible not to be affected in some way, even if only though the reverberation that could be felt in the streets or that percolated through the walls of terraced houses. The Somali Club, the Polish Club, the Palm Beach, the Nigeria Club, the Rialto and the White Club were all crammed into the South End area, while in other parts of the city sound bounded out from the Peppermint Lounge and Sampson and Barlow's restaurant with the famous Casanova Club on the floor above. The Edwardian flocked-wall splendour of the Philharmonic Pub, across the street from Liverpool's classical musical hall, was packed every night with enthusiastic music lovers.

Harold Adolphus Philips, known as Lord Woodbine (self-ennobled and self-named after the cigarettes), was the founder of the All Steel Caribbean band, resident at the White Club. Woodbine had come to Liverpool from Trinidad after arriving at Tilbury Docks in Essex on SS *Windrush* in 1948 along with more than a thousand Caribbean immigrants seeking employment. He was working as a builder by day and a calypso singer by night. One of Woodbine's bandmates, Sugar Deen, came from mixed cultures, his white mother a busker from Scotland who had taught her son to harmonise while his Nigerian father's legacy had been the rhythm of African dance. The enviable dexterity and variety of Woodbine's chords and the richness of Sugar Deen's vocals attracted young art student and part-time musician John Lennon to the club.

In the summer of 1960 John Lennon was living with friend and fellow art student Stuart Sutcliffe at Number 3 Gambier Terrace, in a sprawling Victorian flat that faced the slowly emerging Anglican cathedral. The landlord in this tough and rough place, a few doors down from the safe house that provided a rare sanctuary for gay men, had no extra funds to fix the regular leaks that came up through the flagstones. Johnny Byrne, an Irish writer, crazy for jazz, crazy for poetry, who worked part time down on the docks, lived in the flat above John with fellow poet Spike Hawkins (who before moving to Gambier Terrace had lived in a hedge). Food was sparse. A stale loaf, hollowed out, stuffed with chips and carved like a meatloaf made up their supper. And one year just as they were about to carve the gift of a Christmas turkey their own mangy cat leapt out from the middle of the turkey's guts, where it had been enjoying its own festive feast. But Byrne, Hawkins and any other itinerant residents of Gambier Terrace were strangely content with the deprivation of comfort, 'even though we were all falling to pieces'.[3] It was all part of the satisfaction of working out a means of survival.

Art was at the centre of Stu Sutcliffe's life but he also played the bass guitar passably well and was a member of John's band, the Quarrymen. Lennon himself had only mastered two chords on his guitar, both of which, to Byrne's irritation, he played on repeat. Byrne could not stand rock and roll. Instead, his group of friends had 'long sort of jazzy druggy conversations' through the night. They were not friends with Lennon and his gang; in fact, Johnny Byrne could not stand Lennon either. 'Even with all the pain of his background and all that,' Byrne said, 'there was a type of total brutality in his attitude to people.' When the landlord threw Lennon's treasured paintings into the backyard in vengeance for defaulting on the rent yet again, Byrne retrieved the frames and used them as firewood. And Byrne had 'no time' for the deplorable way John treated Cynthia Powell, his art school girlfriend who had dyed her dark hair blonde to please John. Cyn's patience with her boyfriend's casual behaviour was inexhaustible. Even when Lennon and his band left Cyn for several weeks at a time to play gigs in German cities and to spend days and nights up to no good, she remained loyal. Byrne did not approve.

On Mondays John would go over to the White Club, bringing with him another Quarryman band member, Paul McCartney. Both boys dressed all in black but were conspicuous because young white men were rarely seen in these sorts of places, warned by their parents to stay away from the dangers of the South End clubs. But Lord Woodbine and his mates saw

Lennon and McCartney as a 'sound' pair of lads and became friendly with the two 'tough boys, unwashed sometimes, jumping on to the stage', and were willing to teach them about their music-making and to talk about the opportunities of making it big in the nightclubs of Europe. Sugar Deen even asked John to join him in The Shades, named after the sunglasses the band wore at all times including in the dark, but John resisted the invitation. 'Come down for a jam with the boys,' Sugar would plead. 'No, you're all right, man,' John would tell Sugar. 'We're cool, man. I'm just listening. I'm digging the sound, man.'[4]

John and Paul had met in 1957 when John was playing at a local church fête with the Quarrymen. Detecting a musical soulmate, John did not hesitate before inviting Paul to join his band. But it was song-writing as much as guitar playing that drew them together. Both John and Paul had been inspired by Buddy Holly in particular, not only because he played a Fender Stratocaster guitar but because he wrote his own songs. John and Paul would spend hours together, composing tunes in the tiny lobby that adjoined the front room at Number 20 Forthlin Road, Paul's family home. The council house was part of a pebble-dashed terrace about twenty bus-journey minutes outside the city centre. It was the house from which Paul had left to be a choirboy at St Barnabas Church on the corner of Penny Lane.

Apart from music, there was something else that had created an instant affinity between this pair of lads. Both had adored their mothers. Mrs McCartney, a midwife by profession, was socially aspirational, teased by her younger son for encouraging Paul to speak the Queen's English. She was a slim, capable, house-proud woman with an enviable way on a limited budget of making things look nice.

The inside of Number 20, even smaller than I had imagined, still looks just as Mary would have wished it to. A piano that their father Jim had bought from Epstein's furniture store in town somehow jived and jostled its way into their small sitting room, elbowing in alongside the three-piece suite, the small television set and the standard lamp with the fringed shade. The 1950s linoleum is covered in Persian carpet of varying patterns made up of off-cuts and runners that Mary had collected and stitched together to give an impression of affluent comfort. In the compact kitchen the Formica surfaces, the hygienic and up-to-the minute covering for all 1950s kitchen counters, sparkles with cleanliness. Upstairs the candlewick counterpanes are smoothed to perfection over the beds in the boys' rooms. Only one door remains locked on instruction from Mary and Jim's sons: their parents' bedroom, to which even the keenest of fans is still never permitted entry. The truth is that the interior is an illusion. Nothing of the current decor is original. The house now belongs to the National Trust, which has recreated the McCartney home in every detail from the packet of Lux soap flakes in the kitchen, to the piano, to the mismatched carpet. But it has been so brilliantly done (apparently with the meticulous input of Mike and Paul themselves) that the feel of the place is enough to send any diehard fan faint with nostalgia. I stared at the one tiny patch of wallpaper that is said to have survived after the McCartney family moved away. I felt like Howard Carter looking for the first time into the tomb of Tutankhamun.

I remember the sensation that the Beatles' music first evoked for me whenever I heard it on the radio, a dissolving, a floating away into a private space from which my parents were barred. Paul was my predictable, sweet-faced favourite. John's maverick humour was too strong for me while the other two felt like the back-up pair, necessary to complete the band and the music they made as a foursome. Paul's name was added to the exclusive list of family birthdays (including Shirley's) that I never forgot. I can measure out my life in Beatles songs. I teenaged to *Abbey Road*. I fell properly in love for the first time to the soundtrack of George Harrison's sublime 'Here Comes the Sun'. I learned to smoke to the accompaniment of Paul's 'Hey Jude'. My daughters were married to Beatles music. The Beatles have played to me during the writing of this book. And that day when I was alone in Paul's house, gazing at *his* bedroom, walking down *his* staircase, looking through the window at *his* view of the garden, lingering long in *his* kitchen, I was almost as hesitant to tread on Mary's carpet as I would be to do a handstand on an altar. Closing my eyes I could feel the music in my mind and glimpse the front door through which Paul and John had run to escape their earliest fans in 1963, part of a band on the cusp of meaning everything to so many people all over the world, even to eight year olds like me.

Mary was devoted to her family, her husband Jim, fourteen-year-old Paul and eleven-year-old Mike, and they to her. Her advice to Paul when troubled had always been to 'let it be'.

When Mary left Forthlin Road in October 1956 at the age of forty-seven to go to the hospital she never returned. While the boys were distraught by her sudden death from a far-too-late diagnosis of breast cancer, it was his father's response that hit Paul just as hard. 'That was the worst thing for me, hearing my dad cry,' he said years later. 'It shakes your faith in everything.' And so in 1956 Paul withdrew from the emotion of it all and 'put a shell' around himself, throwing himself into music. In an attempt to distract his sons from his own grief, Jim linked the wireless in the jigsaw-carpeted sitting room up to the boys' bedrooms so they could listen to Radio Luxembourg. He also bought Paul a trumpet for his fifteenth birthday, but Paul had always wanted to sing and freed up his voice by swapping the trumpet for a guitar. The first song he wrote, 'I've Lost my Little Girl', was a song about his mother.

Downstairs in the small front room framed photographs of John and Paul, taken by Paul's brother Mike, hang on the wall of the room in which they used to sit, heads bent together, guitars on laps, mid-composition. Many years later John described the process. 'We wrote a lot of stuff together, one on one, eyeball to eyeball,' he said. 'We really used to absolutely write like that—both playing into each other's noses.'[5] Their joint composition 'There's a Place' recognises this room, a place they could go when they felt 'blue' so that there would be no 'sad tomorrow'.

Two years after Paul's mother died, John had suffered the tragedy that bonded the two lads in a way that neither could have foreseen. The parlour at Mendips, John's Aunt Mimi's house at 251 Menlove Avenue, distinguished not just by a number but a name, was more formal and more genteel than Paul's house and Aunt Mimi was far less enthusiastic about these interminable writing sessions than Paul's dad. John had come to live at Mendips after his mother Julia, known by the family as Judy, had been coerced into relinquishing John's upbringing to her elder sister. Mimi was the sensible sister. Julia was the flighty one. She was a fabulous dancer and revelled in the music that filled the halls and ballrooms of her youth. John's father, Freddy Lennon, was a merchant seaman, often working as a waiter on a passenger ship. He had abandoned Julia, the wife he described as 'an auburn-haired girl with a bright smile and high cheekbones',[6] in 1942 without giving their two-year-old son a chance to get to know him. Julia's childless sister Mimi adored the virtually fatherless baby and insisted to her unreliable and skittish sister that John should be given a stable home with her while Julia jitter-bugged from one unsatisfactory relationship to another. Nonetheless, Julia loved her boy. Sometimes she brought her banjo with her to Mimi's, teaching John the chords. On the afternoon of 15 July 1958 Julia left Mendips, rushing for the bus stop on the other side of the busy main road and failing to notice the off-duty policeman who was driving at speed towards her. Sixty years later the fast-moving traffic can still recreate that dreadful scene with frightening ease.

Long after their first meeting, Paul analysed the particular strength of their relationship: 'We both understood that something had happened that you couldn't talk about – but we could laugh about it, because each of us had gone through it. It wasn't OK for anyone else. We could both laugh at death – but only on the surface.'

Sixteen-year-old John was shattered by Julia's death; it made him into an angry young man. Music was his consolation, and like so many lads steeped in the music coming across the Atlantic, Elvis was his hero. 'We used to go to this boy's house after school and listen to Elvis on 78s; we'd buy five Senior Service loose and some chips and go along. Then this boy said he'd got a new record. He'd been to Holland. This record was by somebody called Little Richard, who was bigger than Elvis. It was called "Long Tall Sally". When I heard it, I couldn't speak. You know how it is when you are torn. I didn't want to leave Elvis. We all looked at each other, but I didn't want to say anything against Elvis.'[7]

Following the well-worn Beatles trail around Liverpool to the small semi-private clubs where they played in the early days, before they were even called the Beatles, offers a committed fan a thrilling chance to time-travel. Lowlands is a handsome Grade II-listed Victorian house in the West Derby district of Liverpool, the home of the West Derby Community Association since 1957. As an indigenous West Derby-ite and now chairman of the West Derby Society, Stephen Guy was determined to help preserve the place and now the thirty-eight-room mansion has been beautifully restored with the help of a Lottery grant and is available to rent for the most stylish of private events, unrecognisable from the dilapidated venue that local groups used in the 1950s and '60s. It was also once home to the legendary Sunday-night Pillar Club, which was always packed even though most adults didn't like their children going to such an overcrowded place. Banned by their parents from wearing drainpipe trousers, these wannabee Teddy boys would hide the illicit 'drainies' in the bushes, ready to wear the following night.

We drank cups of tea in the elegant first-floor study next to Stephen's office at Lowlands and talked about the richness of his Liverpudlian upbringing before he took me downstairs to the large, low-ceilinged basement. The iron columns that gave the club its name are gone now but this eerie underground space once hosted numerous musical legends, mostly unknown at the time except by local fans. As Stephen went to unlock the door to the original stage area, I was alone on the dance floor where music fans had twisted away sixty years ago. Standing in the damp room I fought claustrophobia. I thought about how the ubiquitous cigarettes could have started a blaze from which there would have been no escape except back up the stairs. This was the place where Gerry and the Pacemakers, the Searchers, the Hollies and Billy J. Kramer had all played for up to as many as four hundred music-crazy teenagers. They might have all gone up in smoke.

George Harrison, a school friend of Paul's, had also played his guitar at the Pillar Club. Son of a city bus driver, young George was part of the Les Stewart Quartet when Paul encouraged John to ask his friend to join them, along with Pete Best as the drummer and bassist Stuart Sutcliffe, John's flatmate and fifth member of the Quarrymen.[8] In the summer of 1961, when the Quarrymen changed their name to the Silver Beetles (inspired by Buddy Holly's band The Crickets,) they began playing the occasional night at a club across the street from the Pillar Club. The Casbah took up the basement of a house owned by Pete

Best's mother Mona. Other local bands played there too, and its popularity won it an award for selling more Coca-Cola than any other establishment in Liverpool. Despite the metal railing separating the dance floor from the stage, there was a danger that over-keen fans might invade the band's performance space. John gave the impression of facing off the frequent fights that ensued but it was well known that Lennon was all mouth and, according to Stephen Guy, in a popular Liverpudlian phrase, he 'couldn't punch a hole in a wet Echo'.

Soon the band were once again experimenting with their name, dropping the 'silver' and changing the spelling from Beetles to Beatles, incorporating the neat 'Beat' pun into their final choice, plumping for what writer Philip Norman has described to me as what seemed at the time to be 'so cheesy' and therefore 'a suicidally ill-chosen name'.[9] Brian Epstein had begun reviewing new records for Bill Harry's pop magazine *Mersey Beat*, which had been featuring the Silver Beetles and then the Beatles as cover stories for months. Like most Liverpudlians with an ear to the music scene, Brian knew all about the Beatles. But in order to make his own 'discovery' story more impressive, he later claimed in his 1964 memoir *A Cellarful of Noise* that he had paid scant attention to what was little more than 'a group of scruffy lads in leather and jeans' who hung around the store in the afternoons, chatting to the girls and lounging on the counters. Brian claimed that the first he had heard of the Beatles was on Saturday 28 October 1961 when a customer in the NEMS record store booked one of the shop's listening booths. The requested song, 'My Bonnie', had been recorded by the Beatles as a single that summer in Hamburg by a German record producer, and Brian happened to have a copy. When another couple of girls made the same request two days later Brian exaggerated the 'discovery' story by describing how he had taken a turn in the booth himself. The truth was Brian had long been planning to go along to the Cavern and hear the band that everyone was talking about.

Mathew Street formed part of the network of cobbled streets that led directly into town from the great warehouses at the docks. As a schoolboy Stephen Guy would sometimes find himself in the area at lunchtime. Eager-looking schoolgirls, bunking off lessons, queued outside before going down the eighteen steep stone steps that led to the Cavern. With the twang of an electric guitar cracking like invisible lightning from beneath the street, Stephen would pick his way past the entrance, through 'leaking, squashable, rotting rejected vegetables' as well as piles of 'fades', the Scouse term for fruit past its best or anything a bit 'off'.

On 9 November Brian Epstein described how he 'gingerly' negotiated the slippery steps to find a couple of hundred people jam-packed beneath three condensation-drenched arches in a room reeking of human sweat and yesterday's soup. The adjoining cellars were used for cheese storage, and the aroma of fermenting Cheddar and imported Dutch Edam added to the nasal assault. In this cramped space that John Lennon found 'reminiscent of a railway tunnel', the crowd was almost exclusively made up of girls with 'rapt young faces' who had abandoned the wooden folding chairs and taken to the floor to do what was known by all the locals as 'the Cavern stomp'. The four young men who had hung around outside his shop were, Brian observed, 'not very tidy and not very clean'. In fact, they resembled the dockers with whom Brian was intimately familiar. When Brian arrived the band was already on stage, joshing, smoking, eating, talking, swearing and play-hitting one another. In the intervals between this joky carry-on they went through their playlist in the club where they had been regularly booked, initially as the Quarrymen, since January 1961. The 'vast engulfing sound' seduced Brian into returning. By the beginning of December he had offered to be the Beatles' manager. With the exception of the shop, he had never managed anything before. He was taking a risk and was relieved when his friend Joe Flannery agreed that he would help manage any bookings and negotiate any fees.

Thanks to Brian's tireless enthusiasm and meetings with record labels, the Beatles were accepted for an audition with a top producer at the Parlophone label owned by EMI. Their hopes for a recording contract were not high. They had already failed to convince Decca Records of their marketability as the company regretted that 'guitar groups are on the way out'. Other record labels including Pye, Philips, Columbia and HMV had also turned down Epstein's band. But at Parlophone George Martin, 'a tall thin elegant man with the air of a stern but fair-minded headmaster', was, as John Lennon described it, 'charmed and smarmed' down in London by Brian over the summer of 1962. Thirty-three-year-old Martin had never worked with a rock-and-roll band before. In fact, he wasn't a music producer at all, but he was responsible for the popular BBC Radio *Goon Show*'s records, counting Peter Sellers and Spike Milligan, two of the programme's stars, among his personal friends. This connection with two of John's heroes was more than enough for John to abandon his inherent world-weariness and rate George Martin as 'alright'. Initially unconvinced about their sound, Martin asked the band if they too felt there was something wrong. 'Something with your tie, for a start,' said George Harrison, deliberately misunderstanding the question. Martin was won over, if not by their music then by their charismatic irreverence. As Martin listened to Brian's protégés, 'his long legs crossed, leaning gently on his elbow', he decided to give them a go. He had one proviso. He did not think Pete Best was the right drummer and insisted that Pete was replaced. Pete was the best-looking Beatle and initially the Cavernites were distraught. But Ringo Starr of Rory and the Hurricanes was one of the best drummers in the city and when they heard him work his drumstick dexterity they began to understand why Pete had been kicked out.

By the autumn of 1962, under Brian's inspired guidance, the band had won best group in the Mersey Beat Awards. And their single 'Love Me Do', released in the early autumn, had climbed up to Number 17, almost entirely due to huge sales in and around Liverpool, surpassing all expectations and earning the Beatles their debut television appearance in October on Granada TV's *People and Places* and a royalty of a farthing each per record. On 9 December 1962, despite the gale blowing over the Mersey, George Martin had come up to Liverpool to see the band play in their hometown club. On his way down into the dark mustiness of the Cavern he noticed the slender, red-headed cloakroom attendant. Priscilla White also worked part time hanging up coats at the Jacaranda in Slater Street, where in 1960 she had befriended the Silver Beetles who played there in return for a plate of beans on toast and a Coca-Cola. When Cilla, as her friends called her, jostled her way up on to the stage, her habit whenever she saw a chance to sing with the Beatles, George Martin was intrigued by the sound of her voice. But despite the eminent London producer's enthusiasm, Brian was not about to sign up any girls, let alone hat-check attendants. Instead, he was looking forward to working with George Martin on the planning and recording of the Beatles' first album in the New Year. Brian had also secured them a second appearance on *People and Places* on 17 December, with their second single, 'Please Please Me', set for release a few weeks later.

Before leaving for ten days of engagements in Germany over Christmas the Beatles had played a bumper series of lunch and evening sessions in the Cavern. At the final Liverpool gig they had sung an old Phil Spector composition called 'To Know Her Is to Love Her', and the Cavernites had wept with adoration. Extra-committed fans had even held off buying 'Love Me Do' in case it became too much of a hit and the band became tempted to leave the city. One of their most persistently loyal groupies, known as Polythene Pat for her habit of chewing scrunched-up plastic bags, noticed that during that last song John – tough, mouthy, unsentimental John – had momentarily turned his back to the crowd, suddenly finding his perfectly working amplifier needed immediate attention. It had not escaped Pat that John was as overcome by the emotion of the event as she was. It was as if they both sensed that everything was about to change.

Dressed in pointed grey crocodile shoes, mauve jackets, black shirts and tight trousers, the band, in all its incarnations – the Quarrymen, the Silver Beetles and then the Beatles – had made several visits to Hamburg over the past couple of years, establishing a considerable reputation in the German town. The All Star Club was the seediest of venues, hosting audiences composed of drunken sailors and the women they had met in the street that night and for whose company they paid. The Beatles were always given far longer onstage than at the Cavern and had benefited from the extra time to practise their performance. But while their talent was being polished, the decadence of the city was damaging. In Hamburg they had discovered Preludin, an appetite suppressant containing amphetamines that produced the terrific high they needed to keep them awake during long hours on stage. One of Preludin's side effects was to dry up the saliva. John Lennon dealt with this challenge by drinking a few lagers before heading to the stage, where he often appeared to be foaming at the mouth.

On 1 January 1963 the Beatles had arrived back from Hamburg. They had hoped to kick off the New Year with a gig on 2 January in the small town of Keith in north-east Scotland but the snow meant their flight to Edinburgh had to be re-routed to Aberdeen and the gig was cancelled. However, on 3 January they had made the 150 miles to the Two Red Shoes Ballroom in Elgin, stopping off to have a quick wash in a freezing river. When the young daughter of the Red Shoes' owner met them on arrival she was puzzled that the lads were 'smelling funny, smelling of weeds'. Despite the weather, a halfway-decent audience of two hundred turned up but the following day just fifty miles away in Dingwall the fans numbered only twenty. On 5 January, one hundred miles further along the road in Stirling, one hundred drunken farmers had come to jeer and hurl a coin or two, which had pinged off Paul McCartney's guitar with a satisfying ring.

Outside Scotland the band's prospects were more encouraging. The *Mersey Beat* was no longer the only northern publication paying attention to the Beatles in the early days of 1963. Harry Evans, campaigning editor of the *Northern Echo*, was finding the tedium of covering the relentless bad weather a challenge, even though his reporters tried their best to come up with new angles on the story. Twenty-year-old Guy Simpson worked in the cub branch office of the *Northern Echo* in Bishop Auckland. He had found himself having lugubrious conversations with bored diggers in graveyards where the ground refused to give way to a spade and dead bodies spent their final nights above ground in chilly church crypts waiting for the earth to move. But Guy was also one of the dazzling bunch of young journalists whom Harry referred to as 'the Music Juniors'. Each of these 'Juniors', Philip Norman, David Sinclair, David Watts, John Cathcart and Guy Simpson, had filed such dynamite accounts of the touring bands that Arnold Hadwin, the editor of the *Northern Despatch*, the *Echo*'s stable-mate, persuaded Harry to feature more music for the younger readership in a new dedicated section called the *Teenage Special*. On the day the pop music insert first appeared the sales of the paper shot up by a third.

Harry said he had always 'kept pace' with the thrilling way the musical revolution in the North was happening way ahead of the London scene and might even be giving some of the old American musicians a run for their money. He could hardly have missed the multiplying number of bands giving their own interpretations of Chuck Berry, Little Richard and Fats Domino, and who were filling stages in local clubs, ballrooms, bingo halls, ice rinks and even Doncaster's swimming baths, which had been boarded over to make a stage during the winter months. But Harry's wife Enid was a Liverpudlian and had insisted that the Evans family watch the Beatles' first appearance on Granada TV in October 1962. That spring the Beatles were about to set out on their first nationwide tour as one of the support bands for a current teenage hit singer and Harry was determined that his newspaper would follow their every move.

# Chapter Eighteen

## *A Bunny's tale*

Music was not the only source of inspiration for those in Britain looking enviously and impatiently at changes happening across the Atlantic. But while the contraceptive pill had recently brought new freedoms of choice to women on both sides of the ocean, emancipation had taken a step backwards since the war. In 1950s America women had unwittingly relinquished the authority that had been theirs not long ago. During the war, in the absence of men, they had been encouraged to be strong, to be extraordinary, to run the show and to wear the trousers. But when the men returned women had begun to feel they were expected to revert, ideally in waisted dresses, to their previous subordinate role. It was a suffocating environment: this resurgent conservatism had coalesced with Cold War witch-hunts and the McCarthy communist hearings. In the male world of American politics, women were still required to know their ornamental place. The *Mona Lisa*, the most famous portrait in the world, the ultimate symbol of inscrutability, had gone on show in the nation's capital at the beginning of January for a month. By February half a million people had come to see the picture. The painting had arrived in New York on board SS *France* just before Christmas after Jackie Kennedy, on an official visit to Paris in 1962, had charmed André Malraux, the French First Minister of Cultural Affairs, into lending the masterpiece to the Smithsonian Museum. Amidst the tightest security, the canvas had been settled into its own chauffeur-driven limousine and escorted on the journey down to Washington by an eight-car motorcade. In his welcoming speech on the opening night of the show, President Kennedy had reminded his audience, including Malraux, the guest of honour, of the continued significance of the links between their two countries during this volatile nuclear age. 'Our two revolutions helped define the meaning of democracy and freedom,' he said, continuing, 'today, here in this gallery, in front of this great painting, we are renewing our commitment to those ideals which have proved such a strong link through so many hazards.' Jackie Kennedy, wearing a strapless, full-length, mauve-chiffon gown, had stood silently beside her husband. She had just discovered she was pregnant with their third child, but her secret was not yet out. Despite Leonardo da Vinci's glorious backdrop to Kennedy's remarks, a woman's part in this magnificent future as celebrated by the men in charge appeared to be confined to the decorative.

But by 1962 the last decade had seen a diverse group of American women setting the pace for a new feminist agenda where women of all ages and with backgrounds variously in literature and science, motherhood and marriage, had begun to speak out and write about the urgent need for change. With the environmental alert contained in her book *Silent Spring*, published in that year, Rachel Carson had shown leadership in an area dominated by male scientists. A passive acceptance of the post-war idyll of the meek subordinate housewife was on the wane. The stigma around 'feminism', which the *New Yorker* magazine recently described as once having been seen as 'a refuge and revenge for ugly women', was breaking down.

In January 1963 Gloria Steinem,[1] a twenty-eight-year-old journalist, was working undercover for the glossy entertainment magazine *Show*, investigating Manhattan's latest venue for male 'entertainment'. She chose her grandmother's name, Marie Catherine Ochs or 'Maria', as her alias when she applied to join 150 other women already working as Bunny Girls at the new Playboy Club. This shiny box of plate glass, which the famous *Ed Sullivan Show* called 'the greatest new showbiz gimmick', had taken its place on the skyline of midtown Manhattan in December 1962. Steinem had answered an advertisement recruiting girls who were 'pretty and personable, between 21 and 24'. Her application was successful and she braced herself to learn a Bunny's basic duties, including 'serving drinks, snapping pictures or greeting guests', for which she would be paid 'an attractive' wage of between $200 and $300 a week. The job involved style, excitement and, for young women looking to find their way in the world, the promise of independence and liberation. As a Bunny they would be earning their own living and bridging 'the gap between being girls and becoming women'.

For some Bunnies the enticement of 'glamour' offered by the clubs and by the chance to feature in *Playboy* magazine was irresistibly seductive. Kathryn Leigh Scott, who began working at the Playboy Club at the same time as Steinem, remembered 'something secretly divine about shedding the polo coat and loafers in the dressing room and stepping into the sexy satin Bunny costume and high-heeled shoes'.[2] The mischievous cartoon figure known as a 'Femlin', a cross between a female and a gremlin in thigh-length boots and long gloves and nothing else at all, appeared each month in *Playboy* magazine. The magazine never denied the uncanny resemblance of this sprite to Jackie Kennedy, who shared the Femlin's widely spaced eyes and shiny bouncy hair.

Steinem's interview for the job involved a 'special physical' with Playboy's own gynaecologist and a blood test to check for sexually transmitted diseases. According to Steinem, the Bunny outfit was 'darted and seamed until it was two inches smaller than any of my measurements everywhere except the bust' and was so tight-fitting that 'the zipper caught my skin'. Girls with colds who sneezed regularly and burst out of their costumes were replaced. Steinem felt 'the boning in the waist would have made Scarlett O'Hara blanch', while 'the entire construction tended to push all available flesh up to the bosom'. Some of the girls were numb from the knee up by the end of a working day. Iced drinks were 'accidentally' spilled down their backs. Dark-skinned girls were known as 'chocolate bunnies'. The Bunny cottontail was tweaked as they served drinks. One customer wept tears of laughter when Bunny Gloria rejected his martini-fuelled advances protesting she was a 'virgin' bunny.

Her fake-affronted suitor demanded if she was under the illusion he was there 'for roast beef'. One of the customers suggested Bunny Marie might find her sense of humour in response to one of his jokes.

'If little girls were blades of grass what would little boys be?' he asked. 'Lawnmowers?' she guessed. 'No. Grasshoppers.'

The avalanche of prejudice that Steinem witnessed included dishonesty over pay, as well as humiliating, straitjacketing, uncomfortable clothes. But the worst aspect of all was, of course, the unfettered, unregulated, encouragement of sleazy, male sexual harassment in an adult playground where abuse of women's physicality was just part of the deal. After eleven days, while being praised for doing her job so well, Steinem quit. Her cool account of the experience appeared in two parts and in two consecutive issues of the magazine under the title 'A Bunny's Tale'. Cleverly avoiding overt criticism and, more importantly, any legal objections to the story by the club, Steinem's witty and matter-of-fact report enraged Playboy staff and members, furious at having been duped. 'Men fear ridicule the way women fear violence,' Steinem said. 'If those men thought of feminism at all it was as a historic blip that began and ended with the "suffragettes".'

Betty Friedan was a forty-one-year-old American writer, a graduate of Smith College, a wife, a mother and a housewife. Her book *The Feminine Mystique*, published in February 1963, was based on conversations she had been having with her former female classmates over the previous five years. Those conversations with mostly well-off, married mothers were originally intended as copy for a single magazine article in which Friedan identified 'a strange stirring, a sense of dissatisfaction, a yearning'. But the richness of the material had expanded into a book that spoke to thousands of American housewives with its raising of the previously implicit question: 'Is this all?' The symptoms of the 'dissatisfaction' she had uncovered included fatigue, a propensity to drinking in the daytime, to taking tranquillisers or uppers, and to developing bleeding blisters on their arms, attributed by doctors not to the constant use of detergents but some other psychological condition. Friedan argued that the question of purpose, of what we are doing in a world that favours men, was a question that had lain 'buried, unspoken, for many years in the minds of American women'. One of her biggest targets was the largely male view that marriage, motherhood and the management of the house was the route to female satisfaction.

Even those men who publicly pronounced themselves to be supporters of professional and social gender equality made exceptions when it came to sexual freedom. But American poet Sylvia Plath had never dreamt that her husband, the Yorkshire poet Ted Hughes, would ever behave that way towards her.

# Chapter Nineteen

## *Blown and bubbled and warped and split*

By the winter of 1962 Sylvia Plath was feeling all too keenly the subservience of gender and of men's licence to behave as they wished. During the endless February coldness of this brutal British winter, Sylvia, at the age of thirty, was far from her family in Boston, Massachusetts, the city of her birth. She missed her mother, and she missed her friends. But here in England it was Ted, or the version of Ted that had so recently been exclusively hers, whom she was missing most.

The young American poet had moved back across the Atlantic in 1959 with her Yorkshire-born husband and fellow poet Ted Hughes to live in Britain. They had become the parents of two small children. Through her marriage Sylvia had found herself absorbed into the heart of London's literary society. In 1960 she and Ted had been invited to dinner with the seventy-four-year-old T. S. Eliot at the Kensington flat he shared with Valerie, his young second wife. The evening had been weighted in favour of poets when Stephen Spender and his concert-pianist wife Natasha had joined Sylvia and Ted. Conversation had been of Stravinsky, of Virginia Woolf and of D. H. Lawrence, all of them acquaintances or good friends of Valerie and Tom and of Natasha and Stephen.

Sylvia told her mother that she felt as if she was 'sitting next to a descended God' and that Eliot had 'a nimbus of greatness' about him.[1] But it was as the wife of Ted that Sylvia had thrived over the past few years. She recognised herself as 'one of those women whose marriage is the central experience of life'. Her first sight of Ted at a bookish party in Cambridge in 1956 had been of 'a large, hulking healthy Adam', who spoke to her 'with a voice like the thunder of God' and left her overcome with wanting him, lust-struck as she 'screamed' within herself, 'Oh to give myself, crashing fighting to you'. His arrival, lion-like, in her life, brimming with a love for language that she shared, and glowering with darkness, also awoke in her a sex drive that was addictive, insistent, violent, possessive and insatiable. They had married less than four months later. But in the summer of 1962 after Ted began an affair with Assia, a friend of the couple, Sylvia and Ted's marriage had collapsed. In December 1962 Sylvia and the children had left their home in Devon and moved to London. Her marriage had been all consuming, a relationship of intense, tormenting, reckless, possessiveness, a relationship impossible to sustain. Assia became the detonator that lit the inevitable explosion.

*

Assia Wevill was five years older than Sylvia and worked at an advertising agency. She was half Russian, half German, thrice married, and although she was blessed with a face that was very beautiful, Sylvia was among others who could not help noticing that cleverly draped, loose-fitting clothes often disguised the generous width of her waist. Assia and her husband David, also a poet, had rented Sylvia and Ted's London flat when in 1961 Ted and Sylvia moved out of the city to Court Green a large, thatched house surrounded by fields in the hamlet of North Tawton in Devon. When Ted and Sylvia invited the couple to stay for a summer weekend at a time when the demands of motherhood were not only exhausting Sylvia but restricting her, Sylvia had felt herself boring her husband. Assia arrived in Devon wearing high heels. The absurdity of this affectation struck Sylvia all the more forcibly, she told her friend Jillian Becker, in the light of all the cowpats and especially because Sylvia had never seen her in anything other than flat shoes in London. But Ted's attention was undisguisedly fused to their house guest. In his poem 'Dreamers' he had written of how he found Assia 'slightly filthy with erotic mystery', with her 'soot-wet' eye make-up and Dior-scented flamboyance. And that weekend, on the Sunday, Ted and Assia kissed. And Sylvia saw them, or thought she saw them. She was not sure. She did not wish to be sure. But she knew the signs. Five years earlier, a year after their marriage, she had noticed a look on the face of her idolised husband, 'an odd lousy smile'. And she had followed him one day to the library, bumping into him by chance on a road where boys took girls 'to neck on weekends'. Ted's attention was wholly focused on the 'uplifted doe eyes of a strange girl with brownish hair'. Sylvia had just enough time to take in the 'bare thick legs in khaki Bermuda shorts',[2] before the girl vanished. During the summer of 1962 Ted's new affair had been confirmed when Sylvia answered the telephone only to hear Assia putting on a disguised man-like voice. Sylvia ripped the telephone cord from the wall. Assia herself was both enthralled and appalled by her affair. 'In bed he smells like a butcher,' she told a friend. Undeterred by Sylvia's suspicions, she and Ted continued to meet, often in a white 1950s van lent to them by a friend for that purpose. Assia's husband David waited for the infatuation to fizzle out as Sylvia battled through the summer, gripped with jealousy but unable to let Ted go.

For a while Sylvia's practicality of nature had seen her through. She rode, kept bees on which her father had been an authority, cooked and cared for those she loved, especially her children. Even though – or especially because – they were so young and still at the age, as Wordsworth called it, of 'unrememberable being', Sylvia's sense of duty as a mother took priority over everything, over marriage, over her own poetry, over her own welfare. But when Sylvia found out that Ted and his lover, who she referred to in letters to her therapist friend Dr Beuscher as 'Weavy Asshole', had spent a week together in Spain, the country in which she and Ted had spent their honeymoon, she knew the marriage could not last.

Just before Christmas Sylvia had rented the flat at Number 23 Fitzroy Road in Primrose Hill, an area in which Al Alvarez, the all-powerful poetry editor of the *Observer*, noticed 'gentility was advancing fast'. Front doors were newly painted with warm Mediterranean colours promoted enticingly as 'cantaloupe', 'tangerine' and 'blueberry', and 'everywhere was a sense of gleaming white conversions'. Sylvia's decision to rent two storeys of the brick terraced house with its stucco windows had been made not only for its proximity to the zoo but also because her hero W. B. Yeats, in her view the greatest ever Irish master of verse, had lived there for five years ninety years earlier. As Ted moved to London to be with Assia, Sylvia locked up their house in Devon, remembering to pay attention to the final note she'd written on her calendar to 'turn off gas' before arriving in London. She wrote to tell her mother how her new bedroom, doubling as her study, 'faces the rising sun'. At first she was delighted to be in the city with its 'terrible and fascinating smog' that 'stuffed every crack of London with white cotton wool'. She delighted in shopping for clothes in Dickens and Jones, a 'most fantastic store'. She described to her mother the beautiful wardrobe she had assembled from the Oxford Street shop, courtesy of regular cheques sent to her by Olive Higgins Prouty, her loyal American philanthropic supporter . Sylvia had bought for herself a 'Florence-Italy blue and white velvet blouse, a deep brown Italian velvet shirt, black fake fur toreador pants'.

There were also practical improvements to be made to the flat, including the connecting of a telephone, the fixing up of the electricity supply and the installation of a gas stove. Her new sitting room had been painted 'fresh white', and rush matting covered the floor. She was making her house beautiful, with Japanese and Arabic glass 'in lovely clear colours' and cane chairs. The new clothes and a new hairdo had done wonderful things for her 'shattered morale'. The wrench from Devon and from all the outdoor freedom it had offered her was not as bad as she had anticipated. As Christmas approached the appearance of sunshine on the shortest day of the year, when the light was bright with frost, had 'felt all the more dazzling for its rarity'.

Sylvia had become friends with Al Alvarez. He had met her with Ted three years earlier in London when, in her neat jeans and shirt, her hair in a tidy bun, Mrs Ted Hughes seemed to Alvarez to be 'effaced' by Ted, and firmly 'under the massive shadow of her husband'.[3] To Alvarez himself she was 'rather distant' although friendly enough. Ted dressed in a sombre black jacket, black trousers, black shoes and with his dark hair, appeared to Alvarez to be 'in command'. As Sylvia always wrote under her maiden name, Alvarez was astonished when she explained that she was the author of the poem he had published in the *Observer* a year ago. 'For God's sake, Sylvia *Plath*!' he could not help exclaiming. He had not made the connection.

During that first meeting Alvarez had found not so much a poet as 'a young woman in a cookery advertisement', but over the following two years he had felt a levelling in the balance of literary power between this married couple. He became increasingly moved by the fineness and originality of the poems Sylvia sent him, and told her he thought she would win a Pulitzer Prize. He had begun to believe Sylvia Plath to be the first woman poet worthy of comparison to Emily Dickinson. In the aftermath of her separation Sylvia would drop round to Alvarez's house and read him her latest work, her voice sounding older than her years, drinking a tumbler of whisky, loving the clink of the ice cubes against the glass, the only thing, she said, that tugged at her to go home to America.

Alvarez was the arbiter and kingmaker of British poetic opinion. A discerning critic, his rare slips of judgement included the distinguished Philip Larkin, who in 1962 he accused of 'gentility, neo-Georgian pastoralism, and a failure to deal with the violent extremes of contemporary life'. Larkin apart, Alvarez could singlehandedly establish or demolish a new poet. Sylvia basked in his intellectualism as well as his evident appreciation of her writing. Spending time with Alvarez was compensation for missing Ted. His betrayal had left her suffering from a gnawing, voracious, consuming sense of worthlessness. She had lost her chief mentor, her best critic, lover, admirer, friend, husband. She was fierce with herself, wanting, as Alvarez wrote, 'an A in marriage as well as poetry'.[4] But poets, it had turned out, do not make good spouses. The only way in which love can push poem-making out of the way for a poet of either sex is for a poet to cease writing poetry, to cease to be a poet. And only with the shutting out, shutting down of creativity can the woman subsume the man and the man subsume the woman.

For a while Sylvia had allowed poetry to take second place to love but when love was not enough, or when love did not work, the poetry-making returned. Writing was Sylvia's central means of surviving. In a 30 October 1962 interview with Peter Orr from the British Council she had spoken of being influenced by the American poet Robert Lowell. She had been excited by his 'intense breakthrough into very serious, very personal, emotional experience which I feel has been partly taboo'. And the poems she wrote during those desperate months represented an intense, creative outpouring in which dexterity of language and thought commingled. The creative act of questioning helped clarify, even if it meant giving expression to rage. Through poetry, through the deep-down reaching for communication about how she was feeling, came a new honesty. Poetry was her revolt against the threat of collapse.

And yet in public she was impressively self-controlled. Despite sitting next to the coal stove, cross-legged, undergraduate style, on Alvarez's floor, positioning herself on the 'couple of rugs on the blood-red uncarpeted lino', she was always very neatly dressed. With her distinctive magenta lipstick, her stylishness rarely failed to make an impression. Fellow Cambridge undergraduate Michael Frayn had first come across her when she popped into the offices of *Granta* magazine wearing a white belted gaberdine mackintosh. They discussed a poem she had sent him for consideration by the magazine and they made a plan to meet at her lodgings so she could show him some more for possible publication. She guaranteed him 'great mugs of coffee'. As she left, Frayn could not stop himself from following her out of the door.[5]

When she sat down to telephone Alvarez on Christmas Eve Sylvia had been buoyed by invitations from loyal groups of friends for herself and the children for tea on Christmas Day, for dinner on Christmas Day and for supper on Boxing Day. For some time Alvarez had more than suspected Sylvia was angling to shift their friendship on to another level. But Alvarez was also suffering from the unravelling of a relationship. When his marriage to Ursula Barr, the granddaughter of D. H. Lawrence's wife Frieda, had come to an end in 1960 Alvarez had swallowed a handful of sleeping pills in an unsuccessful attempt to take his own life. He could not give his soul or his heart to Sylvia even though she clearly yearned for both a soul and a heart with which to connect. He was reluctant to encourage her, to allow her to feel her romantic interest was reciprocated in any way. 'I didn't want to go to bed with her,' he said in his essay about Sylvia in *The Savage God*. 'It would have been trouble.' And Sylvia was not his type. 'She was a big girl,' he said, 'with a long face.' It was possible that Sylvia was unaware that a couple of years earlier Alvarez too had been taken with Assia and had pursued her relentlessly.

But he knew Sylvia was all alone with her children that Christmas Eve and when she telephoned he agreed to go round for a drink. He was shaken by her appearance. Ordinarily so neatly dressed and so apparently in control, even in the recent fragmenting circumstances, he was met at the door by a figure who seemed to have lost her way. As Alvarez followed her up the stairs to her small sitting room he was struck by the powerful scent, 'sharp as an animal's', that clung to her hair. Usually caught up in a neat but severe bun, that night it was unpinned, floating round her, resembling 'a tent' and giving her pale face and gaunt figure 'a curiously desolate rapt air, like a priestess emptied out by the rites of her cult'. Despite the efforts she had described to her mother to make the flat lovely, Sylvia had not yet hung any curtains and the place felt empty and cheerless. She had put up a few flimsy Christmas decorations but their insubstantiality emphasised how the forced jollity of Christmas can make those who are sad sadder. She read Alvarez some of her new poems, including 'Death & Co.'. She wanted to discuss the subtlety of the word 'verdigris', which she had used in that poem. When she finally made a move to seduce him Alvarez 'backed off'. He left her alone as he hurried away to a dinner party, knowing he had damaged their friendship, perhaps irrevocably.

But on Boxing Day Sylvia sat at the window in her sitting room mesmerised, even charmed, by the transformation of her London street. The snow had started to fall early that morning, wiping out any lingering traces of the smog as the air became thinned, bleached and clarified by the sharpness of the cold. The British incompetence when confronted with snow baffled and amused Sylvia, who was used to extremes of weather at home in America, but she did not welcome the cold. 'Weather affects me intensely,' she had said in an interview in a BBC interview in August 1962. She was making plans to meet up with her friend Marcia Stern after the snow had melted. 'I do need a spring tonic,' she wrote. 'I am dying to see what you think of my little Frieda and Nick.' Letter writing and letter receiving sustained her. The action of sharing the details of her life, of rendering them absurd and also optimistic, convinced her that things were indeed absurd and also optimistic. That winter her letters to her mother and to her friends in America brimmed with child-love. Her sense of needing and being needed by her two children tethered her to a purposefulness that had been missing a decade earlier when, in a state of deep depression, she had tried to take her own life.

Sylvia had always wanted children of her own. Once she and Mrs Plath had been to visit a friend's new baby and Mrs Plath noticed how her daughter had 'opened the curled hand and stretched out the exquisitely finished little fingers' and Mrs Plath saw 'such warmth, such yearning in Savvy's face'.[6] But parenthood had never been a role Sylvia wished to occupy alone. She knew with a particular poignancy the significance of fatherhood. In October 1962, two days after her thirtieth birthday, Sylvia had recorded some of her poems for the BBC, her otherwise deep and robust voice breaking a little in 'Daddy'. The act of emotional and physical desertion by Ted had reignited her childhood feelings of abandonment. She had been eight years old when her adored father died from the effects of diabetes but it was a decade later that the full impact of that loss struck her, leading to the suicide attempt, hospitalisation and electric shock treatment. Incarceration was something she never wanted to repeat.

As the snow began to fall ever more heavily, Ted had driven down to Court Green, unable to go faster than twenty miles an hour. He had dug up potatoes and gathered the apples they had stored from the autumn and made his way back through the ice to deliver them to Fitzroy Road. But all the while he was being solicitous to Sylvia he had begun to betray Assia. Sylvia's suspicions that Assia and Ted were expecting a child were not unfounded. But Ted did not want any more children and Assia was neither interested nor excited by the idea of motherhood. And then Ted had begun sleeping with Susan Alliston, a twenty-five-year-old secretary who worked at his publishers, Faber & Faber. They had met in the office lift. She showed him the poems she was writing. She was part Welsh. Her hair was like 'dark-bronzed fine wire'. She was made for Ted. At least for now.

A week into the snowfall the persistence of compacted ice had become obstructive to day-to-day living. Sylvia complained to her mother how 'the English being English have no snow-ploughs, so to get from shop to shop one climbs mountains of sludge'. There was something so old fashioned about the sight of the standpipes that Sylvia felt she was caught 'in a limbo between the old world and the very uncertain and rather grim new'. When she forced herself to go out to buy necessary supplies, the man in Sylvia's local chemist reached behind the counter among the throat sweets and the Kleenex and heaved up a six-foot plank of wood, the magical solution with which he scraped a path in the road, and made the slippery pavement outside his shop safe for her. Less amusing was the unavoidable need to buy nappies, milk and bread. When the children were in bed and in the smallest hours of the night, before the morning light, Sylvia wrote poetry by candlelight with freezing fingers. She was anxious about the rent and at times she feared Ted's irregular financial support would somehow dry up altogether and she would have to put Frieda and Nicholas 'in an orphanage and work as a waitress'. She was appalled to learn that the British courts only gave a woman a third of her husband's income as a divorce settlement and less if the woman herself worked. All around her, like the freezing ground itself, coldness and anger became the private territory within which she moved, and she began to feel overpowered by her state of aloneness. Writing to her mother she described the unshakeable flu from which both she and the children suffered. She wrote about the strikes and about how her children went without cooked food. 'There are mad rushes for candles,' she wrote. 'I just need someone to cheer me up by saying I've done all right so far.' Here, in the city, snow, death, anxiety over money, absence of sex, of love, and an insuppressible, raging jealousy had all begun to erode her confidence in her own capability. Writing, the writing of poetry, had always been her saviour and it was to writing that she now clung.

At the end of January 1963 the American poet Robert Frost, one of Plath's heroes, had died at the age of eighty-eight of complications from pancreatic cancer. Some six years earlier she and Ted had heard 'dear, shrewd, funny lovable Robert Frost' when he came to Cambridge University where they were studying and teaching, to read to a packed and enthusiastic hall. While the elder poet was now silent, Sylvia yearned to hear the old, loving, passionate, committed voice of her husband. The tenderness of tone he brought with him on his weekly visits to her London flat was confined to his children. If Ted had abandoned her, he remained loyal to Frieda aged nearly three and Nick aged just one, arriving at Sylvia's new home 'like a kind of apocalyptic Santa Claus', and taking them on trips to the nearby London Zoo as often as the weather would allow. She had chosen the flat in part because it was within the sound of a lion's roar, the zoo a place she and Ted had always loved visiting first as a couple and then with their children.

On 4 February Sylvia wrote to Marcia Stern, her friend at Smith College, Massachusetts, 'Everything has blown and bubbled and warped and split.' That day her unhappiness was not unconnected to the publication two weeks earlier of her autobiographical novel *The Bell Jar*. Fiction had been an adventure for her, a divergence from poetry. This book, set in the oppressive backdrop of 1950s America, had appeared under the pseudonym of Victoria Lucas and in it the heroine Esther Greenwood, witty and enquiring, confronts the complexity of creativity, friendship, yearns to understand love and tussles with identity, sexuality and despair. But although the reviews were respectful they had not been as rapturous as Sylvia had hoped and they had contributed to a depression that had been embedding itself ever deeper since Christmas.

The same day, Sylvia wrote to Dr Beuscher, the therapist in America who had counselled her during her breakdown in 1953 and who Sylvia felt to be 'the wisest woman emotionally and intellectually that I know'. Since her discovery of Ted's treachery the preceding July she had written regularly and at great length to Dr Beuscher. Her letters were filled with the bleak honesty and undisguised rage that she censored in part when writing to her other correspondents, to friends, to her mother. The poems she had completed in the past week were written, she told Dr Beuscher, 'on the edge of madness'. Her letter is full of words and phrases for chilliness as she described how she kept slipping into 'this pit of panic and deep freeze', a despair at her own failure whipping round her 'like a cold, accusing wind' as she confronted 'this dammed self-induced freeze'. She described how coping with dressing, cooking, 'putting one foot in front of the other' had become 'torture'.[7] And she acknowledged that the worst inhibitor of enjoyment of life was her incapacity to love herself.

As her words to Dr Beuscher became ever more desperate her early-morning poems became ever more astonishing. Many years earlier she had written in her journal 'what I fear most is the death of the imagination'.[8] But at the time of her greatest vulnerability it was her imagination that thrived and as she told her friend and fellow poet Ruth Fainlight she was 'producing free stuff I had locked in me for years'. Her writing that New Year was conceived in consciousness but removed from rational, or even irrational, thinking, a Keatsian existence where 'the sense of Beauty overcomes every other consideration, or rather obliterates all consideration'. With the snow lying outside, inside a mind was skating on the thin ice of genius, capable of cracking and giving way at any moment.

# Chapter Twenty

## *Sleeping before dawn*

Sylvia Plath's spirits continued to fall, quietly but unstopping, like loose tiles sliding off the slope of an icy roof. And her physical appearance was worrying her friends and especially her doctor, John Horder. She had recently lost 20lb in weight and had started smoking. She was taking prescribed sleeping pills on a nightly basis. Horder examined her chest, and also the children who seemed unable to shake off the colds they had been suffering from since Christmas. Horder began to visit Fitzroy Road daily, prescribing antidepressants and arranging for Sylvia to start having a series of appointments with a psychiatrist. He was an exceptional medical practitioner whom colleagues praised for his gentle manner that 'never instructed or insisted'.[1]

Her neighbours checked in on her regularly, collectively worried about the increasingly volatile young woman. Trevor Thomas, the elderly artist who lived in the flat below Sylvia, was especially disturbed by her state of mind. On Sunday 27 January she had come to his door 'with red swollen eyes, the tears running down her face and with voice shaken by sobs',[2] telling him she was going to die and asking, 'Who will take care of my children?' She accepted his offer of a glass of sherry and sat with him for a long while, sharing her rage against Assia, 'the scarlet woman, the Jezebel'. But he also felt her to be curiously removed from his presence, appearing wholly uninterested when Thomas confessed that his own wife had disappeared to Spain with another man. The *Observer* was lying open on a chair on a review by Anthony Burgess of *The Bell Jar*. Just as Alvarez had once been surprised by Sylvia's identity, so Trevor was taken aback when Sylvia revealed herself to be its author. He had no idea she was a writer, let alone a poet of such stature.

Sylvia was still waiting for a telephone to be installed in her flat. However, on Thursday 7 February, when most of the telephone lines went down in the icy weather, she managed to make a call from the telephone box on her street corner. But she was exasperated to hear that the young au pair she had just engaged was backing out of their agreement. Immediately Sylvia called her friend Jillian Becker. Asking if she could come straight over with the children to Jillian's house in Islington, Sylvia told her friend she felt 'terrible'. On Sylvia and the children's arrival the two women shared bowls of the chicken soup Jillian had made for her husband Gerry who was too ill in bed with a bad dose of flu to join them. Jillian kept a very watchful eye on Sylvia's nervy behaviour. Encouraged by her robust appetite that evening, Jillian cooked them each a steak 'from a great French butcher in Soho, and mashed potato and salad', thankful that

Sylvia had asked to stay the night.[3] And then Jillian listened. She listened as Sylvia erupted with anger at Ted's cruelty and her contempt for Assia's vanity. She was especially distressed that Ted had taken Assia to Spain, and where it was now warm when Sylvia needed warmth, when the children needed warmth, when all three should be somewhere beside the sea, away from this relentless cold weather. When the very worst of the rage had passed Sylvia finally slept. But despite the sleeping pills she woke again at 3 a.m. asking Jillian if it was time to take another pill. She got back to sleep just before dawn. Jillian was relieved that Dr Horder was arranging his patient's hospital admission as soon as possible. He had told Jillian to make sure Sylvia looked after the children herself. 'She must feel that she's absolutely necessary to them,' he explained. On the evening of Saturday 9 February Sylvia dressed in a smart blue and silver dress, made herself up, curled her hair and went out, leaving her children in Jillian's care. Perhaps she went to meet Ted at the flat. Jillian did not know where she had gone and did not ask. But on Sylvia's return something had happened to calm her. Or something had given her some resolve, some insight about her plans for her future.

Herbrand Russell, the 11th Duke of Bedford, had been president of the Zoological Society of London for forty years and had introduced American bison, deer, antelope, lion and tiger into his private park at Woburn Abbey in Bedfordshire. Not all of them had been hardy enough to make it through the winter. The *Spectator* told the distressing story of a muntjac deer that had escaped from the woods near Woburn. With its sharply pointed cloven hooves and small legs, the animal, no bigger than a large dog, failed to cross the snowy woodland around the park. It was discovered by one of the Duke's park attendants, trapped, still alive but half eaten by a fox and suffering the most agonising sort of half-existence.

In the warmer conditions of the London Zoo in Regent's Park animals and birds were less exposed, well fed and had no reason to resort to savagery for survival. Construction of the new aviary, designed by Princess Margaret's dashing husband, Tony Snowdon, was not yet complete, but progressing well. The future occupants in their temporary accommodation were better protected from the weather than most birds during those icy weeks. Reuben the mountain gorilla, who had arrived in Regent's Park in 1960, had shown encouragingly enthusiastic signs about getting to know a beautiful new female gorilla. But the first of the winter casualties had occurred before the snow had even begun to fall when Reuben succumbed to pneumonia. Soon a couple of zebras at Whipsnade perished in the falling temperatures, although the resident penguins looked as pleased by the unaccustomed appearance of so much snow as children given the keys to a sweetshop.

On Sunday morning, 10 February, when the snow had been on the ground for over seven weeks in Primrose Hill, a robust little huddle of two grown-ups and five children arrived at the Zoo. The place was very empty that day, with attendance numbers down so dramatically that the Zoological Society was facing a £20,000 deficit due to lost revenue, extra costs of food, litter, electricity and gas and the unexpected deaths of animals. In the 'Daily Occurrences' book that logged the Zoo's arrivals and departures as well as the births and deaths, the Departures column listed all the animals that had died since Boxing Day: a beaver, a wild rabbit, an antelope, a hawk eagle, a Humboldt penguin, a golden-naped parrot, a flamingo, a cockatoo, a goat monkey, a white-nosed monkey, a quail, an ibis, a lemur, a ferret, a Madagascar Lovebird, a black Lory from West Papua, a crab-eating racoon, an owl, a hamster and a night heron. There had been much death, far too much death, in the Zoo that winter.

But that Sunday morning, Sylvia remained behind with Jillian Becker and Phyllis, the Beckers' Irish nanny, confident that her children were safe in the care of her close network of friends. Gerry Becker and Nest Cleverdon acted as chaperones to five children: Madeleine Becker aged 1, Julia Cleverdon aged 12, her brother Francis aged 2, Frieda Hughes aged nearly 3 and her brother Nick also just one year old. Sylvia never allowed her children to miss a chance to visit the Zoo. On 15 December she had written to tell Mrs Prouty how Frieda in particular 'was absolutely fascinated by the lions and owls, the new baby elephant and the penguins swimming in their "bath"'. Being with her little girl, watching these animals through her eyes, was like having 'a fresh expanded consciousness'.

Nest's husband Douglas, a bookseller and senior producer of radio drama for the BBC and a great friend of Ted's, had first met Sylvia for lunch the preceding spring when he commissioned her to write *Three Women: A Poem for Three Voices*. Julia, Lewis (aged nine and staying away that night with an aunt) and Francis were the three survivors of Nest's eight pregnancies, and even at the age of twelve Julia was both mature and sensitive enough to know that something was wrong with the young mother of whom her parents were so fond. Gerry Becker, a lecturer in English literature at Hendon Polytechnic, was loved by all the children. He was the driver of his own London taxi-cab and reminded Julia of a 'rambunctious pirate'. She still remembers that morning as a happy one.[4] They returned to the Beckers' home to find Jillian had cooked a traditional Sunday lunch. The whole party sat down to soup, roast lamb 'with all the trimmings' and further courses of salad and cheese and pudding. Wine was drunk. Sylvia was enjoying herself, helping her small son to manage the food on his plate. But she did not laugh. Jillian did not hear her laugh once.

In the evening Sylvia announced she was going home. Frieda had to go to her nursery school the following day. There were clothes to be washed. She had a lunch date with her publisher. No amount of persuasion could entice Sylvia to stay another night, to allow the Beckers to keep her with them, to keep her safe from herself. Wearing his fur hat, a donkey jacket and the butcher's apron that prevented oil dripping on his clothes from the gap in the shaft of the steering wheel, Gerry drove her towards Fitzroy Road. The noise coming from the engine of the old snow-covered machine that 'rattled and roared' was so loud that Gerry did not immediately hear the sobbing coming from the seat behind him.[5] Eventually he stopped the cab and climbed into the back, holding Sylvia's shoulders from across the jump seat as she put her head in her hands. Then the children began to cry too and climbed on to Gerry's knee and for a moment Sylvia, who had once told Gerry that she and Ted 'made love like giants', seemed to feel safe with all three of them, her small family, held together in the cramped space of a taxi-cab, finding comfort in Gerry's weighty, male strength. He begged her to return to his and Jillian's house. 'Jillian doesn't want you to go. I don't want you to go. Come back.' But she was adamant, stern even. 'This is nonsense, take no notice,' she told him. She must go to her own home with the children. He got back behind the wheel. There was nothing more he could say to her. Her mind was made up.

After Gerry had spent a couple of hours with Sylvia, making sure she was able to manage, he left. Dr Horder came to confirm that a nurse would visit the house at 9 a.m. the next day. Later that evening, Sylvia came downstairs and asked Trevor Thomas for some stamps for airmail letters. She insisted on paying him or 'I won't be right with my conscience before God, will I?' Fifteen minutes after she had left and Trevor had closed the door he opened it again to find her standing still and silent in the hallway. She was fine, she told him. She was having a wonderful dream, 'a vision'. As 10 February came to an end, all the emotional intensity with which she invested her early-morning poems, the creativity symbolised in her writing but also in the children themselves, was subdued and exchanged for the meticulous practical care with which she made her essential arrangements. With one part of her in full focus and another broken, incapable of clarity of thought, she went about her business. Trevor Thomas heard her pattering about above him. Having settled her two tiny children in bed, she crept out to post the letters. When they had fallen asleep she poured two cups of milk. She buttered some bread. She left the milk and the bread for her children to find when they woke up. She taped up the spaces around their bedroom door and wadded any remaining cracks with towels, leaving the windows partially open despite the cold temperatures outside. She went downstairs to the kitchen. She folded a cloth that she laid on the open door of the oven. At some point after 5 a.m., probably nearer 6 a.m., when Trevor Thomas was asleep downstairs and her children were asleep in their beds above her, she sat down on the floor beside the gas oven with its four rings and a small grill above and laid her head as far inside the oven's cavity as she could, resting it on the folded cloth. Accumulated gas, scentless carbon monoxide can collect inside an oven without the need for the taps to be turned on but that winter the coldness of the pipes had restricted the usual speed of the flow. So Sylvia turned on the taps. She died in the limbo between the silent dark of the night and the pale beginnings of daylight, that time when the day has not quite begun, bringing with it what Jillian Becker called the 'small consolations', that might breathe life into words and transform them into poetry or breath that might breathe life into the almost dead and help them survive.

Nearly sixty years later, on 11 February 2020, I woke unusually early with a start. Sylvia had been on my mind, filling my thoughts even when sleeping. I watched the dawn blushing the sky above the curve of the hill outside my bedroom window, a brightness strengthening just within the rim of my vision. A storm had been raging across the entire country for two days; it had been uprooting trees in London streets and whipping up waves in the English Channel. The Hastings lifeboat had almost toppled over as it tried to rescue a lone surfer who had braved the bucketing of the huge seas the night before. I watched as an unexpectedly warm sun rose slowly from behind the Downs and within this beautiful luminosity, a blessing after the raging, I heard birdsong for the first time in more than a week. The air was still. The storm had passed.

At about 9 o'clock Myra Norris, the nurse who had been booked by Dr Horder, could not get any response from Sylvia's building. Pipes in the street had burst again and a long queue to call the plumber had formed outside the telephone box. Al Alvarez said that a good plumber cost as much as a side of smoked salmon that winter. Myra also waited in the queue to telephone her office to check she had the right address but looking up from the street she spotted the faces of two children staring down at her from the window. Returning to the house and with the help of a local builder, she managed to get the front door open. Passing the pram in the hall, onto which Dr Horder's telephone number was taped, the overwhelming smell of gas led them straight to the kitchen. The nurse tried to breathe life into the young woman they found lying there, inert, but there was no response even though her body was still warm. Dr Horder came at once. He made the formal identification of the body and registered the cause of death as: 'carbon monoxide poisoning (domestic gas) while suffering from depression. Did kill herself.' Upstairs the children were waiting for their mother to come and find them in their bedroom. They were very cold but alert enough after those meticulous efforts at preventing the gas from escaping upwards had succeeded. However, Trevor Thomas remained unconscious from the fumes that had seeped downwards through the kitchen floor into his flat below, unaware for most of the day of what had happened in the flat above his.

Three weeks after the review of *The Bell Jar* had been published in the *Observer*, the same newspaper carried its author's obituary written by Al Alvarez. Describing the 'intensity of her genius', he explained how she had explored 'that narrow violent area between the viable and the impossible, between experience which can be transmuted into poetry and that which is overwhelming'. This man who had admired her writing almost before any other, the man to whom she had longed to become closer, considered her 'the most gifted woman poet of our time'. He reflected that 'the loss to literature is inestimable'.

In the weeks that followed, Sylvia's friends from Smith College in Massachusetts were determined that the circumstances of her death should not be allowed to eclipse her life, to diminish her as a person, nor to cloud the vibrancy of her writing. They put up a plaque carrying the words, 'I write only because there is a voice within me that will not be still.' Alvarez felt that Sylvia's action on 11 February might have only been a 'cry for help' that fatally misfired. Had she failed to imagine the consequences involved in removing herself as her children's primary source of love? Had she forgotten momentarily what it was for a parent to abandon a child, a child to miss a parent, the subject about which she had written with such first-hand power in her October 1962 poem 'Daddy'? How could it possibly have been that the vitality of her children and the absolute dependency that connected her to them and them to her was not powerful enough to hold her to life? The survival of the children was the only gain in an act of multiple loss: the loss of Sylvia's life, her children's loss of their mother, a mother's loss of a daughter, a husband's loss of a woman he had once loved perhaps not wisely but too well, and the loss of words, so many more words, to the richness of literature.

Arthur Miller described his wife Marilyn Monroe in his memoir *Timebends* as 'a whirling light to me, all paradox and enticing mystery, street-tough one moment then lifted by a lyrical and poetic sensitivity that few retain past early adolescence'. He suggested that suicide might not only be an act of self-destruction but a demonstration of hatred for someone else. In China suicide victims would hang themselves from the doorway of those who had mortally offended them. If a desire for revenge was part of Marilyn's motive for taking her life in August 1962, then Miller agonised over the identity of her tormentor. As a husband he hoped he could absolve himself. One of the chief sources of Sylvia Plath's final and fatal despair was easier to distinguish. That morning, instead of turning the intense mental energy outwards in the creative act of writing a poem she had turned it inwards, and in a sense it suffocated her. Perhaps she had suffered a sort of heart attack of the brain, a catastrophic failure of the wiring of the mind, or a sense that only with the most final of all finalities would the love that had been denied her in life become hers. Perhaps only another poet would have been able to express in words such a transcendent paradox.

In his poem 'East Coker', Sylvia's hero T. S. Eliot wrote:

> Love is most nearly itself
> When here and now cease to matter.

# Chapter Twenty-one

## *Hitting number one*

On 11 February 1963 the Beatles were in the Abbey Road studios not very far from Fitzroy Road, recording ten tracks for their first album. *Please Please Me* was packed with songs overflowing with optimism, songs celebrating love. The band was on the brink of fame, their reputation breaking Liverpool's geographical boundaries fast. The week before the recording session Maureen Cleave, arts correspondent for the London *Evening Standard*, had published a piece about the band whose 'physical appearance inspires frenzy'. Maureen Cleave's old university friend, Gillian Reynolds, born and bred in Liverpool, had spent months urging Maureen to go and see this pop group who 'look beat up and depraved in the nicest possible way', and were driving their audiences wild with excitement. Eventually Maureen had made her way north where music was not the only art form attracting attention. Poet and playwright

Adrian Mitchell had observed in the *Daily Mail* how 'Liverpool seems to be overflowing with talent'. Alun Owen's gritty, award-winning television plays inspired by life as a young man in Liverpool, including *No Trams to Lime Street*, were much admired by John Lennon. The new television series *Z-Cars*, set in a fictional district 10 miles outside Liverpool, was on everyone's TV set and lips. But it was one particular pop band that was causing more excitement than anything else.

Other performers in the Grafton Ballroom on the night of Maureen's visit had included the wildly popular Gerry and the Pacemakers, Sonny Webb & the Cascades and the Hilton Showband. But it was the Beatles who Maureen had come to see, and within moments of meeting them she was enchanted. For one thing they spoke in their own accents, rather than adopting a fake American twang like fellow Scouser Billy Fury, a former Mersey tugboat hand. Of the four Beatles, Cleave found George Harrison, 'handsome, whimsical and untidy', the most attractive. Ringo Starr, the replacement drummer for the handsome Pete Best, was 'ugly but cute'. And Paul McCartney, with his 'round baby face', told her that John, with his 'brutal upper lip', was 'self-confident because he was too blind to see all the nasty little faces in the audience not enjoying it'. Paul explained to her that their humour was based on 'anything that other people don't laugh at – death for instance or disease'. But Maureen Cleave thought they were 'more fun than anyone else', soon finding herself at the mercy of their teasing. In an interview in 2009 she still remembered how 'they might put your coat in the wastepaper basket, offer to marry you, seize your notebook and pencil, pick you up and put you somewhere else, demand you cut their hair'.[1] In hotel rooms, 'John's favourite game was shuffling his feet on the carpet, then touching you on the cheek to give you a mild electric shock'. All four Beatles were preoccupied with hair. When Ringo joined the band the first thing he was told was: 'Get your hair down.' Some observers thought they wore wigs but Lennon told Maureen that 'if that's the case mine's the only wig with real dandruff'. Above all, Cleave was struck by an irresistible audacity and an honesty about these lads that was at odds with other entertainers whose transparently faux altruism was expressed in wanting nothing more than to buy houses for their mothers. John Lennon told Cleave the truth: the Beatles 'all want to get rich so we can retire'.

A week after Maureen Cleave's visit, the group made their second appearance on the regional programme *People and Places* and sang 'Please Please Me'. Even though numbers of television viewers had continued to rise as snow continued to discourage Saturday nights spent in the pub, the Beatles audience outdid all others, swelling to one and a half million. But if their fame was growing, fortune remained elusive. Three days later, as their friend and roadie Neil Aspinall was struck down with flu, the band lugged their own sound equipment into the town-hall ballroom in Whitchurch in Shropshire. That evening their pre-recorded, first appearance on the number-one pop programme *Thank Your Lucky Stars* was broadcast. The programme was essential viewing for music fans and for followers of Janice Nicholls, the chirpy resident teen critic from Birmingham who awarded bands top votes with her catch phrase, 'I'll give it foive.' The ubiquitous Andrew Loog Oldham had also been at the recording at the ABC studio with Mark Wynter, famous for singing 'Venus in Blue Jeans' and whom Oldham was looking after on behalf of Wynter's record label. The other artists that day were Petula Clark, clarinettist Acker Bilk and the Chris Barber Jazz Band. But even after hearing the Rolling Stones at the Crawdaddy and recognising genius in the 'dead eyes' of Bob Dylan, Oldham had not been prepared for the sound of 'Pentecostal joy' that he heard that night. 'Please Please Me' 'exuded a "fuck you, we're good and we know it" attitude' that took pop music to another level, giving Oldham a 'pop epiphany'. After the recording, Oldham went to speak to Lennon. Oldham wanted the name of the band's manager. Lennon jerked his thumb towards the elegant figure of Epstein, who Oldham saw 'radiate success in his expensive overcoat, paisley scarf and haughty demeanour'. Epstein grudgingly acknowledged to Oldham how his band could do with a bit of 'promotional' help in London, a word he spat out 'as if getting rid of phlegm in his throat'. London had been so resistant to Epstein's advances on behalf of his clients that he had not forgiven the up-itself attitude of the capital. For £5 a week Oldham set about talking to any journalist that would give the Beatles 'plenty of ink'.

Meanwhile, the four Beatles remained as close as friends could be. Nothing could dent their delight in larking about with each other or indeed their elation at simply being lucky enough to be alive in 1963. With Neil Aspinall at the wheel, the Beatles and their equipment would be jammed into the grey and maroon Commer van, scrawled all over – as George described it – 'with girls' names, and things like "I love you, John"', to travel on icy roads between sweaty ballrooms. One day in the high winds their windscreen suddenly blew out. As Aspinall guided the van along the precarious roads, heading straight into the gales, the four Beatles climbed into the back, lying horizontally on top of each other like mattresses in the story of the princess and the pea, taking it in turns to swap positions as every few miles a Beatle on the bottom of the pile moved up to the top. Like a pack of penguins, or a tangle of otters, body warmth kept them from freezing.

As the Beatles pushed their way through the snow to reach the concert halls, Harry Evans was keener than ever to cover stories about the local bands and to publish pictures that did not include the ubiquitous shot of a snowball fight or a graveyard. In early February 1963 George Carr, the *Northern Echo*'s deputy chief photographer, braved the dreadful weather in the newspaper's decrepit Ford Popular on a double mission to rescue people trapped in the snowstorms in the Pennines and to bring back some good images. Fifteen-year-old printing assistant Ian Wright was a hardy youth and volunteered to go with George. Weighting the back of the car with bags of coal to stop the tyres from sliding on the ice, piling the back seat with hessian sacks for wedging beneath sliding tyres and armed with a thermos and sandwiches, Wright and Carr set off with George's ancient plate camera. Not only did the pair succeed in mounting a terrific rescue operation to release the trapped cars, but they also brought back atmospheric shots of drivers and cars buried in the snow. Harry was surprised to discover that young Ian had taken the snowy photograph he liked best of all. When he was called into the editor's office, Ian mentioned his passion for pop music and was rewarded with Harry's encouragement to follow the other photographers who were tracking the bands, especially the group that Harry and his wife Enid had long been keeping their eye on. On Saturday 9 February Ian Wright heard that the Beatles were playing in Sunderland. As Ian was too young for a licence to drive the office car, he bicycled for three hours with his camera swinging from the handlebars as he negotiated the thirty or so miles in the atrocious weather from Darlington to the Sunderland Empire. Leaving his old rusty bike in the care of Don the Doorman, Ian settled himself down for the show. Brian Epstein had smartened up the appearance of the Hamburg and Cavern ruffians and four neatly suited young men with cleanish hair bounced on to the stage, chatting, laughing, having fun in front of the lavishly draped faux-silk curtains. Ian knew the Beatles' music but he had never heard them play. After a set that included 'Love Me Do', 'All My Loving', 'Please Please Me', 'Twist and Shout', 'Roll over Beethoven' and 'Mister Postman', Ian rushed backstage.[2]

Hospitality in these venues was minimal. Male bands shared a single chaotic dressing room in which to change in and out of their stage clothes and relax after the show. Everyone smoked. George was known for simultaneously juggling three cigarettes, a bacon butty and a brimming cup of tea. The 'amenities' in the dressing room comprised a sink, one cold tap and a bar of soap. The mirror above the sink was scrawled with pan-stick obscenities and the tap was essential when the sweaty artists returned from the stage and stripped down to their string vests for a good rinse. Given the mile-long queue for the single backstage lavatory and urinal, the sink also offered an alternative convenience. The stink from the sink and a thousand stale cigarette butts thickened the air. The noise in the room was dense with the clamour of girls who had managed to blag their way backstage, shouting above music that blared from a portable record player as Ray Charles, Chuck Berry and Bo Diddley merged with the post-performance din.

As Lennon answered Ian's knock on the changing-room door, the newly fledged cameraman suggested photographing the four guys inside the old-fashioned theatre lift. Pushing back the metal concertina-grille doors, Ian took just one shot as a 'flash the size of a Bentley headlamp' temporarily blinded the four of them. As the Beatles began to move off, rubbing their eyes, Ian shouted, 'Stop, stop, I need your names,' suddenly confused about which Beatle was which. Warming to the young photographer, Lennon asked Ian to send a copy of the picture to his Aunt Mimi, who was making a scrapbook of clippings and photographs of the band so that when the excitement was all over she would have something to prove that her John had once actually done something. Ian assured him he would. After Ian's photograph of the Beatles in the lift appeared in the new Teenage supplement under the caption 'On Their Way Up', Harry advised Ian to keep the negative somewhere safe, just in case it had some future value. When John Lennon saw the photograph, he was convinced that Wright had taken the band 'out of the darkroom and into the spotlight'.

On 2 February the band had joined Helen Shapiro in Bradford for her month-long nationwide 'pop package', taking days off from the tour here and there to fulfil their own pre-booked engagements.

Sixteen-year-old Helen, the current pop-star sensation with her trademark twelve-inch-bouffant hair, lived in London in an east-end council flat with her father, a machinist in a clothes factory, and her mother, who sewed buttons on jackets. At the beginning of her singing career there had been some discussion at home about changing Helen's surname in order to avoid any anti-Semitic comment. But Norrie Paramor, her producer at EMI, thought 'Shapiro' sounded distinctive and that 'most people wouldn't know about it being Jewish'. They had to be careful. The 'wrong' religion could be as hazardous to a star's career as sexual choice or, like John (who was still with Cynthia) being romantically 'unavailable'. With her hair held in place by can after can of spray, Helen had reached the zenith of pop stardom aged just fifteen, with a run of appearances at the London Palladium. Her beautiful deep voice, which had encouraged her school-friends to call her 'foghorn', had taken 'You Don't Know' to the top of the charts in the summer of 1961. Helen had become Britain's top female singer when her first number-one hit was followed by another. 'Walking Back to Happiness' hit the top of the charts in the autumn of the same year. With frocks so horizontal with starch that Joanna Lumley would have given her school's entire sugar supply to own just one, Helen was now earning twice as much as the Prime Minister. The programme notes informed her fans that she had just left Clapton Park Comprehensive, where she had won a medal as captain of the netball team. As she explained in her memoir, *Walking Back to Happiness*, fans felt encouraged to write to this 'completely unspoiled' young woman whose ambition was to be rich enough for her parents to retire. But the Palladium gigs were interrupted because Helen was a smoker. Her attempts to keep the habit from her family had been successful until one day her agent offered her a 'ciggie' in front of her parents while at her Auntie Jean's house and the secret was out. In the middle of the Palladium appearances she went down with laryngitis. To her shame and disappointment, Helen was ordered by the doctor to rest her voice and she was replaced by Russ Conway, a clean-cut, nicotine-averse thirty-seven-year-old pianist with a safe sort of 'Palladium appeal'.

In the autumn of 1962, Helen had flown with her parents to New Zealand and the start of her first world tour, unable to sleep in case she squashed her hair on the headrest and disturbed her 'crowning glory'. She had then left New Zealand for America. For a London schoolgirl this new world was 'mind-blowing'. She was booked on to the prestigious Ed Sullivan programme on 28 October, the national TV chat show that could make or break a star. At first she confessed to being 'exhilarated by the bigness and the differentness' of New York, by the glass buildings soaring above her, by the salt-beef sandwiches and cheesecake, by the televisions in people's bedrooms. But then Ed Sullivan's producer told her that her dress was wrong. And he gave her a choice of song that she felt to be wrong. And then Ed Sullivan thought it was 'clever' to imitate Helen's London accent. For Helen the whole thing was a bit of an anticlimax, especially as her visit had taken place slap in the middle of the Cuban Missile Crisis and she was terrified of the imminent prospect of nuclear weapons blowing up Manhattan. She felt 'too young to die'.

In early February Helen was joined by eleven other acts appearing nightly on a month-long tour of the ballrooms and cinemas in Britain's second cities. Her popularity had begun to ebb and her record label hoped to put her back up in the charts. Two of the handful of black singers on Britain's white-dominated pop scene were on the bill: Danny Williams, known as 'Britain's Johnny Mathis', and Kenny Lynch, a singer and songwriter of middling success from East London, whose parents had been born in the Caribbean. In addition, Helen was joined by the Kestrels, a successful backing group of four from Bristol, and the Beatles, sold to Helen as a 'promising' band from Liverpool. She had loved the 'rhythm and blues feel' of 'Love Me Do', which felt 'like a shot in the arm'. But when she saw Paul McCartney setting up the three Vox amplifiers they used to turn the sound up she explained they wouldn't be necessary because her audiences sat silently and paid proper attention. Paul carried on with his set-up.

The groovy Beatles in their leather jackets and Cuban-heeled boots were not much older than Helen but they treated her like a little sister, calling her Helly and joshing and teasing and protecting her. She soon realised that she far preferred travelling between sessions in the bus with the lads to her own chauffeured limousine. Trundling along the snowy roads between the northern towns, with John pulling what Helen called his 'cripple face' at passers-by who stared through the windows, the Beatles and Helen entertained the managers and roadies with impromptu renditions of 'Keep your Hands off my Baby'. Deliberately embarrassing the star of the tour was their way of showing her how much a part of the gang they considered her to be. They persuaded Helen to let them practise their signatures on her promotional pictures. She was still trying to keep her ciggie habit from the public when in front of a group of fans, the Beatles offered to sign her Peter Stuyvesant packet. But the fun began to ebb for Helly when fans began to scream for the Beatles and not for her. Her own current single 'Queen for Tonight' had only made it to Number 33 while 'Please Please Me' was edging ever higher towards the top. A trade magazine ran a headline asking, 'Is Helen Shapiro a has-been at 16?' It was as if she had been 'punched in the stomach'. John was instantly reassuring. Pay no attention to that rubbish, he told her. 'You'll be going on for years.' If he didn't fancy a girl he was nice to her and because Helly held no romantic interest for John or any of the other Beatles she earned all their affection and respect.

Sometimes the Beatles went to the back of the coach to write a new song. At the beginning of the tour Kenny Lynch would join them, but he soon became fed up with their lack of cooperation.[3] 'I'm not going to write any more of that bloody rubbish with those idiots,' he announced, as he stormed back down the aisle watched by Roger Greenaway of the Kestrels. 'They don't know the music from their backsides. That's it! No more help from me!' he snapped, leaving them on their own to complete a new song, inspired by the romantic letters page in the *New Musical Express* and which they called 'From Me to You'. After a few gigs the running order was changed and the Beatles were moved up to close the first half of the show, edging out the Red Price Band, the Honeys, Dave Allen and Danny Williams. 'Please Please Me' became their finale as they bussed between Doncaster, Wakefield, Carlisle, Coventry, Taunton, York, Shrewsbury, Southport, Sheffield and Hanley, with a resounding National Anthem rounding off each performance.

A week into the tour, when they had all finished their sessions at the ABC cinema in Carlisle, the cast of the Helen Shapiro pop package went across town for a drink in the Crown and Mitre hotel. The local golf club was having a late-night 'do' when a fan spotted Helly and her co-stars in the lobby and against Helen's and the Beatles' better judgement persuaded them to join their party in the banqueting suite. Kenny Lynch and the leather-jacketed Beatles were twisting away on the dance floor with sixteen-year-old Helen and the long-dressed ladies of Carlisle when Bill Berry, the captain of the golf club, appeared with a face flushed to match his name. He was incandescent with anger, blood pressure and drink. Huffing and puffing about the gate-crashing of his exclusive soirée by such an ill-dressed and, Helen suspected, wrong-coloured bunch of ruffians, he opened a side door and threw them out into the snow. News of the incident hit the papers but the publicity did the Beatles no harm. 'Please Please Me' was making its way steadily up all the charts, although the top slot in *New Musical Express*, the chart that really counted, still evaded them.

After the Sunderland gig the Beatles took a couple of weeks off from the Helly tour and joined Cilla Black, the Hollies and the Swinging Blue Jeans for an eight-hour rhythm and blues marathon in the Cavern, before dashing down to London on Sunday 10 February for the recording of their album. They stayed in Chelsea at the hotel across the square from WH Smiths next to the Royal Court Theatre. Joshing about during a promotional photograph session in the King's Road organised by Andrew Loog Oldham they were snapped by Cyrus Andrews pushing their snow-frosted car out of a drift in Sloane Square. And as Oldham accompanied them to interviews with the *New Musical Express* and *Disc* magazine, they never stopped being themselves. John was 'a cute lout, laconic and rude', Paul in contrast 'bopped, weaved and almost curtsied'. George was as Oldham predicted 'already to the manor born' and finally the delightful Ringo remained 'nimble and droll' throughout. But some of the energy that usually lit up their faces on stage was missing from the larky photographs. They looked exhausted. George Martin hoped they would make it through the recording session. Two singles into his working relationship with the band, Martin was pleased that John and Paul's compositions were becoming a bit more 'cerebral',' and began to wonder if real success was within their grasp. There was no question about the charm and musicality and seductiveness of the Beatles' performances, but what struck Martin was the originality and exceptional joy of McCartney and Lennon's songwriting.

At 10 a.m. the band began recording the album's fourteen tracks, of which eight were original compositions. Apart from taking a tea break to pose for another Oldham-fixed photo opportunity, this time with the fashionable Terry O'Neill, they did not wrap up till 10.45 p.m. By the end of the session John's voice was barely there. Orange and red tins full of Zube throat sweets, bottles of milk and a carton of cigarettes were on hand to get him through 'Twist and Shout', the final belter, in one take. And although the sound that came out was slightly raspy, the band and George Martin knew it was all the sexier because of it.

On 12 February the Beatles raced back up north. Having completed two sets in the Azena Ballroom in Sheffield, they changed out of their sweaty suits into polo necks to be driven to Lancashire by roadie Aspinall for their next engagement. Even in the best weather the beautiful crossing through the Pennines, driving at 1,680 feet above sea level around hairpin bends and blind summits, presents a challenge. Two weeks before the Beatles' van negotiated the terrifying route, the local *Glossop Chronicle* had reported how a thick, 200-foot high snowdrift hanging dangerously over Snake Pass 'had been blasted free by four hundred lb of gelignite', as all around, just as in Wordsworth's 'Prelude' 'every icy crag tinkled like iron'. Eventually Aspinall and the band arrived safely at Oldham's Astoria Ballroom. Another ballroom. Another town. Another concert. But something shifted that night. That charm, that gut-shaking head-shiver that Maureen Cleave had noticed – 'a signal to the audience to scream even louder' as soon as Paul joined George at their shared microphone – was becoming familiar. Audiences had begun to anticipate Paul's arousing habit of holding his lips so close to the microphone that he appeared to be on the point of kissing it while John's eyes would meet those of his fellow bandmates in cool, quasi-flirtatious amusement. That evening in Oldham, when a crowd numbering twice the hall's capacity of eight hundred had turned up, a telegram had arrived backstage from Morris Kinn, publisher and owner of the *New Musical Express*. Tony Prince, the nineteen-year-old

Trying to make sense of the 'new-fangled' fashions in Mary Quant's shop Bazaar on London's King's Road

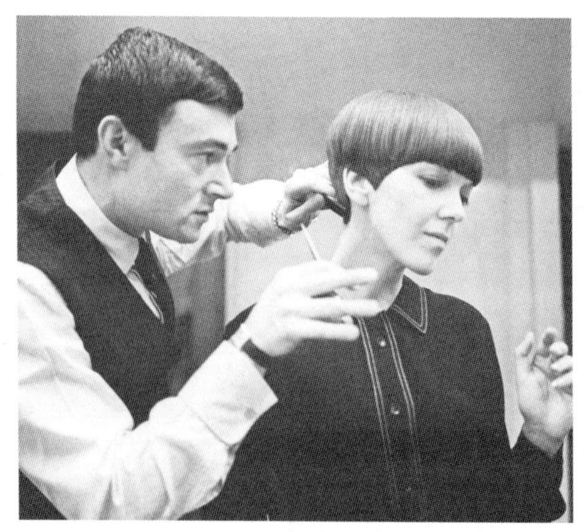

Vidal Sassoon cutting Mary Quant's hair into his distinctive five-point bob

'Dandy' Kim Waterfield, the King's Road's pied piper

The Beatles playing Liverpool's Cavern Club in 1962 before Ringo Starr replaced Peter Best as drummer

Teenage pop star Helen Shapiro rehearsing for Granada TV's *Ready Steady Go!* with two members of her original support band, John Lennon and Ringo Starr

John F. Kennedy, Jacqueline Kennedy, André and Madeleine Malraux and Vice-President Lyndon B. Johnson welcome the Mona Lisa to Washington DC, January 1963

Sylvia Plath and Ted Hughes on their honeymoon in Paris, 1956

Sylvia Plath with her two precious children, Frieda and Nicky, in early summer 1962

Frenzy on stage at Oldham's Astoria Ballroom at the moment Beatlemania truly began, February 1963

Captain Eugene Ivanov, the maybe-only-once Russian lover of Christine Keeler

Dr Stephen Ward with his 'little baby' Christine Keeler and two of her friends at Spring Cottage, Cliveden

The notorious property dealer Peter Rachman

Christine Keeler's boyfriend Johnny Edgecombe in custody

Christine Keeler's stalker 'Lucky' Gordon and the investigative journalist Tom Mangold

The Flamingo Club in London's Soho where Edgecombe and Gordon famously fought over Christine Keeler

*That* swimming pool at Cliveden

Best friends Mandy Rice-Davies and Christine Keeler on their way to the trial of Stephen Ward in the summer of 1963

John Profumo after confessing to lying to the House of Commons in June 1963

Mandy Rice-Davies holding court, outside court, July 1963

Police holding back demonstrators protesting about unemployment outside the House of Commons, March 1963

Juliet, Harold, and Philippa Nicolson with Juliet and Adam's sister Rebecca aged one week at Sissinghurst in April 1963

resident DJ at the Astoria listened as Paul shushed the crowd in the dressing room and read the telegram aloud.[4]

'Congratulations, the Beatles. "Please Please Me" is Number One on the *NME* charts!' Paul and the rest of the room were momentarily silent, absorbing the news.

'Fuck me,' said John.

In Oldham, news of the chart position had spread not only to the ticket holders inside the ballroom but also to some two thousand ticketless fans outside, whom the local police were trying to keep in check. At first there was a 'carnival' atmosphere as Tony Prince went on stage to introduce the band to what suddenly felt like an audience behaving as 'hot gospellers of a new religion'. As the foursome ran on to the stage, their heads bent in an attempt to avoid the 'forked fingernails and shrieking fans', Tony took up his position 'perched at the side of Paul's amplifier'. All at once a girl with a determined expression broke through the fragile human barrier formed by the Astoria's amateur security team: moonlighting café owners and market stallholders proved incapable of preventing the fan from throwing herself around George's neck. Tony saw fear flicker on George's face. Droplets of sweat bounced off Paul's Hofner Violin Bass as John, eyes distended, stuck his chin out and stroked 'six strings for a B flat'. The group struck up and in that moment Tony knew that 'the whole fucking world was wonderful'. Only Ringo, behind his drums and a little removed from the battlefront, managed to remain semi-calm as he began to bash away at his skins. As the half-hour set kicked off with 'Love Me Do', another woman hurled herself on to the stage, the zip in her black, skin-tight sleeveless dress already wrenched apart, her bra and naked back exposed to the audience as enraged fans, furious at her proximity to the band, went wild. Bodies were crushed against the platform. Girls fainted and were brought to relative safety outside the dressing rooms. Others pretended to faint in the hope that they would be 'rescued' in the same way. Backstage, the St John's Ambulance team were making their way along heaps of semi-conscious girls. The Beatles were energised to the point of ecstasy. At every chorus Paul and George shook their hair ever more vigorously, their long fringes reminding journalist Philip Norman of a 'Grenadier's busby'. At the end of the set John vanished. Tony saw him emerge minutes later from the lavatory zipping up his flies. Moments afterwards the lavatory door opened again and a young girl, adjusting her skirt, slipped into the room. As John swallowed two white 'Prellie' tablets with the help of a Scotch and coke, the world of pop music shifted up a gear.

That night the Beatles' dressing room was jam-packed. John McCann, an old friend of Paul's father from the Cotton Exchange, had not been able to get a ticket for the Oldham concert but being a top-class salesman he had blagged his way backstage, name-dropping his connection to Jim McCartney. The McCann family had been committed Beatles fans ever since Jim had tipped John off about Paul appearing on Granada TV's *Scene at Six* two months earlier. Spotting a golden opportunity to introduce the band to his family, McCann suggested the Beatles might like to come back to his house in the Coppice, about ten minutes' drive away, for a cup of tea. Neil Aspinall could bring them over in the van. John Lennon was hungry.

He said yes, he would definitely come as long as a plate of 'cheese sarnies' would be waiting for him.

Liz McCann, the eleven-year-old daughter of Paul's dad's 'old mucker', was at home with her brothers and sisters when their father arrived with news of the imminent appearance of some unexpected guests. The two youngest children, Frances aged six and Martin aged four, had already been sent to bed but Liz and her siblings, Phil aged fourteen, Cath aged twelve, and Steph aged nine, were all still up. While her schoolteacher mother Mary rushed to the kitchen to make the sandwiches, Liz could barely allow herself to *think* about what was about to happen.[5] Sixteen-year-old Pat Costello was also in the McCann house that night. She earned pocket money by doing ironing for Mary and, to the envy of the McCann children, had just got back from the concert. John McHugh, a fourteen-year-old 'cheeky chappy' schoolboy who lived next door was well known at the McCanns for his peculiar habit of using the word 'bill' at the end of every sentence, as a way of emphasising what he wanted to say. And in the way that news about a once-in-a-lifetime chance has a habit of spreading, no one was surprised to see John appear in the McCanns' hallway. Suddenly Neil Aspinall and four leather-jacketed Beatles were squashing into the McCanns' front room, a glowing coal fire burning in the large Victorian fireplace.

For Liz, with every detail embedded in her memory, that night remains one of the most unreal and thrilling of her life. As George twirled one of Ringo's drumsticks, the others, impeccably mannered, admired the sideboard loaded up with a huge plate of roast lamb sandwiches (there being no chance to buy any cheese so late at night) and one of Mary's delectable home-made chocolate sponge cakes. As they made themselves at home, chatting about Everton football club, chatting about their first album which was coming out the next day, the four boys bewitched this room full of strangers who perched on the arms of the sofa and chairs, sitting as close as they could get to their mesmerising guests. Ringo had taken the big chair and was particularly sweet to Liz as she sat at his feet while he asked her questions about the life of an eleven-year-old schoolgirl. The other three Beatles and Aspinall were all jammed up on the sofa opposite her with John McHugh from next door standing in front of them holding court. Hearing about his keenness on the music scene, one of the Beatles asked young John whether the rest of his family wanted to come in from next door.

'Do they, bill!' John M replied, at which the Beatles started to laugh and play around with John's favourite expression. Did Paul want another piece of cake?

'Did he, bill!'

Did George think he could manage another of Mary's sandwiches?

'Did he, bill!'

However, much as Liz was touched by Ringo's solicitousness, her eyes were on no one but Paul. In his green crewneck sweater, she knew in *that* moment, with *that* Beatle sitting on *her* sofa 'the dawning of her adolescence' had begun to shine.

Brian Epstein now employed two girls in his office to deal with fan mail and a fan club in the south of England had been opened to ease the load in the north. Information about the boys personal likes and dislikes informed fans that Ringo's favourite food was steak and chips, Paul's car of choice was the Ford Classic (in Goodwood Green), George's greatest dislike was 'black eyes' and John's favourite movie director Ingmar Bergman. Derek Adams, a journalist on the *Sentinel* and the *Derby Evening Telegraph*, shared fish and chips with them and gave a detailed account of the eating habits of all four. Paul smothered everything in ketchup, George drank his tea from a saucer, John ate chip sandwiches and Ringo's chips were sprinkled with sugar. But not a word was written about their private lives. No mention was made of John's shotgun marriage to Cynthia Powell in the summer of 1962 or about her advancing pregnancy. No mention was ever made of any of Paul's girlfriends either, including Dot Rhone, a sixteen-year-old shop assistant whom he had met at the Casbah and had encouraged to dye her brown hair blonde, the colour of Paul's fantasy woman, Brigitte Bardot. Not a whisper was heard about how Dot had become pregnant in 1960 with seventeen-year-old Paul's baby, and how Paul thought he would have to give up music and get a proper job. When Dot sadly had a miscarriage at three months, Paul continued to play music but no longer continued to see Dot. He had moved on to Iris Caldwell. Iris's brother, Rory Storm, was the lead singer with the Hurricanes, the band that Ringo had left when he replaced Pete Best as the Beatles' drummer. Paul had met Iris in the scrum of the Cavern and for a while he hung out at her house where he would roll up his trouser legs and ask Iris's mother Vi to give his naked legs a comb. The feeling relaxed him. But early in 1963 Iris had been dumped too. And meanwhile there were enough blonde Brigitte Bardot lookalikes in every town they played in to stop him missing Dot or Iris and to maintain the myth of an unattached Beatle.

Two days after they had eaten their tea in Liz McCann's house, the Beatles returned to Liverpool for Valentine's Day. That night the Meteorological Office announced that temperatures were probably about to rise the length and breadth of Britain. A thaw was on the way. The father of Stephen Guy's classmate Sandra McLeod was the official photographer at the almost 2,000-seater Locarno ballroom in Liverpool's West Derby Road. McLeod's shop and studio was just down the road from the Locarno, opposite the Hippy (as everyone called the Royal Hippodrome), which had almost 3,000 seats. The opportunity for photographers to land a scoop on visiting performers was boundless. That night the audience in the Hippodrome went wild when Ringo Starr announced that each Beatle had received more than thirty Valentine cards. The next day Sandra came to school with a professional glossy picture taken by her dad of herself and her best friend posing with a dishevelled young man in a collarless jacket and drenched in sweat, his arms draped round the two girls. That picture of Sandra, her mate and Paul McCartney was the raunchiest thing Stephen and Sandra's schoolmates had ever seen. For the next few weeks Stephen filled his notebooks with sketches of the Beatles and listened to them on the wireless speaking in accents that 'came from the bottom of the ocean floor'. John's accent was the most distinctive, sounding like a slowed-down record, a 'very old-fashioned working-class voice' that Stephen had never come across in Liverpool. Stephen could not get enough of it.

*

News that the snowfall had been interrupted was welcomed everywhere, but especially in Dartmoor where a farm that had been cut off for sixty-six days, immersed in 20-foot-high drifts, was finally liberated by the army. On Skye the gradual warming of the air combined with the lowest rainfall for thirty years and the effect of the grass shrivelling before the frost eventually melted contributed to a fire covering a seven-mile stretch of land. In Derbyshire the decrease in snowfall meant the Chatsworth shoot could go ahead. A large house party that had assembled for the weekend of 22 February included Hugh and Antonia Fraser.[6] On Saturday evening, in black tie and long dress, the guests came downstairs to the drawing room where the Duchess of Devonshire was waiting.

'Henry is bringing us some entertainment,' she explained. 'There's something awfully good on television that I want to show you.'

With an ear to the ground and a passion for Elvis, the Duchess had already seen the Beatles on their first outing on *Thank Your Lucky Stars*. And although Elvis held on to his foremost place in her heart, she had to admit she had been smitten. 'Dinner might be a little late tonight,' she told the hungry, puzzled diners, who knew it was far too early in the evening to be watching *TW3*. And as the bacon on the grouse began to crisp up in the Chatsworth kitchen, Henry the butler opened the doors to a small recess that led into the chapel. Removing the television from its hiding place, the butler wheeled the set into the centre of the room, positioning it within sight of John Singer Sargent's ethereal portrait of three sisters in floating white dresses, the granddaughters of the 8th Duchess. Soon the black-and-white screen burst into life and the sound of the programme's jaunty theme tune filled the drawing room. Billy Fury was on first, his hair flicked up into a stiff Elvis quiff. And then four smiling young men appeared with swingy, long-fringed haircuts, dressed in severe collars, tightly knotted ties and dark suits with velvet collars. Under the Epstein sartorial regime, the black leather of their Hamburg days had been banished in favour of shiny suits from Burton Tailoring. The band had also long been forbidden by their management to make V-signs, swear or smoke during performances. Belching into the microphone and thwacking each other mid-song were also banned. As they kicked off with 'Please Please Me', high heels beneath the long evening dresses in the Chatsworth drawing room began to tap. Behind the door to the butler's pantry Henry's shiny shoes began to tap. Soon the great house was filled with the sound of tapping feet. Some thought that even the dainty feet of the Acheson sisters appeared to move. A surprising concession to their old habits crept into the end of the performance as the band bowed deferentially to their audience just as Epstein had taught them to do. Secretly John Lennon was not keen on this outmoded instruction but felt he must acquiesce if the band were to have a choice of 'making it or still eating chicken on stage', an anecdote from the slovenly habits of their early, pre-Epstein Cavern gigs that was already becoming part of his own folklore.

The reprieve in the weather was not set to last. Diesel froze in the tanks of two hundred London buses on 23 February, the day the Beatles arrived in Coventry to resume touring with

Helly, and trains coming south from Manchester were stopped in their tracks as coal and points and signals all iced over. Gale-force winds had blown on thirteen days of the month in Scotland and for nine in England and Wales, while fog had been recorded somewhere in England and Wales on every single day of February. That week, Garth Christian had written to *Country Life* to record how fieldfares and redwings were invading urban gardens and railway cuttings. And although 'this winter might not be the first occasion on which a bittern has been found in a London bus queue', he could not remember any previous year in which a kestrel had descended to a Sussex bird table beside a kitchen window. When the kestrel began to peck the fat provided for a bold flock of long-tailed tits, Christian remained astonished by the unprecedented intimacy between birds and men in recent weeks, 'one of the most striking features of this strange winter'.

Undaunted by the cold, the Beatles continued to speed up and down the country, completing their stint with Helly on 3 March at the Gaumont Cinema in Hanley, Stoke on Trent. Meanwhile, Cynthia Lennon, her marriage to John still a secret, had hardly seen her husband over the past few months as she waited in Liverpool for the spring to arrive and with it, just like my own mother, the birth of her child.

# Chapter Twenty-two

*Swimming in a warm pool*

On Wednesday 6 March after sixty-three consecutive days of frost, Britain woke up to a warmer world. The country was basking in its first frost-free night since before Christmas. The thaw had been gradual as different pockets of the country had been liberated from the harshness of the winter over the preceding few days. In Scotland and the North of England, heavy rain coincided with the steady melting and resulted in extensive flooding. On 7 March the water levels in the River Kent in Kendal rose ten feet. But further south the temperatures in London that week reached a balmy sixteen degrees, the highest since 25 October 1962. Long lost milk bottles were found leaning drunkenly against doorsteps, released from their snowy hiding places. Ladybirds appeared on windowsills and spiders emerged from webs that had once glistened in the chill and were now shimmering in the sunshine. On 6 March at

Sissinghurst, Harold's daily diary entry, which had shrunk along with his increasingly empty life over the past few months to nothing more than a few lines, described the purple and white petals of the crocuses in the orchard, which were at last 'beginning to unfurl'. Little by little a national realisation developed that 'The Great Freeze' as the newspapers were now calling the past ten weeks, was over at last. The ice had finally broken. The time had come for music and dance.

On Tuesday 12 March the Queen Mother and her younger daughter, Princess Margaret, stepped out, jewel-laden, on to Covent Garden's ice-free pavements on their way to a Gala Performance at the Royal Opera House. *Marguerite and Armand*, Sir Frederick Ashton's new ballet, had been written for forty-three-year-old Margot Fonteyn and twenty-four-year-old Rudolph Nureyev. Ashton had been inspired not only by Alexandre Dumas's *La Dame aux Camélias*, but by his own response to the young Russian dancer from Eastern Siberia. There was 'a physical intensity and a sexual impulse' about Nureyev, he said, 'that charged the atmosphere with electricity'.[1] Cecil Beaton had designed the set as well as the costumes for the ballet. He had not taken to the wild-eyed, hollow-cheeked dancer, alarmed by Nureyev's rawness, his untamedness. 'He has no pity, no concern for others,' he wrote in his diary. 'He is ruthless.' During their costume design meeting in his house in Kensington, Beaton felt 'very much as if I had brought an animal from the woods into my room'. He feared Nureyev might even attack his furniture and that his cherished house might be 'reduced to a shambles'.

Beaton was either ignorant of or threatened by Nureyev's complex nature. Ballet-crazy Rachel Pritchard, who lived in Rhodesia, had seen another side of the dancer.[2] She had been spending the Christmas holidays with her family in a flat in London's Ennismore Gardens. At the age of seven she already knew all about the famous Russian who had taken the flat above – her father Leslie had told her the romantic story of his defection, and a friendship had sprung up between the blonde-haired child and the reclusive exile as they passed one another coming in and out of the building. One snowy morning Rachel had found a wrapped parcel on her doorstep containing a beautiful vase made of shiny paper. The present from the Russian became one of her greatest treasures. But no such sweetness of nature revealed itself to Beaton. At the dress rehearsal for the ballet Nureyev had snipped the waiter-like tails off his performance jacket because they flapped annoyingly as he moved. Failing to understand how male dancers were driven mad by anything that flipped and flapped behind them, impeding the smoothness of each jump, Beaton was irritated. To make things worse, Fonteyn had behaved like a prima donna, rejecting the hat he had created for her and refusing to accept the red camellias that had been stitched on to her gown at his instruction. There was some small comfort for Beaton when he was told that the gala performance had ended with twenty-one curtain calls. He hoped that this enthusiastic reception was not only intended for the dancers but for the costume designer too. At least he knew he could have counted on the loyal applause of the Queen Mother.

British theatre was thriving, especially after the founding in 1962 of a British National Theatre, a proposal that had been under discussion for more than a century. In 1939 George Bernard Shaw had furthered the cause, asking, tongue in cheek, whether the English people really wanted a National Theatre. Of course they don't, his answer teased. 'They never want anything,' he said. 'They got the British Museum, the National Gallery, and Westminster Abbey, but they never wanted them,' he said, before delivering his punchline: 'Once these things stood as mysterious phenomena that had come to them, they were quite proud of them, and felt that the place would be incomplete without them.'[3] But despite funding problems, location questions and world wars, the National Theatre idea kept coming back until finally, in the summer of 1962, the dearest and long-campaigned-for wish of Laurence Olivier, the country's most famous actor, had come true. He was to become the National Theatre's first Artistic Director and the Old Vic would provide a home for the theatre until something more permanent could be found.

Since early December 1962 Olivier had been playing the part of Fred Midway in David Turner's *Semi-Detached* at the Saville Theatre in London. Riskily, Olivier had adopted a thick Midlands accent, alienating the critics who had difficulty in understanding his blunted vowels. The reviews were tepid. Although his stage wife, Mona Washbourne, tried to cheer him up by pronouncing the critics stupid, Olivier was not used to tepid. The glow of praise had instead been focused on twenty-eight-year-old Eileen Atkins who played Olivier's daughter in the play. Eileen had been so amazed to land a part in the West End alongside such a superb cast that she had nearly fainted during the first rehearsal. But the morning after press night

Olivier paid Eileen a visit in her dressing room. 'Critics aren't always stupid,' he told the astonished young actress. 'They have discovered Eileen.'[4] Despite this unusual display of humility, the attacks had not done Olivier's temper any good. Luckily the National Theatre project had afforded him the self-belief he needed in order to begin the New Year with gusto.

While Nureyev's youthfulness was a reminder of Cecil Beaton's own private and painful preoccupation with ageing, Olivier's elevation had further exacerbated Beaton's irascible mood. In his private notebook of August 1962, he had admitted to being filled with 'resentment and anger' at the news of Olivier's appointment, even though he knew Olivier was 'the most suitable man for the job'. Beaton's own 'ruthless ambition' had flourished unabated with the years, but recently he had been forced to confront the reality of ageing. The Edwardian world into which he had been born and from which he derived his sense of himself was crumbling as fast as he was. In August 1962 at the age of fifty-eight, Beaton had filled several pages of his notebook with regret about 'becoming aged, aged, aged', lamenting how 'one does not feel old or look old in gradual stages. One disintegrates in a series of jarring jolts.' He felt he had become 'the hangover' of his youth 'without the charm or the vitality'.

Beaton was right. Youth was in the ascendant and with approaching spring talk of sex was filling the air. Sex remained an uncomfortable topic for Harold Macmillan. The Prime Minister may well have chosen not to read *Private Eye*'s 'Lunchtime O'Booze' columns that March, which described how 'Miss Gaye Fun-Loving' and her friends had attended parties given by a 'Dr Spook' with guest lists including a Soviet spy and an unnamed government minister. The latter had offered his resignation to the Prime Minister 'on personal grounds'. The offer had been rejected. As ever, *Private Eye* was only just ducking the threat of libel, hovering as close as it legally dare to the truth of a story that would threaten Macmillan's tenure at Downing Street.

This was a story in which an innocent young woman was caught up in an appalling patriarchal cover-up and abused and almost destroyed by those in positions of privilege. The drama involved John Profumo, the Secretary of State for War and a married man. Profumo had been accused of having an affair in the summer of 1961 with a nineteen-year-old model named Christine Keeler, a quasi protégée of osteopath Stephen Ward. She was also rumoured to have slept with a senior naval attaché at the Soviet Embassy. Profumo denied vehemently any suggestion that Keeler might have compromised the nation's security by passing on confidential information between her two lovers. But was he telling the truth? And who was protecting him? And what was Christine's version of the tale? The story had every possible ingredient of a plot cooked up by Ian Fleming. Press and public fascination in this irresistible combination of a beautiful young woman, the British aristocracy and Russian espionage was eclipsed only by the opportunity to attack the attitude of entitlement that politicians had been getting away with for centuries. The Labour leadership election on 14 February had strengthened the opposition's confidence. The Conservatives, especially the frontbenchers, were aware that

Harold Wilson, new to the post with 60 per cent of the party vote behind him, was not going to let the crimes and misdemeanours of the Government go unchallenged. By the middle of March the electrifying tale of the model and the government minister and its potential to empower whole sections of society to confront the old order was reaching its climax.

Christine Keeler had arrived in London aged seventeen, leaving behind the pair of railway carriages on the banks of the Thames in Berkshire that had been her childhood home. Having tried unsuccessfully to end a pregnancy with the help of a pen and a knitting needle, she had recently recovered from the birth and subsequent death of a baby son, the child of an American GI. The city also provided her with the escape route from the sexually threatening volatility of her stepfather and his temper. Christine had found a job as a showgirl in Murray's Cabaret Club in Beak Street, Soho, where her whispery voice, her beautiful, inscrutable face and her alluring figure made her one of the club's most popular dancers. Men found her dynamite. Even though the girls were compelled to carry out their shifts topless, the dancers had to be careful how they moved because bouncing breasts were considered too much of a temptation. And even though touching was forbidden, Christine knew Murray's was little more than a 'visual brothel'. Dressed to mimic the moment Antony fell for Cleopatra, Christine wore an outrageously elaborate jewelled thong and a sumptuous satin cloak that fell open at the front. Chunky gold bracelets reached from her wrist to her elbow, and her long legs ended in dizzying heels. A heavy jewelled headpiece was balanced on her chestnut hair from which a vast paste emerald dangled. She was unashamed not only of enjoying her appeal but of admitting it. Sexuality was her currency.

She had made friends with several of the other girls at the club, especially the flamboyant go-getting, try-anything, blonde-haired, Welsh-born Mandy Rice-Davies. Together they moved, Mandy said, 'in the kind of world where the normal code of morals has no place; where there is no dividing line between good and bad, only that between a gay time and boredom'.[5] Brought up in Solihull, Mandy had wanted to be treated with respect since the age of nine after seeing the way people behaved towards Princess Margaret when the Queen's sister visited the Birmingham Brownies in 1953. Ambitious, irreverent and very pretty, Mandy had adorned the bonnet of a car as 'Miss Austin Mini' at London's Earl's Court Motor Show in 1959 before landing herself a job as a dancer at Murray's. One night Christine had introduced her to an old boyfriend, property tycoon Peter Rachman, one of the owners of the club. But although Rachman was generous to Mandy, it was not only the flat in Bryanston Mews, the white Jaguar saloon (Mandy's favourite colour for cars) complete with a helpful, forged driving licence (because Mandy did not know how to drive), the Arab mare, the £4,000 fur coat, the jewellery and the £100 'pocket money' each week that made her fond of him. As well as finding him hugely sexy and his 'aura of power' exciting, she also felt 'genuine affection' for the man, and believed he felt the same about her.

At 2 a.m., at the end of their evening shift, the two friends would change out of their performance clothes and dash along the street to one of the other nearby clubs. There was a good choice. At the huge Marquee in Oxford Street, with its stripy tent-like canopy, a new band had been attracting some attention since the summer, not all of it favourable: the Rolling Stones were viewed as a bunch of scruffy housemates from the less glamorous end of the King's Road, who many at the Marquee thought were chancing their luck by playing rock and roll in a jazz club. At the Roaring Twenties in Carnaby Street, resident DJ Count Suckle, a Jamaican stowaway who had arrived in Britain in the 1950s with his own home-made, wardrobe-size loudspeakers, was formidable in both size and influence. He drew in the crowds with his vast record collection from the Caribbean and the United States. But the Jamaican Ska sound at the Flamingo was Mandy and Christine's favourite, with performers like Terri Quayle and Georgie Fame and the Blue Flames. From midnight onwards the Flamingo became known as the All-Nighter, with its special licence to stay open at weekends until 6 a.m. Distinctive for being a venue that welcomed a mixed-race clientele, Georgie Fame described how the club had been wildly popular with 'black American GI's, West Indians, pimps, prostitutes and gangsters' since its launch in 1958. Regulars included American boxer Cassius Clay on his visits to London and Jamaican musician Syco Gordon. Syco would walk in 'smoking ganja, taking pills and all these beautiful girls were so nice. We'd start making friends with them and start dancing. White and black would mix together. Like brother and sister. We loved dancing. We never had fights down there.'[6]

Christine Keeler had first met Stephen Ward at Murray's Club in 1959. He was the son of a vicar and his Irish wife and had spent part of his youth in Hamburg, a translator by day and a frequenter of the raunchy German clubs by night. On returning to England he trained as an osteopath, becoming professionally indispensable to the great and the good. In the privacy of his treatment rooms in Wimpole Mews, off Marylebone High Street, Stephen Ward pulled and pushed limbs and backs and buttocks, tending to the aching bones of Winston Churchill, Elizabeth Taylor, Ava Gardner and members of the Royal family, including Prince Philip, Princess Margaret, Lord Snowdon and Princess Alexandra. Lord Astor, known to his friends as Bill, had suffered a riding accident in 1956 and was among the patients who would hobble into Wimpole Mews and emerge with a spring in their step. Ward was also a wonderful amateur draughtsman and would make quick but expert pencil sketches of his clients. With what Mandy Rice-Davies called his 'large fish-like eyes which were almost hypnotic in their effect on men and women alike', despite being partially hidden beneath his thick glasses, he had a tantalising smile and a beautiful speaking voice that made you 'feel important'.[7] His pleasingly trim figure was always beautifully dressed in expensive, perfectly cut suits. He was tremendously popular, a wonderful raconteur and brimming with what Mandy called 'easy charm'. But while in his professional life he adhered to the highest standards, out of working hours his very private private life was something else. He had a touch of the outsider about him and cultivated an image of complexity and subtlety. He was as seductively manipulative of minds as his hands were of needy aching joints.

While Christine initially found Stephen magnetic, she soon detected something of a 'spider and fly manner' about him that disconcerted her.[8] When she and Mandy turned up for the first time at one of Stephen's famous London parties with a guest list comprising a 'barrister, a barrow-boy, a writer, a motor salesman, a peer, and always, for some reason, a steady stream of pretty girls', they could not understand why all the male guests were wearing 'socks and nothing else'. Furthermore, the girls noticed how several of the naked partygoers had 'wheals across their backs and buttocks. Others had shocking bruises'. And they were startled to find that no one was paying attention to a couple making love in full view 'on a beautiful antique French divan'. Retreating to the kitchen, Mandy and Christine demolished a bowl of caviar, a large platter of smoked salmon and all the liqueur chocolates they could manage before leaving a scene that Christine felt was 'all too kinky' for either girl, 'the snake pit, masquerading under the title of High Society'. Being more of a voyeur, Stephen was not particularly interested in sex himself but more in making political, social and sexual connections between members of his own huge acquaintance. According to Mandy, he saw himself as 'an international go-between with power to negotiate on both sides of the Iron Curtain'. Politically he was a sympathiser of the left and according to Mandy 'given half a chance would talk for hours about the beauties of the communist system'. He had long been known to the Government intelligence agency and had made clear to them the strength of his friendship with Eugene Ivanov, the Soviet naval attaché. Ward had introduced Ivanov to members of High Society, including Lord Astor and Princess Margaret, who wanted nothing more to do with the tipsy Russian after he enquired whether the Queen's sister dyed her hair. Stephen Ward hoped to ingratiate himself with MI5 by offering to help persuade Ivanov to defect and work for Britain's Security Services. But Ward himself invited suspicion within MI5 for what historian Richard Davenport-Hines in *An English Affair*, his superlative account of the Profumo story, has described as his 'otiose meddling'. Britain's wider political establishment also distrusted the osteopath. William Shepherd, a Conservative backbencher, thought Ward's voice had 'a phoney, almost homosexual intonation', a view that was shared by other parliamentary colleagues.

Lord Astor had offered Ward the use of a timber-framed cottage a few yards from the banks of the Thames at Cliveden, Astor's beautiful estate in Berkshire, in exchange for a peppercorn rent. Cliveden is and always has been a Gatsby sort of escapist retreat, a place far away from the noise and the tiresome restraints of a busy world. Even now, as a hotel, it remains a haven fit for a princess. Pulling up the car on a crunch of gravel, you are greeted by white-coated house staff at the porticoed entrance. In summertime the scent of just-mown grass drifts through the open windows accompanied by the clip-clip of secateurs as the gardeners smooth the hedges into perfect symmetry. Willow trees sway in the breeze, and statues populate the garden. Three goddess-like figures emerge from the marble Fountain of Love, hovered over by a gang of lichen-draped cupids.

In the 1960s, wedged between the vegetable garden and the tennis court, sat the swimming pool. The Astors sometimes tied a water polo net across the width of the pool and just in front of the changing hut with its tiled hexagonal roof an upturned Corinthian capital had been placed as a bench for spectators. My grandfather Harold once spent the weekend at the house in 1936 and concluded that the outside decor was 'like living on the stage of the Scala theatre in Milan'. But in the summer of 1961, a quarter of a century after his visit, Christine Keeler wasn't in a position to criticise the theatrical drama of her surroundings. In her own words, she was 'a mixed-up lovesick young girl' who simply enjoyed herself as a frequent guest, driving down to Spring Cottage with Stephen in his white Jaguar, looking forward to her weekend where men and girls drifted 'like moths among the whisperings and the champagne and the stars'.[9]

On the weekend that would give the Cliveden swimming pool its enduring notoriety, Christine had forgotten to pack her swimming costume. She made do with a black swimsuit she found in the bathing hut that 'was a bit old fashioned and was tight around my bottom'. In the pool she 'couldn't get going' in the ill-fitting suit so she took it off, believing herself and Stephen to be alone. But, having dressed for dinner in black tie, Bill Astor and one of his weekend guests, John Profumo, had decided to take a stroll through the garden. Jumping out of the pool as they approached, Christine realised that Stephen had kicked her bathing suit out of reach as a tease. She grabbed 'a sad square of towelling', the only covering she could lay her hands on, before, as she later described, finding herself being chased around the pool by Her Majesty's Minister for War.[10] The chase came to an abrupt end as, in full evening dress, the two wives arrived. Together they made quite an entrance. Lady Astor, aged thirty-two, formerly Bronwen Pugh, was nearly six foot tall and as the face of the designer Balmain, had been one of the leading models of the 1950s. She was five months pregnant. Valerie Hobson, the beautiful, well-known stage and film actress had married John Profumo almost ten years earlier. Famous for her part in the comedy whodunnit *Kind Hearts and Coronets* in 1949, she had completed her final theatrical performance as Anna in *The King and I* in Drury Lane before retiring at Profumo's insistence to become his wife. John Profumo was widely known to have what Mandy considered to be 'a roving eye' and was frequently criticised by Valerie for wearing his trousers so tight that an unambiguous bulge was plainly visible, some might say flaunted, beneath the zip. He was a slick seducer, a master of timing. As Antonia Fraser, whose husband Hugh Fraser was a fellow MP and Secretary of State for Air, put it, 'he knew when to brush his hand on your arm or accidentally touch your breast'. Old habits die hard. Thirty years later Profumo, a one-time parliamentary colleague of my father's, came with some friends to see the garden at Sissinghurst. For a moment I found myself alone with him when suddenly he pinched my bottom.

At Cliveden in the summer of 1961, the day after Christine met Profumo, the large house party congregated around the pool in glorious sunshine included the President of Pakistan and cartoonist Osbert Lancaster. Stephen and Christine had been the first to arrive. Stripping to a small pair of bathing trunks, Profumo invited fellow house guest Ivanov to race him down the length of the pool. It was a classic boys-show-off moment in front of a girl they both wanted to impress. Ivanov won – not only the race but also the reward of giving Christine a lift back to London. But the pair did not leave before Profumo had taken a note of Christine's telephone number.

Some fifteen months later MI5 learned that Profumo and Christine had done more than catch each other's eye. For Christine the power-buzz of landing a minister felt, she said, like 'fucking Marlon Brando'. Within days of meeting they were making love wherever they could find any privacy. Sometimes they met in Stephen Ward's flat, sometimes they found time to be alone in Profumo's car and once in the house he shared with Valerie and their young son David. Profumo appealed to her not only because he was a government minister but because after they had made love, and it was the 'after' that mattered most to her, he was 'kind and loving'. But after Ivanov had given her the lift back to London, she had been unable to resist the handsome Russian either, even if it was after rather a lot of whisky and even though it was just the once. Whether this encounter actually resulted in the consummation that Christine later claimed it had is still open to debate. Christine's word was never contradicted by Ivanov. And certainly the fling with Profumo lasted a few weeks longer, but in August 1961 Christine received a letter on War Office-headed writing paper in which Profumo apologised that they would not be able to meet for a while. Christine had no idea that he had been officially warned off seeing her. Signed simply 'love J', the letter began with one word: 'Darling'.

# Chapter Twenty-three

*As the ice cracked*

By the Christmas of 1962, over a year after the ending of her on-off affair with John Profumo, Christine Keeler had moved on. A tempestuous relationship with a thirty-one-year-old Jamaican dealer known as 'Lucky' Gordon had been followed by another with an Antiguan called Johnny Edgecombe. The two men became rivals for Christine. Both had significant pasts. Lucky had done a spell in Wandsworth Prison for assault, smash-and-grab robbery and forging cheques. Edgecombe (known by Christine as the Edge) had also done a few months in jail after working his passage across the Atlantic as a teenage pantry boy and posing as an African prince who pocketed precious rings from upmarket jewellers. He had explained to the jewellers that the rings would enhance his own crown jewels.

When an obsessively jealous Lucky informed the police about Edgecombe's small illegal drinking club in Notting Hill and held Christine hostage for two days, threatening her with a knife, Edgecombe took revenge. Confronting Lucky with a flick knife at the Flamingo Club in October 1962, he had slashed Lucky's face from his forehead, down the side of his cheek to his mouth. Half blinded by his own blood, Lucky screamed his own intended recrimination as Edgecombe and Christine managed to escape. A few weeks after Lucky's wound had healed, he went round to Mandy Rice-Davies's flat and asked her to hold out her hands in the shape of a bowl. At first she thought he was filling her palms with 'black seeds' until she realised that the shrivelled pellets were the dried-up stitches from Lucky's face, a gift to Christine 'with his love'. As a disgusted Mandy threw the shrunken threads into the bin, Lucky informed Mandy that Christine would soon receive double the number of stitches in her own face.

After finishing with both men and finding herself without a full-time boyfriend, Christine had been spending most of her time hanging out with Mandy at Stephen Ward's London flat. Christine's relationship with Stephen had not become any less complicated. His term of endearment for her was 'little baby' and at times she did indeed feel childlike under his care. He had a way of making her do anything he asked and she was not sure she trusted him. But although Mandy was her teammate, their partnership a bulwark against a treacherous world, she was leaning on Christine's friendship more than ever. Peter Rachman's death from a heart attack on 29 November 1962 at the age of forty-three had knocked Mandy sideways. She had swallowed thirty sleeping pills and had still not returned to her usual effervescent self and Christine was worried. Ten days before Christmas the girls were getting ready to go out shopping. Christine was hoping that spending a little money on themselves might cheer her friend up. Mandy was fixing her hair and Christine was smoking a cigarette in the bathroom when there was a ring on the doorbell followed by a shout from outside. Suspecting that Christine had got back together with Lucky, Edgecombe had arrived in a taxi in a jealous fury. Mandy yelled down to him from the window that Christine was out. She had gone to the hairdresser, Mandy said. Suddenly the sound of gunfire came whistling through the open window as Edgecombe fired several shots at the front door, aiming to dislodge the lock. There was a momentary silence before Mandy leaned out to see if Edgecombe had left, but three more bullets pinged up at the glass. Ducking down out of sight she saw that Christine had already 'spun the numbers' on the telephone dial. The police arrived within minutes. Edgecombe had vanished but the police investigation was just beginning. And they wanted to speak to both girls. Furious at this legal intervention in her life, Christine feared that the press attention such an incident might attract would lose her the two modelling jobs she had just landed, one with best-selling Knights Castile soap and the other with Scottish Whisky. The press were sure to ask questions about the propriety of a twenty-year-old white girl having sex with a black man. The free-and-easy inter-racial socialising that took place at the El Rio and behind the closed doors of the Flamingo Club would not find acceptance in the streets or the courts outside.

*

By January 1963 the press had indeed become intrigued, not by the shooting incident itself but by rumours of a story behind the story of the shooting. Christine was always extremely short of cash and this together with her regular enjoyment of cannabis contributed to some dodgy decision-making. As the ricochet of Johnny Edgecombe's gunshots faded, Christine's story reached the desk of Reg Payne, the editor of the *Sunday Pictorial* (shortly to be renamed the *Sunday Mirror*) after Christine had succumbed to financial persuasion and shared with Reg the details of her love life. She explained that communist-sympathiser Ward had asked her to extract details of America's plans to supply nuclear weapons to Germany from Profumo and to pass them on to Ivanov. She did not divulge that this fictitious scenario had been a running joke between herself and Ward. She was unaware that Ward himself had suggested to MI5 in July 1961 that Ivanov had asked him for such information. And then, from her handbag, Christine produced Profumo's 'Darling' letter. Intimacy blazed from the headed notepaper. Chequebook journalism was the way of doing things. Money bought talk. The newspaper offered her £1,000 for the story, with £200 upfront and the bulk payable on publication. As the cash went into the handbag together with the letter, the *Pictorial* filed away a copy of the document for use when the time was right.

Although the events of the Cuban Missile Crisis and the immediate spectre of war with Russia had gradually receded from the front pages by the end of 1962, a new danger with spies and reds beneath elite beds had flared up once again in the New Year. On 23 January Glencairn Balfour Paul, the First

Secretary at the British Embassy in Beirut, had given a dinner for a few journalists with whom he had been on friendly terms. Included on the guest list were Eleanor Philby and her husband Kim Philby, the former head of the Soviet department of MI6 and now working in Beirut as the *Observer*'s correspondent for the Middle East. Although the weather was dreadful that day, Eleanor was looking forward to the party, a rare chance to be sociable and also to enjoy the delicious puddings made by the excellent Embassy cook. When her husband, once a fine-looking figure but now a man in alcoholic decline, left their apartment in the early afternoon to brave the belting rain, they had agreed to meet that evening at the Embassy. But Philby was not waiting for her when she arrived. Nor did he appear in time for the trifle. As evening turned into night Eleanor became increasingly anxious, frightened that her husband had been in an accident. When she eventually returned to their apartment there was still no sign of him. Unbeknown to her, Philby was on board the *Dolmatova*, a Russian cargo ship, the Hammer and Sickle flying from its stern, which had left Beirut harbour that very night, bound for Odessa. Philby was on his way to join double agents Guy Burgess and Donald Maclean for a life in Soviet Russia. No public announcement was made about the defection of a third man, and the Government was determined that the double identity of Philby as a KGB mole should remain hidden. One week later Christine's one-night-stander, Captain Eugene Ivanov, left London to return to Moscow. Given the rumours around his association with Keeler and hers with Profumo, as well as government jitters over Philby, Ivanov's presence in Britain was no longer considered desirable or secure.

Although the *Sunday Pictorial* suspected it might be on to something huge the editor still feared that publication of the 'Darling' letter and the unravelling Keeler story might bring a lawsuit from John Profumo. But rumours were spreading.

On 28 January Profumo had been questioned by Sir John Hobson, the Attorney General, by Sir Peter Rawlinson, the Solicitor General, and by Martin Redmayne, the Chief Whip, about his relationship with Keeler. While confirming a glancing friendship with the 'model', explaining that 'my wife and I met Miss Keeler at a house-party', he denied completely any sexual impropriety and any knowledge of her former romantic liaisons with either of the West Indians, Lucky Gordon and Johnny Edgecombe, or with Captain Ivanov. Seeing Profumo's shocked response to the allegations, Hobson was convinced of his colleague's innocence. Selwyn Lloyd, the former Chancellor and Profumo's friend, also believed him. Harold Macmillan also believed him. Or chose to believe him. A gentleman, a sitting Minister, a Member of Parliament, had given his word. Confiding in his diary, Macmillan hoped that the muddle with the girl, if there was one, was nothing more than 'a silly scrape'.

On 29 January Thomas Corbally – a slick American private investigator masquerading as an advertising executive, a great friend of Stephen Ward, a swimmer in the silky waters of the Cliveden pool and host to sex orgies in his own flat in Mayfair – had given a small lunch party. He had been asked by the American ambassador David Bruce (who had in turn been asked by the Prime Minister) to sleuth out any information Ward might have about his friend Christine Keeler. Stephen Ward, Thomas Corbally and Alfred Wells, personal secretary to Bruce, sat down at a discreet upstairs booth at Simpson's restaurant in Piccadilly. Garrulous, drama-loving Ward spilled the beans that his friend Christine had slept with Profumo, and also repeated as fact his joke that Christine had extracted Government secrets from Profumo and passed them across the pillow to Ivanov. Ward piqued further interest by confirming to this new audience the existence of the now well-thumbed 'Darling' letter. He did not know Christine had already sold the story to the *Sunday Pictorial* or that his own role in the saga was being moulded into that of pimp and threat to the nation's security. He was contacted by Tom Mangold, tenacious and sympathetic journalist on the *Daily Express*, which newspaper Mangold himself described as 'a broadsheet with the brain of a tabloid'.[1] The *Express* had become very interested in the story after the *Pictorial*, running scared, had shared with them the 'Darling' letter. But the *Express* was not ready to publish the letter either.

Ward's revelations were passed to Clive Bossom, the Parliamentary Private Secretary working for Hugh Fraser, the Secretary of State for Air. In the summer of 1962 Bill Astor had offered Hugh and Antonia Fraser the use of another cottage on the Cliveden estate and the Frasers had spent the autumn of 1962 redecorating the place. But a combination of the winter weather and Antonia's advancing pregnancy meant they could publicly confirm that they had never even spent a night at the cottage. They felt fortunate that their private lives were therefore not linked in any way to the goings-on at the great house. However, they had long known the truth about Profumo's relationship. They had once been witness to Christine and John's recklessly indiscreet behaviour at the Cliveden pool, where Christine had gaily splashed while John 'mooched about'[2] around the edge unable to keep his eyes off her. And knowledge of the relationship had not been confined to the Cliveden houseguests. It was out there in what Antonia described as 'a White's Club sort of a way', the kind of information that would curl its way like cigar smoke around the leather armchairs of London's most exclusive Gentlemen's clubs. It seemed 'everyone' knew something of the story. As rumours of the Profumo scandal reached Washington, Antonia Fraser visited the American capital with her husband and having been lent Mrs Kennedy's swimsuit, swam in the same White House pool with which the alliterative interns, 'Fiddle and Faddle', were so familiar. That same week at an al fresco dinner party given by journalist Joe Alsop, Antonia was flattered to be invited to take a seat beside the President. Despite his own relaxed attitude to marital fidelity, Kennedy was perfectly capable of judging others and of expressing moral judgements on promiscuity and immoral behaviour when it suited him. He was intrigued by rumours that were flying around about Government Minister John Profumo. 'Drugs, threesomes, blacks – that's pretty way out,' he remarked to Antonia. 'Here in Washington we raise a cheer if anyone can get it up at all.' Antonia, fully aware of the priapic propensities of the President as he had briefly shared a flat with Hugh Fraser after the war, kicked herself for a long time afterwards for not making the comment that hovered on the tip of her tongue: 'But we hear, Mr President, that you personally don't have a problem.'

Even before Christmas there had been open chat in certain circles. Diana Wood, the wife of the Minister for Power, had attended a dinner party in Eaton Terrace in December '62.

Sitting next to Osbert Lancaster, the *Daily Express* cartoonist, she was perplexed to hear him blurt out, 'Of course it's absolutely dreadful about Christine Keeler.'[3] As a Cliveden houseguest in the summer of 1961, Lancaster had seen the original swimming pool encounter himself. Years later, Diana Wood remembered not having 'the remotest idea what he was talking about'. Coincidentally her eleven-year-old son Edward had been joined at Sunningdale prep school by David Profumo, John and Valerie's seven-year-old son. All boys were told 'on pain of death' not to mention Christine Keeler, and when Edward was caught with a drawing of Christine in the nude he was treated with the contempt the school felt he deserved. He has never forgotten the shame he felt.[4]

And all the while Harold Macmillan was trying to suppress the rumours, at least in his own mind. In his diary he was still reassuring himself that John Profumo was part of a society 'where no one really knows anyone and everyone is darling'. But by early March the whispers were seeping out ever faster, spilling over the safe boundaries of parliamentary meeting rooms, the dining rooms of Chelsea and the clubs of Pall Mall and into an ever-widening domain. At first Christine had enjoyed the drama of being the centre of attention, but the novelty began to pall. Coverage in the press meant 'you lose your identity', she wrote, 'not just your individuality but what makes you *you*'. She did not know who to trust because whenever she trusted anyone she found herself 'used or betrayed'. Meanwhile, Stephen Ward was pressurising the *Sunday Pictorial* with legal threats not to run Christine's version of the story. He had himself to protect.

The story was also close to breaking across the Atlantic. In March, without mentioning any names, *Time* magazine wrote 'on the island where the subject has long been taboo in polite society, sex has exploded onto the national consciousness'. Back in Britain the *New Statesman* asked, 'Are Virgins obsolete?' The *Daily Herald* wondered, 'Are we going sex crazy?'

And then, on 8 March, under the heading 'That was the Government that was', the incriminating hot potato, the 'Darling' letter, finally emerged in print. The *Westminster Confidential* was a political pamphlet published by American journalist Andrew Roth, for which circulation was so small that Roth had risked publication in the hope of getting away with it. But that tiny circulation included George Wigg, Labour MP for Dudley and former Minister for Defence. Wigg had it in for the Tory government and sensed an opportunity for attack might be opening up as the previously nervous, respectful, established media prepared to move fast.

On 14 March in an apparently unconnected development, Johnny Edgecombe's trial for the previous December's attempted shooting in Wimpole Mews was due to begin at the Old Bailey, but the star witness had vanished. The mainstream newspapers were hoping Christine's evidence might have included a passing mention of Profumo's jealousy of Edgecombe or the identification of Wimpole Mews as the venue for her assignations with Profumo and Ivanov. But Christine was nowhere to be seen. She had been expecting to exchange legal heat for Spanish warmth but the weather at the villa in the small village near Alicante she had rented with Paul Mann, a shirt salesman friend of Stephen Ward's and the latest in the interminable line of men to get in on the Christine Keeler act, had turned out to be freezing. All Christine's hopes for a 'spot of sand and sangria' had been dashed as they sat in the weak sunshine playing whist and bridge. She had jumped at the offer of a lift from two passing matadors on their way to Madrid, where she and Paul hit the city's nightclubs, danced the twist and where life became a bit more holidayish. Meanwhile, at the Old Bailey Johnny Edgecombe's possession of a gun had brought him a seven-year jail sentence, imposed, the Edge was convinced, as the result of racial prejudice. The British establishment could not tolerate a Government Minister 'sleeping with the same chick as a black guy', he said. If he had been white he felt the whole case 'would have blown over'.[5]

Coincidentally, public interest in the Vassall case and in spying had been reignited yet again when two national journalists, Reginald Foster of the *Daily Sketch* and Brendan Mulholland of the *Daily Mail*, were imprisoned in Brixton for refusing to name sources for their revelations about the homosexual clerk. When on 15 March the *Daily Express* ran two lead stories adjacent to one another on their front page, concerning the 'Vanishing Model' and John Profumo's offer to resign from the Cabinet, connections between the two items were glaringly implicit. Macmillan persisted in seeing the Profumo fuss as one of 'morality'. The story had been inflamed, he believed, by a press who relished the goings-on at Cliveden, where the 'raffish and disreputable set that centres round Lord Astor' congregated.[6] He further comforted himself that unlike Vassall, Profumo at least had got himself entangled with a woman and 'thank God, not boys'.

On 21 March, high up in the public gallery of the House of Commons, David Dimbleby, a young news reporter and son of the leading broadcaster Richard Dimbleby, was watching proceedings. After dinner with some friends he had made a spontaneous decision to go along to Westminster by himself to listen in on the late-night session. There were no security checks, not even a request for ID, as Dimbleby walked through the halls and took his seat.[7] The popular speaker, Sir Harry Hylton-Foster, in his knee breeches, silk stockings, buckled shoes and silk gown, was presiding. Known for his winning ability to turn anger into laughter, this session was proving a bit of a challenge even for Sir Harry. Despite the lateness of the hour, Members of Parliament, in their black jackets, waistcoats and striped trousers, were in hot debate about the collusion, obfuscation and freedom of the press and the individual. They were discussing the Vassall case and the jailed journalists. The debate on the green benches then took a new turn as George Wigg, recently promoted as Harold Wilson's advisor on security matters, chose not to beat about the bush. Wigg was vociferously anti-appeasement and felt 'contempt for political pacifists and fence sitters'. He was well known for his intolerance of incompetence and for those who occupied positions unworthy of them. Apart from the *Westminster Confidential*, there had been no explicit mention in the press of Profumo's association with Christine Keeler – the threat of libel action still holding the newspapers at bay, but only just: their coverage of the Edgecombe trial had been extensive and suggestive. But as George Wigg rose to speak he was not prepared to let what he perceived as the journalists' collective failure of nerve continue.

'There is not an Honourable Member in the House, nor a journalist in the press gallery, nor do I believe there is a person in the public gallery, who, in the last few days, has not heard rumour upon rumour involving a member of the Government Front Bench,' Wigg began.[8] Up in the public gallery collective breath was held as Wigg edged closer to his point. 'That being the case, I rightly use the Privilege of the House of Commons – that is what it is given to me for – to ask the Home Secretary, who is the senior member of the Government on the Treasury Bench now, to go to the despatch box – he knows that the rumour to which I refer relates to Miss Christine Keeler and Miss Davies and a shooting by a West Indian – and, on behalf of the Government, categorically deny the truth of these rumours.'

The uttering of those two names aloud had the impact of a bishop expleting a string of four-letter words from his cathedral pulpit. This was the moment when the political elite and their cover-up of the Minister for War's indiscretions felt more threatened than ever before. Having trusted in the gentlemen's mantra of 'never tell', a traitor had suddenly emerged in their midst, determined to have his day.

At 11.35 p.m., as David Dimbleby leaned in closer over the gallery railing, Barbara Castle, redheaded Labour MP for Blackburn and ally of George Wigg, was the next to speak.

'It would suit the book of many people no doubt to deplore the avidity with which the Press is at this moment pursuing the question of where Miss Christine Keeler has gone, the missing "call girl", the vanished witness,' she began, continuing, 'Is it the pursuit of sensationalism for its own sake, or could it be that there is public interest at the back of the agitation by the Press?' Barbara Castle was getting to the heart of the matter. She wanted to know if there were 'people in high places' who knew where Keeler was, her implication being that Keeler had been 'conveniently' hidden. It was not the whereabouts of a missing witness that mattered but the suggestion of a connection between Keeler and a Government Minister.

Henry Brooke, Home Secretary, had nowhere to hide except in silence as he found himself openly challenged to deny the rumours that had been swirling around Westminster throughout the winter months like wind-gusted snowflakes. He refused to engage. His comments were brief.

'I do not propose to comment on rumours which have been raised under the cloak of privilege and safe from any action at law,' he said. 'The Honourable Member for Dudley [Mr Wigg] and the Honourable Member for Blackburn [Mrs Castle] should seek other means of making these insinuations if they are prepared to substantiate them.' In an attempt to defuse the tension, Reginald Paget, the Member for Northampton, suggested the whole scandal was a matter of inconsequence. 'A minister is said to be acquainted with an extremely pretty girl. As far as I am concerned I should have thought that was a matter for congratulation rather than enquiry.'

But Mrs Castle persisted. She wanted to know: 'What if there is something else of much greater importance?'

At twenty-two minutes past one on the morning of 22 March the new Labour Leader Harold Wilson, who had held himself back from openly joining the interrogation, ended the evening's business by urging the Home Secretary to hold an inquiry into press legislation. And those up in the public gallery and in the chamber of the House itself knew that this was a debate simply postponed and far from concluded. That same evening John Profumo had dined at the Other Club, Winston Churchill's own favourite, and on returning to his house in Chester Terrace near Regent's Park, had taken a sleeping pill. At 3 a.m. seven-year-old David heard a 'disconcerting deep sway of male voices' below his bedroom window[9] as his father was roused from druggy unconsciousness by the leader of the House of Commons. Fumbling for clothes, insisting to Valerie that he 'must have a clean shirt', struggling as he tried to insert his cufflinks, Profumo made his way to Westminster in the car sent by the Chief Whip and presented himself in the Chief Whip's office. Waiting for him was Iain Macleod, the Leader of the House; William Deedes, the Minister without Portfolio who advised the government on public relations, and Martin Redmayne, the Chief Whip. The question Macleod asked Profumo was short and to the point.

'Did you fuck her?'

Denying any such activity just as he had denied it to everyone who had pressed for a confession so far, Profumo was helped by the men in the room to prepare a statement. He went home. Despite having barely slept, Profumo returned once again that morning to the House. He arrived looking like what our nanny Shirley would have called 'death warmed up'. At 11 a.m., after morning prayers and before a debate on the Estate Agents Bill, John Profumo, sitting beside the Prime Minister, rose to make a short personal statement:

> My wife and I first met Miss Keeler at a house-party in July 1961, at Cliveden. Among a number of people there

> was Dr Stephen Ward, whom we already knew slightly, and a Mr Ivanov, who was an attaché at the Russian Embassy. The only other occasion that my wife or I met Mr Ivanov was for a moment at the official reception for Major Gagarin at the Soviet Embassy. My wife and I had a standing invitation to visit Dr Ward. Between July and December, 1961, I met Miss Keeler on about half a dozen occasions at Dr Ward's flat, when I called to see him and his friends. Miss Keeler and I were on friendly terms. There was no impropriety whatsoever in my acquaintanceship with Miss Keeler.[10]

Before leaving the chamber the Minister added that he would take legal action against anyone who made any more 'scandalous allegations'. As he sat down Harold Macmillan clapped him warmly on the back in approval. And that seemed to be that. Except for one thing. Open laughter had accompanied this statement of innocence. The denial had not fooled a single person present. Everyone, even Harold Macmillan, knew John Profumo had slept with Christine Keeler because, as Antonia Fraser remarked, 'Why wouldn't he?' The failure to tell the truth, to hide behind the privileged protection afforded the ruling class, had prevailed at the beginning of the winter. As the ice cracked, lying could no longer be tolerated. The cat was out of the bag.

That afternoon Profumo left London for Sandown Park Racecourse where, photographed in the company of the Queen Mother, he watched the runners in the Grand Military Gold

Cup before dancing the evening away at Quaglino's in the arms of his loyal wife to the tune of 'The Green Leaves of Summer'. The following day Profumo's denial, rather than 'lancing the boil' as the *Daily Telegraph* claimed it had done, had inflamed it. George Wigg gave an interview to the BBC's *Panorama*, outlining the security threat that had emanated from Keeler's affair with Ivanov. Still using the 'missing witness' line, the *Daily Express* devoted several of their inner pages to photographs of Christine, from which, as Lord Denning would later comment, 'most people would infer her calling'.

The same paper interviewed Mandy Rice-Davies, who claimed (untruthfully it emerged later) that she had slept with Lord Astor. *Time* magazine wrote how 'leggy, red-headed Christine Keeler' had been acquainted with 'top names in London's political, social, diplomatic and show business worlds'. Mary Whitehouse, the teacher from Shropshire, joined in the outrage. She knew of fourteen-year-old schoolgirls who were simulating sexual positions during their school milk break and were planning careers in prostitution, explaining how Mandy and Christine had inspired them. Another girl was thrilled to know that 'getting engaged', as Mandy had been to Rachman, was the qualification for intercourse. These were the shocking limits to which the media coverage of the Profumo case had stretched! Mrs Whitehouse was writing at once to Sir Hugh Greene, the director-general of the BBC, to demand some means of healing the damage done.

Meanwhile, Christine was making her way back from Spain, speeding through the French countryside escaping the mob of British journalists who were in pursuit. She had agreed a deal with the *Daily Express*, who had paid her £2,000 for an exclusive and had advertised the upcoming interview with a photograph of Christine in knee-high boots and a tight sweater. On 28 March, bronzed and wearing a chic, tight-fitting, above-the-knee dress and a sheepskin jacket, Christine returned to London. She had just celebrated her twenty-first birthday. She professed to be amazed at all the fuss that greeted her. She told the *News of the World* that Mr Profumo and his wife were both 'friends' of hers, 'a friendship no one can criticise'. She attributed all the attention to envy. 'Many people consider me photogenic,' she admitted. 'If I had been fifty-two and a housewife in Surbiton,' she speculated, there would have been 'no such trouble'. On the same day Christine was facing the music, the Queen flew back to Britain with Prince Philip, descending the steps of the aeroplane, hatted, pearl-decked and gloved after their two-month tour of Australia and New Zealand. Both of these women now looked forward to the challenges of the spring with the straitjacket of a lifetime's duty to her country confronting one and entrapment by the establishment a likely prospect for the other.

# Chapter Twenty-four

## *After the clocks changed*

On the last day of March the clocks went forward, lengthening the night-time curfew. Here was the marking of the seasons, the unmistakable sign of transition, the next episode in the unfolding narrative of the year, when winter finally came to an end and changes beneath the earth that had been incubating for so long were at last ready to reveal themselves. While my mother remained in London in case her baby arrived early, we returned to Sissinghurst for the Easter holidays, thankful that our local railway station had not been on Dr Beeching's recently published list of closures. In the garden we reclaimed the air-raid shelter that smelled of new earth and where forgotten-about potatoes had sprouted, finding warmth far below the surface. On the shelf where I kept my spare comb and the small trowel, lay the stiff body of a field mouse. We took the trowel and buried him beneath an apple tree in the orchard, marking the spot with a little cross made of twigs.

In the orchard the first tight buds of blossom were just discernible on the branches of the apple trees. This sense of time passing and of life opening up again felt to me like the final section of Prokofiev's *Peter and the Wolf*. It is the moment when the wolf has been captured at last and the entire orchestra comes together to acknowledge in one glorious exhilarating movement that the danger has passed and a new freedom has arrived.

During those ten weeks of winter, when suspicion and suggestion had hung over the behaviour of ministers of Her Majesty's Government, the stranglehold of hypocrisy had been loosened. Over the subsequent months as the long weeks of hardship started to melt into our memories, the stories of the winter continued to play themselves out.

At successive points during the summer of 1963, four of the men at the centre of the Profumo scandal found themselves trapped: Lucky Gordon, Stephen Ward, John Profumo and Harold Macmillan. Exasperated by Lucky Gordon's persistent attention, Christine accused him of giving her the black eye she had probably received during a fight with the brother of her latest flatmate. Lucky was arrested. And then to his horror, Ward was accused of living off immoral earnings acquired through pimping the two models, Christine and Mandy. The machinery to entrap Ward had been set in motion long ago, but he realised too late that he had become the establishment's scapegoat for his relatively innocent part in the whole affair.

Ward was deserted by all his friends and clients in high places, even Bill Astor, who notified him that his tenancy of Spring Cottage had been cancelled with immediate effect. But the worse treachery lay with Roger Hollis of MI5. By making a move on Christine during the Cliveden weekend, Profumo and his libido had inadvertently messed up the honey trap that MI5 and Ward had planned for Ivanov.[1] If Hollis had chosen to make Ward's planned collaboration with MI5 public he could have saved Ward from prosecution. But Hollis's overriding priority had been to stop incriminating Profumo. An attempt at the end of March by Ward to reach the Prime Minister himself and explain his part in the whole saga had been blocked. As a result Ward was stitched up, framed as a symbol of how Britain was going down the drain, with prostitutes, immoral earnings and communists all playing their part.

After spending a few days in Venice with her husband, ostensibly to get away from the relentless attention of the press, Valerie Profumo concluded she could no longer condone her husband's deception. Unlike John F. Kennedy's ever-acquiescent wife, Valerie had seen and heard and experienced enough. Profumo was left with no option other than to agree that the game was up. On 4 June, ten weeks after deceiving the House of Commons, John Profumo finally admitted to the Prime Minister that he had slept with Christine Keeler and lied about it, and resigned as a Minister and as a Member of Parliament. At the time he was not condemned for the way he had behaved towards Christine, nor for his infidelity, nor for his possible betrayal of his country. Profumo's guilt, it was generally agreed, lay in his deception of the House of Commons. Fleet Street now found itself liberated from the threat of libel and the story of a Member of Parliament and his affair with a model became the trigger for an all-out attack on the moral depravity at the heart of the political establishment. On 11 June 1963 *The Times* editorial declared that 'eleven years of Conservative rule has brought the nation psychologically and spiritually to a low ebb'.

During those frenetic midsummer weeks Lucky Gordon's assault case came to court, and Christine's evidence brought him a three-year jail sentence. At the same time Stephen Ward was also preparing for his trial, with Christine, yet again, serving as a key witness. The following month, just as the jury was finding him guilty, Ward was being carried, unconscious, out of his front door on a stretcher, having taken an overdose. He died the following day. The corruption endemic in the police force, the Home Office, MI5 and the aristocracy had known no limits.

The final act of the drama of this tragic story of imprisonment, ruin and death came at the end of the year. In December 1963 Christine Keeler was put on trial for having perjured herself during Lucky Gordon's trial. Jeremy Hutchinson QC defended her. He found her 'to have grown entirely weary with life' and that her voice 'had lost any joy'. Hutchinson saw in front of him not a perpetrator but a 'victim of circumstances and of a kind of unquenchable male desire'. The media's representation of this young woman as a wrecker of lives had, in his view, to be reversed. It was Christine whose life had been wrecked. But there was no pity in court for this young woman who had been abused since her early teens. She pleaded guilty and was imprisoned for nine months. Meanwhile, Profumo began working as a volunteer at Toynbee Hall, a charity that looks after the disadvantaged and the poor in the East End of London. He never returned to politics. And as I saw for myself thirty years later, his presence in a room never failed to prompt whispers, penetrating stares and even an advisable degree of wariness if one was a young woman. Valerie remained faithful to him until her death in 1998. Profumo died eight years later.

Jeremy Hutchinson QC believed the Profumo scandal brought about an awareness of sleaze at the heart of the ruling institutions that would never be tolerated again. More than half a century later he was convinced that there was 'a real sense that the old deference which had been an intrinsic part of life had gone'.[2] Richard Davenport-Hines sums up the immediate post-Profumo period succinctly: 'Authority, however disinterested, well-qualified and experienced, was increasingly greeted with suspicion rather than distrust.' The behaviour within the country's fundamental edifices including the Government, the police and the press had all been exposed in ways from which they could never recover. Truth-telling and fairness was beginning to gain the upper hand.

In September 1963 Lord Denning published his report about the Profumo scandal, concluding, 'It was the responsibility of the Prime Minister and his colleagues, and of them only, to deal with this situation: and they did not succeed in doing so.' Neither Christine Keeler nor Mandy Rice-Davies ever escaped the public sensationalism that had engulfed them both during the winter, spring and summer of 1963. For the rest of their lives, through successive marriages and relationships, their names were forever associated with The Profumo Affair. Mandy was the more resilient of the two. At the launch party of her published memoirs on the last day of 1963, the author wore 'a high-fronted black dress with hardly any back' and explained her disappointment that although she had written 'about four times as much they had to cut out most of the best bits'.[3] Christine had been 'enmeshed in a net of wickedness', as Lord Denning said in his report, the victim of a level of physical and emotional manipulation that continued unabated. Such abuse of women, especially young women, persisted for decades at the hands of predators all over the world before reaching another turning point in unacceptability even as I was writing this book. But in 1963 the emotional, physical and prejudicial abuse of women had been exposed and an irrepressible movement to condemn such behaviour had begun.

The credibility of Harold Macmillan and his government was destroyed by the scandal. The affair was the final toppling block in the precarious structure of an ageing and out-of-touch administration. In a Gallup poll conducted that summer, 67 per cent of those surveyed thought Macmillan was failing to ensure the security of the country. Profumo apart, the emotional stress of handling the nuclear threat, Vassall, Philby, de Gaulle, the trade unions and the weather over the single period of six months had weakened the Prime Minister both politically and physically. After the paralysis imposed by ice and snow lifted, the bubbling anger of unemployed members of the coal and shipping unions boiled over. In the biggest demonstration since the 1930s, an estimated seven thousand unemployed northerners gathered in

Parliament Square at the end of March threatening to force themselves through a straining chain of policemen. As helmets were kicked about in the scrum, the demonstrators tried to break into the chamber of the House of Commons, policemen were knocked to the ground and manure was hurled in their faces. On 27 March a reporter from the *Guardian* encountered a crowd that included 'apprentices, foremen, old age pensioners, a child in a pram, mill girls, foundry men, Labour MPs, trade unionists, wood workers' carrying banners with slogans saying 'We want work', 'Forty hour week means full employment' and 'Sack the Tories, not the workers'. But of the ten local MPs only three agreed to meet and discuss the causes and solutions to the problem. By July the high levels of unemployment had dropped back: from 4 per cent in February to 2.1 per cent, with much of the blame laid on impossible working conditions in the dreadful weather.

But in October 1963, with his health increasingly precarious, Macmillan resigned as Prime Minister from his hospital bed where he was being treated for prostate problems. He was succeeded by his titled Foreign Secretary, Lord Home. Tony Benn had long thought the appointment would be a 'godsend' to the Labour Party since Home was 'completely overrated' by his own party.[4] Even though the noble Lord had disclaimed his title and reverted to his commoner name, Sir Alec Douglas-Home, the Labour Leader Harold Wilson attacked the appointment for its 'Edwardian Establishment mentality' as he prepared to fight for the top job at a General Election the following year.

The Conservative government remained in office but barely in power for one more year until the election in October 1964 when Harold Wilson walked through the Downing Street door with a majority of just four seats. As he entered Number 10 he carried with him the same conviction that Harry Evans had voiced throughout the winter of 1962–3 that 'something *could* be done and something *should* be done'. Over the next six years, and after a second election brought Labour a healthily increased majority, the Wilson government amassed an astonishing portfolio of far-reaching reforms. The year 1967 was a particular milestone in which the Sexual Offences Act decriminalised homosexuality and established a path of social inclusivity that would culminate in the legalisation of marriage between same-sex couples in 2014.The contraceptive pill was also made available on the National Health Service in 1967 regardless of marital status, and abortion became legal in Britain. The abolition of the death penalty was passed in 1965. And during the same Labour term of government the desperately inconclusive fight against racism became a central issue when the Race Relations Act was passed in 1965, outlawing direct discrimination on grounds of race, colour and ethnic origin. Not since the Labour Prime Minister Clement Attlee's government set up the National Health Service in 1948 had a leader put the people so definitively at the forefront of his policies. With Harold Wilson's election to the Labour leadership in January 1963, his dedication to the socialist movement began to gain credence with the public, bringing with it a social revolution that had seemed unthinkable during Macmillan's increasingingly archaic Conservative administration.

During the winter of 1962–3 questions about the way we are governed, and the way we lead our lives, both at home and within the wider world, had been highlighted and prised open for debate. The special relationship between Britain and America not only endured but deepened, while a full decade after Macmillan had been rebuffed by de Gaulle, Britain became a member of the EEC on 1 January 1973, retaining its membership of the European community until 2020. It remains to be seen how much longer it will take for the recognition of mankind's destruction of the planet, identified so long ago by Rachel Carson and Harry Evans among others, to take priority on the agendas of world leaders.

When I met Harry Evans some sixty years after he had set out to eradicate the 'Teesside smell', he remained just as energised. Sitting in his club in London on a day when the skies felt almost as gloomy as those dominated long ago by chemical smog, Harry's lifelong impatience about 'getting something done' – he thumped the table in unabating indignation – startled fellow members of the club dozing in their leather armchairs. His brilliant investigative work while editor of the *Sunday Times* from 1967 to 1981 came thanks in part to the discussions and risks taken during the winter of 1962–3 concerning the freedom of the press and other media. The licence to explore and to print or air the previously unprintable had been encouraged by the campaigning energy of young journalists up and down the country, and above all by the satirical movement. By the end of the 1960s the political enfranchisement that was extended to eighteen-year-olds was accompanied by the expression of individuality – in an exuberant freedom to dress as one pleased and in a joyful musical explosion that would be felt across the world for decades. The frozen winter of 1962–3 had concentrated minds. Ten weeks of extraordinary weather had produced an unprecedented paradox: paralysis had effected release.

Harold Wilson was a Beatles fan even though at the beginning of the winter few outside the North-West of the country had heard of the band. Scruffy, local groups from way up north were not paid much attention by a generation still listening to the music of the 1950s. By the end of the winter to admit your ignorance of the Beatles was like saying you had never heard of Henry VIII or cornflakes or God. Over the winter of 1962–3 John, Paul, George and Ringo (the order in which each of them had joined the band) collectively played more than eighty live shows up and down the country. They had also landed a number-one single, released their first album and appeared on numerous television and radio programmes. They had signed tickets, programmes, postcards, shirts and any number of cigarette packets. When Ian Wright, the young photographer from the *Northern Echo*, had caught up with them at the City Hall in Newcastle on 23 March, John Lennon had been ebullient, remembering their encounter in the lift in Sunderland. 'Now then, Wrighty, me Aunt Mimi got those photographs. You gotta take some more of 'em. C'mon, we're number one in the charts . . . Get a picture.' A couple of weeks later the Beatles spent the afternoon at Paul's house in Forthlin Road, making tea, gardening, ironing, putting out the milk bottle empties and being photographed by distinguished Hungarian Dezo Hoffmann doing 'normal' things. They had knocked Cliff Richard off the top of the national charts and were beginning to find it almost impossible to walk down a street in any town in Britain without causing a riot.

At 6.40 a.m. on 8 April in Sefton General Hospital, Liverpool, Cynthia Lennon gave birth to a son called Julian, weighing 6 lb 11 oz. John was still away touring, and did not meet the baby until 11 April, when the new mother remembered seeing him arrive 'like a whirlwind, racing through the doors in his haste to find us. He kissed me, then looked at his son, who was in my arms. There were tears in his eyes: "Cyn, he's bloody marvellous! He's fantastic."'[5] But the window in Cyn's room looked out onto the corridor and as soon as the news spread that John Lennon was in the hospital the collective noses of patients and staff alike were pressed against the glass. It was obvious that John couldn't stay long. Cynthia remembered how her husband had hugged her before signing dozens of autographs on his way out. 'I was disappointed that we'd had so little time together,' she wrote with her usual quiet patience and understatement. But there were priorities in John's life and neither Cynthia nor the baby was at the top of that list. In August the Beatles released their single 'She Loves You', which became the fastest selling single ever. By the end of the year they were the most famous pop group in the world and soon America's monopoly of making the coolest sounds on the planet was eclipsed. In November the Beatles played at the Royal Variety Performance where the Queen Mother and Princess Margaret were once more fulfilling their regal mother/daughter duties. The ever-subversive John Lennon invited the occupants of the cheap seats to clap their hands while the others (with a nod to the royal box) should show their appreciation and 'rattle your jewellery'. Afterwards, in a somewhat apologetic tone, John explained, 'It was the best I could do.' The band agreed never to play that gig again.

In February 1964 they flew to America where, according to Cyn, there was 'pandemonium' at the airport as 'screaming, sobbing girls held up "We Love You, Beatles" banners and hordes of police, linking arms in long chains, held them back.' This was the beginning of what became known in America as 'The British Invasion', as the hero status of Elvis, along with all Joanna Lumley's other beloveds, gave way to four lads from Liverpool. The band's irreverence was still at the core of their popularity. They had overturned the conventions, the expectations, the requisites for a pop group. They became the best-selling musical act of all time. The songs they wrote that came from a myriad different cultures and traditions influenced in their turn myriad cultures and traditions across the world. Their willingness to experiment, to shake things up, was the hallmark of their sound as well as of their age. They appealed across the classes, across the generations, across the races. They broke every barrier. The Beatles were responsible for transforming the world's musical, even cultural focus, for dislodging America's dominance and making Britain the pre-eminent leader of what was cool, new, exhilarating. Above all, they were the embodiment of an incandescent celebration of how wonderful it was to be young and to be alive in 1963. They were the voice of their generation.

In Kent that spring, under Shirley's care, Adam and I would bike up to the village for a slap-up tea with Aunt Pun, passing the ancient, wooden parish stocks in the village with the unvarying threat that we would be put inside the trap and left there 'till the cows come home' if we didn't stop dawdling. Wheeling along the newly snow-free lanes, we were eager for the high tea that was waiting for us, spread out on a flowery tablecloth. Ham sandwiches, early radishes and tiny lettuces dug up moments before from beneath the incubating cloches of an abundant vegetable garden sat beside a fluffy Victoria sponge cake and chunks of home-made pink and white coconut ice. Lemonade was poured from a bottle that fizzed on release of the metal catch. In a universe that could feel uncertain, there was something about the baking of cakes, the smell of new bread, the orderliness of the tea table that made Mill Lane feel like the least threatening place in the world to be.

Harold had begun to venture out of his cottage in the early April sunshine and into the garden. Having returned from America in the middle of February he had been depressed to find that the atrocious weather had not lifted in Kent. In February giant blocks of ice were still jamming the sea at Sheerness and frozen patches in the River Medway remained pink and blue, flushed by the dyes that made their way downriver from the paper mills upstream. On two consecutive mornings Harold had tumbled out of his bed and landed hard on the floor. The experience had frightened him and prompted an appointment with a doctor recommended by concerned friends in America. On 25 February he had arrived in the Harley Street consulting rooms of Sir Charles Symonds, president of the neurological and psychiatric departments of the Royal Society of Medicine. He subjected Harold to 'a detailed and extended scrutiny', concluding that he would slowly but eventually recover from his state of depression. Harold was less convinced, 'bored', he wrote in his diary, 'by the black shadow that haunts my every step'. Seeking a second opinion he went to his GP, who diagnosed Harold's condition as 'shock'. He prescribed a course of Vitamin D injections to be given at three-week intervals. For a while Harold had remained 'terrified' by his unhappiness, however, on 3 April, despite the disappointingly late blooming of the daffodils, he sat down in front of the television set in the cottage and found a reason to smile. Oxford, his alma mater, had romped home in the annual Oxford and Cambridge Boat Race. Even Harold acknowledged in his diary that he had 'cheered and cheered'.

A week later back in London Adam and I woke up on 10 April to find an envelope drawing-pinned to the bookcase on the top landing in Limerston Street. There was a message in capital letters in my father's handwriting.

> Your sister arrived in the hospital in the middle of the night. Both Mumma and baby are well.

On Easter Day, Sunday 14 April 1963, we returned to Kent and Adam and I picked two garden 'tuzzie muzzies', Harold and Vita's wartime expression for a raggle-taggle nosegay. One was for Hadji to celebrate the beginning of spring, our adored grandfather who was to live for another five years, the person who had taught us, his grandchildren, the way to love. And the other was for our mother, who was bringing our little sister Rebecca home for the first time.

The winter of 2019–20 was not quite over as I neared the end of writing this book, but daffodils were unfolding their trumpet heads in our garden and outside my window the forsythia had begun to blossom. Suddenly the earth felt lit up by yellow flowers. Sixty years before the winter of 1962–3 the century had just turned and with it the old Victorian regime was dying. Sixty years after the winter of 1962–3 the world turned again, a little more sharply than it should have, unbalancing the stability we take for granted and throwing everyone into a state of profound shock. Just two weeks after I had marvelled at the return of the forsythia, the planet drew in its breath. In December 2019, on a world map shown on every single news channel, a tiny red dot indicated a town in the heart of China, a million, million miles away from England, as the place where a brand new strain of a deadly virus had emerged, one that targeted the lungs, the enabler of breath, of oxygen and of life itself. Eight weeks later the dots had spread, and much of the world map was coloured red. In the autumn of 1962 many felt we were teetering on the edge of absolute destruction with nuclear weapons capable of wiping out mankind. And now, in the spring of 2020, the coronavirus, constantly visualised on screens as a spiky globe, an exotic species of underwater coral, a logo of frightening change, made us feel we were once again staring into the abyss, looking over the rim. The merest nudge of a memory, of what we might lose, what our children might lose, what we might have already lost, a glimpse of a photograph taken only last summer, the playing of a song that we had danced to when all was well, when our existence was intact, unthreatened, dislodged our equilibrium and we tried not to weep.

But at the same time we tried to remind ourselves that the brink can shift. The flat horizon over which many believed we might have toppled in the fifteenth century became unexpectedly curved as the great explorers found the planet to be spherical. In the middle of March 2020 the first lambs were born overnight in the farm two fields away from the room where I write. The country lanes were silent not this time because of the muffling of snow but by the absence of traffic. The world was in lockdown. The skies were blue, blue, blue, devoid of aeroplanes, not through mankind's choice, but for its survival. And the birds were going crazy in the sunshine. Nature seemed to have forgiven us not for doubting but for threatening its resilience and had returned once again with an astonishing beauty. The sun felt restoring, sustaining, life empowering. I walked through the ploughed fields that surround us, my back to the sun. I could feel the warmth reaching me through the material of my coat, as if a hand had rested itself there, remaining steady, however jerky my pace. The constancy of that warmth was incredibly comforting. The clichés were there. I was surrounded by, immersed in, 'the newness of everything' that had so moved playwright Dennis Potter in the spring of 1994, just a few weeks before his death. Momentarily dazzled, even blinded by the glare, I suddenly found the outline of the trees, the defiance of the emergent blossom, the song of the thrush, of nightingales, to be sharper, louder, lovelier than I ever remembered. The clichés were valid. The ragged ends of winter had been snipped into shape or cleared quite away.

In the early spring of 2020 as the Easter weekend approached, there was a feeling as people across the world reached out to one another, whether in conversation on the telephone, on the internet, even in letters arriving in the post, that after a time of challenge and of very real collective fear we would once again move forwards. The future might take a new form. As Lucy Winkett, Rector of St James's Piccadilly in London, so beautifully put it during a BBC Radio *Thought for the Day* in the spring of 2020, 'our stubborn messy humanity finds new ways to be itself'. We might become kinder, more tolerant, begin to understand better the value of our planet Earth and start to love those we love even more fiercely. A reshaping of our ways of doing things also took place in 1962–3, not despite but because of the apparent stillness of that snowy winter. Attitudes began to shift. Old ways, or what came gradually to be perceived as wrong ways of doing things, began to be frozen out of existence and replaced with the recognition that there was a new and better way of living life. Perhaps every half-century or so we need an intervention that is outside our control, an uninvited pause in order for resurrection to take place.

# Acknowledgements

The inestimably marvellous Lord Hennessy was the first person I spoke to about the idea of this book and it was his encouragement that convinced me that it was a book worth writing.

Philip Norman has shared with me his incredible knowledge of the period, directed me to gems of information and been an unmatchable adviser as well as the greatest of cheerleaders.

Julia Samuel's wisdom about human nature has lit me along the way.

Rachel Wyndham's constant encouragement has been the mark of true friendship.

Tom Grant's guidance through labyrinthine legal stories, his meticulous reading of the typescript and suggestions for stories of the period have been invaluable.

Liz Bussey's insight and her ability to listen are gold dust.

I have had the most generous and illuminating conversations with so many people about the winter of 1962–3, among them: Michael Ann, Peter Asher, Dame Eileen Atkins, Jonathan Chiswell Jones, Julia and Francis Cleverdon, Robin Clewley and Richard Vegas and David McTague, David Dimbleby, Matthew Engel, the late Harry Evans, Ros Ford, Antonia Fraser, Michael Frayn, Jo and Dave Gardiner, Stephen Guy, Nicky Hessenberg, Barry Humphries, Bernard Ingham, Richard Ingrams, Simon Knight, Richard Lipsey, Joanna Lumley, Liz McCann, James Macmillan Scott, Thomas Pakenham, Lionel Pelling, Tereska and Mark Peppe, Tony Prince, Diana Reich, Hazel Roscoe, Martin Seeley, Bishop of St Edmundsbury and Ipswich, Guy Simpson, Lucy Sisman, Beryl Smith, Linda Stearns, Paulene Stone, Claire Tomalin, Joanna Trollope, Liz Wharfe, Diana Wood, Edward Wood, Carola Zogolovitch.

And I would also like to thank for their help in infinite ways: Patricia Anker, Desmond Banks, Sally Bedell Smith, David Bernstein, Kildare Bourke-Borrowes, Jilly Byford, Paul Calkin, Julie Campbell, Keggie Carew, Dinah Casson, William Dalrymple, Claire Durbridge, Helen Marchant, James Fox, Belinda Giles, Alexandra Harris, Catherine Knight, Claudia Lipsey, Antonia Lloyd, Christopher Meyer, Alan Moses, Bill Nicholson, Virginia Nicholson, Vanessa Nicolson, Cate Olssen and Nash Robbins, Arthur Parkinson, Seymour Platt, Sarah Raven, Sayre Robinson Horley, Joanna Rowlands, Fiona Shelburne, Lizzie Spender, Mary Taylor, Amanda Terry, Aly Van Den Berg, Rachel Van Der Steen, Lucy Wheeler, Susanna White, The Reverend Lucy Winkett and Klara Zak.

A huge thank you to Flora Macmillan-Scott for her stellar picture research.

The archives and archivists at several collections have been beyond helpful: Naomi and Stewart Tiley at Balliol College, Oxford archives; Hugo Vickers and also Kathryn McKee, Special Collections Librarian at St John's College, Cambridge; the staff of the London Library; Sarah Broadhurst at the London Zoo; Nino Strachey at the National Trust; Simon Osborne at the National Trust; Masie Glazebrook and Marie Aylmer and Ian Hislop at *Private Eye*; Oriole Cullen, Jenny Dyson, and Stephanie Wood at the V&A Museum.

At Curtis Brown I would like to thank Cathryn Summerhayes for getting me so smoothly to the starting point.

The meticulous attention, care and energy shown me by my amazing agent Clare Conville at Conville and Walsh is inexhaustible as well as her ability to make everything such fun. And Darren Biabowe Barnes at the agency has been hugely helpful.

I am blessed to be published by the wonderful Chatto & Windus team, including Greg Clowes with his enviable editorial insight, Clara Farmer, Charlotte Humphery, Cecile Pin, Rosie Palmer, Lily Richards and Anna Redman Aylward who have all looked after me and the book so beautifully. Above all I am indebted to Becky Hardie, the most perceptive and most committed publisher, editor and friend I could ever dream of having.

Bean and Miles are the very best of loyal supporters.

My brother Adam has an unerring understanding of what I want to say and knows instinctively how to guide me towards saying it. His praise sandwich means everything.

Imogen, Gabriel, Orlando and Gus are my magical life enhancers.

The unflagging love of Charlie, Clemmie and Flora has melted away the sometimes impossibly frozen and lonely process of writing. This book is for these three beloveds.

# Bibliography

## Autobiography and Biography

Autobiography

*The Unexpurgated Beaton: The Cecil Beaton Diaries as he wrote them*, Cecil Beaton, Weidenfeld & Nicolson 2002

*The Benn Diaries,* Tony Benn edited by Ruth Winstone, Hutchinson 2017

*Daring to Hope: The Diaries and Letters 1946–1969,* Violet Bonham Carter, Weidenfeld & Nicolson 2000

*Grace: A Memoir*, Grace Coddington, Chatto & Windus 2012

*The Way We Wore: A Life in Threads*, Robert Elms, Indie 2014

*Downing Street Diary: The Macmillan Years 1957–63*, Harold Evans, Hodder & Stoughton 1981

*My Paper Chase: True Stories of Vanished Times. An Autobiography*, Harold Evans, Little, Brown 2009

*Sex, Sense and Nonsense: Felicity Green on the 1960s Fashion Scene*, Felicity Green, ACC Editions 2014

*Secrets and Lies: The Trials of Christine Keeler*, Christine Keeler with Douglas Thompson, John Blake publishing 2019

*The Ritz and the Ditch: A Memoir*, Diana Holderness, Stone Trough Books 2018

*My Life as Me: The Memoirs of a Privileged Childhood*, Barry Humphries, Michael Joseph 2003

*More Please: An Autobiography*, Barry Humphries, Viking 1992

*Full Marks for Trying: An Unlikely Journey from the Raj to the Rag Trade*, Brigid Keenan, Bloomsbury 2016

*Dawn: A Charleston Legend*, Dawn Langley Simmons, Wyrick and Company 1995

*The Bunny Years: The Surprising Inside Story of the Playboy Clubs*, Kathryn Leigh Scott, Gallery Books 2011

*John*, Cynthia Lennon, Hodder & Stoughton 2005

*Absolutely*, Joanna Lumley, Weidenfeld & Nicolson 2011

*The Cat-Walk*, Cherry Marshall, Hutchinson 1978

*Timebends: A Life*, Arthur Miller, Grove Press 1987

*Long Life: Memoirs*, Nigel Nicolson, Weidenfeld & Nicolson 1997

*Confessions of an Actor*, Laurence Olivier, Weidenfeld & Nicolson 1982

*Who's In, Who's Out: The Journals of Kenneth Rose: Volume One 1944–1979*, D. R. Thorpe (ed.), Weidenfeld & Nicolson 1988

*Promise of a Dream*, Sheila Rowbotham, Verso 2002

*Diary of a Teddy Boy: A Memoir of the Long Sixties*, Mim Scala, published by Mim Scala 2000

*Fast and Louche*, Jeremy Scott, Profile Books 2002

*Memoirs of a Black Englishman*, Paul Stephenson OBE and Lilleith Morrison, Tangent Books 2011

*Whatever Happened to Sex?*, Mary Whitehouse, Wayland Publishers 1977

*Quant by Quant: The Autobiography of Mary Quant*, Cassell & Co. 1966

## Biography

*The Macmillan Diaries Volume II: Prime Minister and After, 1957–1966*, Peter Catterall (ed.), Macmillan 2011

*So Farewell Then: The Untold Life of Peter Cook*, Wendy E. Cook, Harper Collins 2006

*Foul Deeds and Suspicious Deaths around Brighton*, Douglas d'Enno, Wharncliffe Books 2004

*T. S. Eliot: An Imperfect Life*, Lyndall Gordon, Norton 1998

*Jeremy Hutchinson's Case Histories*, Thomas Grant, John Murray 2015

*How Very Interesting: Peter Cook's Universe and All That Surrounds It*, Paul Hamilton, Peter Gordon and Dan Kieran and Friends (eds), Snow Books 2006

*Betjeman: The Bonus of Laughter*, Bevis Hillier, John Murray 2004

*I Read the News Today, Oh Boy: The Short and Gilded Life of Tara Browne, the Man who Inspired the Beatles' Greatest Song*, Paul Howard, Picador 2016

*Churchill*, Roy Jenkins, Macmillan 2001

*The Macmillan Years: 1957–63 The Emerging Truth*, Richard Lamb, John Murray 1995

*Harold Nicolson: A Biography. Volume II 1930–1968,* James Lees-Milne, Chatto & Windus 1981

*Ian Fleming*, Andrew Lycett, Weidenfeld & Nicolson 1995

*Goldeneye: Where Bond was Born: Ian Fleming's Jamaica*, Matthew Parker, Penguin Random House 2014

*Bob Boothby: A Portrait*, Robert Rhodes James, Hodder & Stoughton 1991

*Supermac: The Life of Harold Macmillan*, D. R. Thorpe, Chatto & Windus 2010

*Cecil Beaton*, Hugo Vickers, Weidenfeld & Nicolson 1985

*Lovers and Strangers: An Immigrant History of Post-war England*, Clair Wills, Allen Lane 2017

*Harold Wilson: The Authorised Life*, Philip Ziegler, Harper Collins 1993

## History and Social History

*Jeremy Thorpe*, Michael Bloch, Little, Brown 2014
*The Neophiliacs: The Revolution in English Life in the Fifties and Sixties*, Christopher Booker, William Collins 1969
*Swinging Sixties: Fashion in London and Beyond 1955–1970*, Christopher Breward, David Gilbert and Jenny Lister (eds),V&A Publications 2006
*Class in Britain*, David Cannadine, Yale University Press 1998
*Silent Spring*, Rachel Carson, Penguin Classics 2000
*1963: That Was the Year That Was*, Andrew Cook, The History Press 2013
*Girl Trouble: Panic and Progress in the History of Young Women*, Carol Dyhouse, Zed Books 2013
*The Feminine Mystique*, Betty Friedan, WW Norton 1963
*That Was Satire That Was: The Satire Boom of the 1960s*, Humphrey Carpenter, Victor Gollancz 2000
*Arlott, Swanton and the Soul of English Cricket*, Stephen Fay and David Kynaston, Bloomsbury 2018
*Rinkagate: The Rise and Fall of Jeremy Thorpe*, Simon Freeman with Barrie Penrose, Bloomsbury 1996
*From the Closet to the Screen: Women at the Gateway Club 1945–85*, Jill Gardiner, Pandora Press 2003
*All Dressed Up: The Sixties and the Counterculture*, Jonathan Green, Jonathan Cape 1998
*Days in the Life: Voices from the English Underground, 1961–1971*, Jonathan Green, Heinemann 1988
*Winds of Change: Britain in the Early Sixties*, Peter Hennessy, Allen Lane 2019
*The Abolition of Britain: From Winston Churchill to Theresa May*, Peter Hitchens, Bloomsbury 2018
*The Life and Times of Private Eye*, Richard Ingrams (ed.), Allen Lane 1971
*Modernity Britain: Book Two. A Shake of the Dice 1959–62*, David Kynaston, Bloomsbury 2014
*1963: Five Hundred Days*, John Lawton, Hodder & Stoughton 1992

*Youthquake: The Growth of a Counter Culture through Two Decades*, Kenneth Leech, Sheldon Press 1973

*1963: The Year of the Revolution,* Robin Morgan and Ariele Leve, Harper Collins 2013

*The Pendulum Years: Britain and the Sixties*, Bernard Levin, Jonathan Cape 1970

*Ready Steady Go!: The Smashing Rise and Giddy Fall of Swinging London*, Shawn Levy, Doubleday NYC 2002

*A Spy Among Friends: Kim Philby and the Great Betrayal,* Ben Macintyre, Bloomsbury 2014

*Very Heaven: Looking Back at the 1960s,* Sara Maitland (ed.), Virago 1988

*Private Eye: The First 50 Years*, Adam MacQueen, Private Eye Productions 2011

*How Was it for You? Women, Sex, Love and Power in the 1960s*, Virginia Nicholson, Viking 2019

*A Very English Scandal,* John Preston, Viking 2016

*Never Had It So Good: A History of Britain from Suez to the Beatles*, Dominic Sandbrook, Little, Brown 2005

*Sex Before the Sexual Revolution: Intimate Life in England 1918–1963*, Simon Szreter and Kate Fisher, Cambridge University Press 2010

*Patriots: National Identity in Britain 1940–2000*, Richard Weight, Macmillan 2002

**Weather**

*Weatherland: Writers and Artists Under English Skies*, Alexandra Harris, Thames & Hudson 2015

*The Long Winter: A Guardian Pamphlet* Geoffrey Moorhouse (ed.), Guardian 1963

*The Sussex Weather Book*, Bob Ogley, Ian Currie and Mark Davison, Froglets Publications Ltd 1991

*A Winter Remembered: Events Recalling the Winter of 1962–3 and its Effect on the Railways of Dartmoor*, Robert E. Trevelyan, Ark Publications (Railway) 1998

**Fiction and Poetry**

*Offshore*, Penelope Fitzgerald, Harper Collins 1979
*On Chesil Beach*, Ian McEwan, Jonathan Cape 2007
*Ariel*, Sylvia Plath, Faber & Faber 1965
*The Bell Jar*, Sylvia Plath, William Heinemann 1963
*The Skating Party*, Marina Warner, Weidenfeld & Nicolson 1982
*Orlando*, Virginia Woolf, Hogarth Press 1928

**Music**

The Beatles

*One Two Three Four: The Beatles in Time*, Craig Brown, Fourth Estate 2020
*The Love You Make: An Insider's Story of the Beatles,* Peter Brown and Steven Gaines, Macmillan 1983
*A Cellarful of Noise*, Brian Epstein, Souvenir Press 1964
*Standing in the Wings: The Beatles, Brian Epstein and Me*, Joe Flannery with Mike Brocken, The History Press 2013
*Forgotten Liverpool: Remarkable Mersey Tales*, Stephen Guy, Buxton Press 2013
*Mersey Beat: The Beginnings of the Beatles*, Edited and introduced Bill Harry, Omnibus Press 1977
*The Beatles in Liverpool*, Spencer Leigh, Omnibus Press 2012
*John*, Cynthia Lennon, Hodder & Stoughton 2005
*The Beatles Day by Day: 1962–1989: A Chronology*, Mark Lewisohn, Harmony Books 1987
*The Beatles Tune In*, Mark Lewisohn, Little, Brown 2013
*Paul McCartney: Many Years from Now*, Barry Miles, Secker & Warburg 1977
*Shout: The True Story of The Beatles*, Philip Norman, Elm Tree Books/Hamish Hamilton 1981
*Paul McCartney: The Biography*, Philip Norman, Weidenfeld & Nicolson 2016

*Walking Back to Happiness*, Helen Shapiro, Harper Collins 1993
*Liverpool: Pevsner Architectural Guides*, Joseph Sharples, Yale University Press 2004

Other Music Makers

*Dylan on Dylan: Interviews and Encounters*, Jeff Burger (ed.), Chicago Review Press Inc. 2018
*Chronicles: Volume 1*, Bob Dylan, Simon & Schuster 2004
*Bob Dylan: Stories Behind the Songs 1962–1969,* Andy Gill, Carlton Books 1998
*Bob Dylan and the British Sixties: A Cultural History*, Tudor Jones, Routledge 2019
*Slowhand: The Life and Music of Eric Clapton*, Philip Norman (Clapton), Little, Brown 2008
*The Stones*, Philip Norman, Elm Tree Books/Hamish Hamilton 1984
*Stoned*, Andrew Loog Oldham, Secker & Warburg 2000
*The Royal Ruler and the Railway DJ: The Life and Times of a Radio Luxembourg DJ and the Boy in the Eastern Bloc Who Couldn't Live Without It,* Tony Prince and Jan Šesták, DCM Publishing 2016
*Life*, Keith Richards, Weidenfeld & Nicolson 2010

**John F. Kennedy**

*Once Upon a Secret: My Hidden Affair with JFK*, Mimi Alford, Hutchinson 2012
*Grace and Power*, Sally Bedell Smith, Aurum Press 1994
*America's Queen*, Sarah Bradford, Viking 2000
*Harold and Jack*, Christopher Sandford, Prometheus Books 2014

**John Profumo**

*Beautiful Idiots and Brilliant Lunatics: A Sideways Look at Twentieth Century London*, Rob Baker, Amberley Publishing 2015

*An English Affair: Sex, Class and Power in the Age of Profumo*, Richard Davenport-Hines, Harper Press 2013

*Scandal: A Study of the Profumo Affair*, Clive Irving, Ron Hall and Jeremy Wallington, Heinemann 1963

*The Truth At Last*, Christine Keeler with Douglas Thompson, Sidgwick & Jackson 2001

*An Affair of State: The Profumo Case and the framing of Stephen Ward*, Philip Knightley and Caroline Kennedy, Jonathan Cape 1987

*Bringing the House Down: A Family Memoir*, David Profumo, John Murray 2006

*The Mandy Report*, Mandy Rice-Davies, Confidential Publications 1963

*Bronwen Astor: Her Life and Times*, Peter Stanford, Harper Collins 2000

**Sylvia Plath**

*The Savage God*, Al Alvarez, Weidenfeld & Nicolson 1971

*Ted Hughes: The Unauthorised Life*, Jonathan Bate, William Collins 2015

*Giving Up: The Last Days of Sylvia Plath*, Jillian Becker, Ferrington 2003

*The Death and Life of Sylvia Plath*, Ronald Hayman, William Heinemann 1991

*A Lover of Unreason: The Life and Tragic Death of Assia Wevill*, Yehuda Koren and Eilat Negev, Robson Books 2006

*The Unabridged Journals of Sylvia Plath,* Ed. Karen V. Kukl, Faber & Faber 2000

*The Silent Woman: Sylvia Plath and Ted Hughes*, Janet Malcolm, Picador 1994

*The Letters of Sylvia Plath. Volume II 1959–63*, Peter K. Steinberg and Karen V. Kukil (eds), Faber 2018

*Bitter Fame: A life of Sylvia Plath*, Anne Stevenson, Viking 1989

*Sylvia Plath: A Biography*, Linda W. Wagner-Martin, Simon & Schuster 1987

## Articles

Notes made during the London Smog in December 1962 by Richard A. Prindle MD, Archives of *Environmental Health: An International Journal*

'JFK File Hidden Illness Pain and Pulls', *New York Times* 17/11/2002

'The December Smog: A First Survey', Arnold Marsh, *Journal of the Air Pollution Control Association*, Volume 13 1963 Issue 8

# Permissions

Extracts from *Four Quartets* by T. S. Eliot reproduced by permission of Faber & Faber Ltd

Extracts from *Letters of Sylvia Plath* by Sylvia Plath reproduced by permission of Faber & Faber Ltd

Extracts from *Collected Poems* by Ted Hughes reproduced by permission of Faber & Faber Ltd

# List of Illustrations

All photos and images, unless otherwise stated, are the copyright of the author.

Plate Section I

*Every effort has been made by the publishers to trace the holders of copyright. Any inadvertent omissions of acknowledgement or permission can be rectified in future editions.*

# Notes

## Introduction

1 *Lovers and Strangers: An Immigrant History of Post-war Britain* by Clair Wills

## Chapter 1

1 Conversation with the author 2019
2 Richard A. Prindle MD (1963), Notes Made During the London Smog in December, 1962, *Archives of Environmental Health: An International Journal*, 7:4, 493–496, DOI: 10.1080/00039896.1963.10663572
3 Conversation with the author
4 Conversation with the author 2018
5 *My Paper Chase: True Stories of Vanished Times* by Harold Evans
6 *Silent Spring* is now credited with being a major catalyst in launching worldwide awareness of the man-made dangers our planet faces

## Chapter 2

1 Conversation with the author 2019
2 *My Life As Me: The Memoirs of a Privileged Childhood* by Barry Humphries
3 *That Was Satire That Was: The Satire Boom of the 1960s* by Humphrey Carpenter
4 *British Culture and the End of Empire (Studies in Imperialism)*, Stuart Ward (ed.), Manchester University Press, 2001
5 *That Was Satire That Was*
6 Ibid.
7 *The Neophiliacs: Revolution in English Life in the Fifties and Sixties* by Christopher Booker
8 *Whatever Happened to Sex?* by Mary Whitehouse
9 Speech in November 1961 at a dinner for BBC TV's 25th anniversary

## Chapter 3

1 On 2 March 1963
2 Hutchinson immediately lodged an appeal and the conviction was successfully overturned in May 1963.
3 *Dark Secret: Sexual Aversion*, BBC2, Thursday 8 August 1996
4 *The Brian Epstein Story*, John Savage, BBC4's *Hidden Lives* 2007
5 *Standing in the Wings: The Beatles, Brian Epstein and Me* by Joe Flannery with Mike Brocken
6 https:/vimeo.com/29252375
7 *One in Twenty: A Study of Homosexuality in Men and Women* by Bryan Magee, Secker & Warburg, 1966
8 *A Lesbian History of Britain: Love and Sex Between Women Since 1500* by Rebecca Jennings, Greenwood World Publishing, 2007
9 10 January 1963

10 *A Very English Scandal* by John Preston
11 Ibid.

**Chapter 4**

1 www.historicalgeographies.com
2 Parliamentary Archive HC Deb 19 July 1962 vol 663 cc635-41
3 *Very Heaven: Looking Back at the 1960s*, Sara Maitland (ed.)
4 *Diary of a Teddy Boy: A Memoir of the Long Sixties* by Mim Scala
5 *The Mandy Report* by Mandy Rice-Davies

**Chapter 5**

1 *The Macmillan Diaries Volume II: 1957–1966*, Peter Catterall (ed.), 7 December 1962
2 Conversation with the author 2019
3 *Supermac: The Life of Harold Macmillan* by D. R. Thorpe
4 *The Macmillan Diaries Volume II: 1957–1966*, Peter Catterall (ed.)
5 *Macmillan: A Study in Ambiguity* by Anthony Sampson, Allen Lane, 1967
6 'England, Whose England?', *Encounter*, July 1963
7 'The Medical Ordeals of JFK', Robert Dallek, *Atlantic* magazine, December 2002
8 *The Secret Letters of Marilyn Monroe and Jacqueline Kennedy* by Wendy Leigh, Thomas Dunne Books, 1967
9 Interview, Sally Bedell-Smith, 30 January 2002
10 *Once Upon A Secret: My Hidden Affair with JFK* by Mimi Alford
11 JFK Library June 10 1964
12 *Once Upon a Secret*

**Chapter 6**

1 Pseudonym for Roger Longrigg
2 3 December 1962

3 *Sissinghurst: An Unfinished History* by Adam Nicolson, Harper Press, 2009
4 After five years of intense negotiation the National Trust took over the ownership of Sissinghurst in 1967.
5 *Dawn: A Charleston Legend* by Dawn Langley Simmons
6 *Diaries and Letters 1945–1962* by Harold Nicolson, Collins, 1968
7 *Harold Nicolson: A Biography Volume II 1930–1968* by James Lees-Milne
8 *Diaries and Letters 1945–1962*

**Chapter 7**

1 Conversation with the author
2 *The Times*, 27 December 1962
3 Conversation with the author 2020
4 *Basildon, Canvey Southend Echo* 22 January 2018
5 Conversation in 2020 between the author and James Macmillan-Scott, Sticklepath resident in 1962
6 *The Times*, 28 December 1962

**Chapter 9**

1 *Diary of a Teddy Boy* by Mim Scala
2 *Ready Steady Go!: The Smashing Rise and Giddy Fall of Swinging London* by Shawn Levy
3 Conversation with the author 2019
4 *Stoned* by Andrew Loog Oldham
5 *Quant by Quant: The Autobiography of Mary Quant*

**Chapter 10**

1 *The Cat-Walk* by Cherry Marshall
2 Cranleigh School Website
3 *The Oldie*, November 2016

4 *Fast and Louche* by Jeremy Scott
5 Ibid.
6 Conversation with the author 2019
7 Hugo Williams in the *Spectator*, 2001
8 *I Read The News Today, Oh Boy: The Short and Gilded Life of Tara Browne, the Man who Inspired the Beatles' Greatest Song* by Paul Howard
9 *I Read The News Today, Oh Boy*

**Chapter 11**

1 *Stoned* by Andrew Loog Oldham
2 *Invisible Now: Bob Dylan in the 1960s* by John Hughes, Ashgate 2013
3 *Daily Mirror*, 12 September 1963
4 *Bob Dylan: Stories Behind the Songs 1962–69* by Andy Gill
5 *Chronicles: Volume 1* by Bob Dylan

**Chapter 12**

1 Obituary, *Daily Telegraph* 2002
2 *Basildon, Canvey Southend Echo*, January 1963
3 *Country Life*, January 1963

**Chapter 13**

1 Conversation with the author 2019
2 BBC News at One website, 8 January 2010
3 *Business Live* magazine, 4 January 2013
4 Letter to the author 2019
5 Conversation with the author 2019
6 Matthew Engle became the *Guardian*'s prize-winning sports (and political) journalist and visited Australia many times, in the sunshine.
7 Conversation with the author 2020

8 Conversation with the author 2020
9 Conversation with the author 2019

## Chapter 15

1 *Supermac: The Life of Harold Macmillan* by D. R. Thorpe
2 *Daring to Hope* by Violet Bonham Carter, diary entry 18 February 1963
3 Ibid., diary entry 9 February 1963
4 *Macmillan Diaries*, 28 January 1963
5 *Ian Fleming* by Andrew Lycett
6 *Goldeneye: Where Bond was Born: Ian Fleming's Jamaica* by Matthew Parker
7 Parliamentary Archive, HC Deb, 22 January 1963 vol 670 cc40–50
8 *The Benn Diaries*, Tony Benn edited by Ruth Winstone
9 *Who's In, Who's Out: The Journals of Kenneth Rose, Volume 1*
10 Parliamentary Archives, HL Deb, 19 February 1963 vol 246 cc1267–364
11 Ibid., cc389–416

## Chapter 16

1 *Harold Nicolson: A Biography* Vol 2 by James Lees Milne
2 Conversation between the author and Linda Stearns 2020
3 Conversation with the author 2019
4 Conversation with the author 2019
5 Conversation with the author 2019

## Chapter 17

1 Conversation between the author and Stephen Guy
2 Conversation between the author and Liverpool historians Robin Clewley, David McTague and Richard Vegas

3 *Days in the Life: Voices from the English Underground, 1961–1971* by Jonathon Green
4 *Standing in the Wings* by Joe Flannery with Mike Brocken
5 *Playboy* magazine. Interview with John Lennon by David Sheff, September1980
6 *The Beatles, the Biography* by Bob Spitz
7 Maureen Cleave, 'Recollections', *Daily Telegraph* 2009
8 Stuart left the band in July 1961 to continue painting. He died of an aneurysm aged 21 in 1962.
9 John's later explanation about the visionary 'flaming pie' was just one made-up story he told in answer to the interminable question of how the band chose its final name.

**Chapter 18**

1 *Show: The Magazine of the Arts*, May 1963 and June 1963
2 *The Bunny Years* by Kathryn Leigh Scott

**Chapter 19**

1 *The Letters of Sylvia Plath. Volume II*
2 *Ted Hughes: The Unauthorised Life* by Jonathan Bate
3 *The Savage God* by Al Alvarez
4 *Observer*, 4 January 2004
5 Conversation with the author
6 Sylvia Plath, *Letters Home*, 348
7 *The Letters of Sylvia Plath. Volume II*
8 Ibid.

**Chapter 20**

1 Obituary, *The Times*, 20 June 2012
2 *The Silent Woman: Sylvia Plath and Ted Hughes* by Janet Malcolm
3 *Giving Up: The Last Days of Sylvia Plath* by Jillian Becker

4 Conversation with the author
5 *Giving Up: The Last Days of Sylvia Plath*

## Chapter 21

1 *Daily Telegraph*, 14 December 2009
2 www.classicbands.com Gary James Interview
3 *The Beatles, Day-by-Day, Song-by-Song, Record-by-Record* by Craig Cross, iUniverse, 2005
4 *The Royal Ruler & the Railway DJ* by Tony Prince and Jan Šesták
5 Conversation with the author 2019
6 Conversation with the author 2019

## Chapter 22

1 The Rudolph Nureyev Foundation, www.nureyev.org
2 Conversation with the author 2020
3 GBS speech made in 1938 at the Ceremony of the Twig and the Sod. www.nationaltheatre.org.uk
4 Conversation with the author 2020
5 *The Mandy Report* by Mandy Rice-Davies
6 *Beautiful Idiots and Brilliant Lunatics: A Sideways Look at Twentieth Century London* by Rob Baker
7 *The Mandy Report*, op. cit.
8 *The Truth at Last* by Christine Keeler with Douglas Thompson
9 *The Great Gatsby* by F. Scott Fitzgerald
10 *The Truth at Last* by Christine Keeler and Douglas Thompson

## Chapter 23

1 *Keeler, Profumo, Ward and Me*, BBC2, January 2020
2 Conversation with the author 2020

3 *The Ritz and the Ditch: A Memoir* by Diana Holderness
4 Conversation with the author 2020
5 *Black Scandal* by Johnny Edgecombe, Westworld International, 2002
6 Macmillan Diary, 15 March 1963
7 Conversation with the author 2020
8 Parliamentary Archives HC Deb, 21 March 1963, vol 674 cc682–771
9 *Bringing the House Down: A Family Memoir* by David Profumo
10 Parliamentary Archives, HC Deb, 22 March 1963, vol 674 cc809–10

**Chapter 24**

1 *Keeler, Profumo, Ward and Me*, BBC2, 11 February 2020
2 *Jeremy Hutchinson's Case Histories* by Thomas Grant
3 *Guardian*, 1 January 1964
4 *The Benn Diaries*
5 *John* by Cynthia Lennon

# Index